GLOBALIZATION AND ANTIGLOBALIZATION

The International Political Economy of New Regionalisms Series

The International Political Economy of New Regionalisms Series presents innovative analyses of a range of novel regional relations and institutions. Going beyond established, formal, interstate economic organizations, this essential series provides informed interdisciplinary and international research and debate about myriad heterogeneous intermediate level interactions.

Reflective of its cosmopolitan and creative orientation, this series is developed by an international editorial team of established and emerging scholars in both the South and North. It reinforces ongoing networks of analysts in both academia and think-tanks as well as international agencies concerned with micro-, meso- and macro-level regionalisms.

Globalization and Antiglobalization
Dynamics of Change in the New World Order

Edited by

HENRY VELTMEYER

ASHGATE

Published by
Ashgate Publishing Limited
Gower House
Croft Road
Aldershot
Hants GU11 3HR
England

Ashgate Publishing Company
Suite 420
101 Cherry Street
Burlington, VT 05401-4405
USA

Ashgate website: http://www.ashgate.com

British Library Cataloguing in Publication Data
Globalization and antiglobalization : dynamics of change in
    the new world order. - (The international political economy
    of new regionalisms series)
    1. Globalization 2. International economic relations
    3. Economic development 4. Imperialism 5. Latin America -
    Economic conditions - 1982- 6. Asia - Economic conditions -
    1945-
    I. Veltmeyer, Henry
    337

Library of Congress Cataloging-in-Publication Data
Globalization and antiglobalization : dynamics of change in the new world order / edited by
Henry Veltmeyer.
        p. cm. -- (The international political economy of new regionalisms series)
    Includes bibliographical references and index.
    ISBN 0-7546-3489-2
        1. Development economics. 2. Globalization--Economic aspects. 3.
    Globalization--Social aspects. 4. Imperialism. 5. Anti-globalization movement--Asia. 6.
    Anti-globalization movement--Latin America. I. Veltmeyer, Henry.
    II. Series.

    HD82 .D38945 2003
    337.5--dc21   2002036804

ISBN 0 7546 3489 2 (Hbk)
ISBN 0 7546 4487 1 (Pbk)

Reprinted 2005

Printed and bound by MPG Books Ltd, Bodmin, Cornwall

Contents

PART III: THE DYNAMICS OF ANTIGLOBALIZATION

List of Tables

List of Abbreviations and Acronyms

AFTA	Asian Free Trade Area
AGM	Anti-Globalization Movement
AMPG	Annual multifactor productivity growth
APEC	Asia-Pacific Economic Cooperation
ASEAN	Association of Southeast Asian Nations
CCS	Central Capitalist State
CFR	Council on Foreign Relations
CONAIE	Confederation of Indigenous Nations of Ecuador
ECLAC	Economic Commission for Latin America and the Caribbean
EZLN	Ejército Zapatista de Liberación Nacional
FARC	Fuerzas Armadas Revolucionarias de Colombia [Revolutionary Armed Forces of Colombia]
FDI	Foreign Direct Investment
FTAA	Free Trade Area of the Americas
GEF	Global Environmental Facility
GNP	Gross National Product
IFIs	International Financial Institutions
ILO	International Labour Organization
IMF	International Monetary Fund
LAFTA	Latin American Free Trade Agreement
MNCs	Multinational Corporations
MSC	Multipler Service Contract
MST	Landless Rural Workers Movement
NAFTA	North American Free Trade Agreement
NGO	Nongovernmental Organization
NICs	Newly Industrializing Countries
ODA	Overseas Development Assistance
PCS	Peripheral Capitalist State
PPP	Plan Pueblo Panama
SAP	Structural Adjustment Program
SEZ	Special Economic Zone
TC	Trilateral Commission
TNCs	Transnational Corporations
TPL	Trade Policy Loan
TSIR	Third Scientific Industrial Revolution
UNDP	United Nations Development Programme
UNRISD	United Nations Research Institute for Social Development
WBG	World Bank Group
WEF	World Economic Forum
WSF	World Social Forum
WTO	World Trade Organization

List of Contributors

Paul Bowles is Professor of Economics at the University of Northern British Colombia (UNBC), Prince George, BC. He has published on various aspects of globalization and regionalism as well as the political economy of China's reforms.

Noam Chomsky is Professor of Linguistics, Massachusetts Institute of Technology (MIT). Author of numerous works in diverse fields including *9/11* (2001) and *11/9/2001* (2002).

Gian Carlo Delgado-Ramos is a Member of the Seminar 'El Mundo Actual' of CEIICH at the Universidad Autónoma de México (UNAM) and author of *La Amenaza Biológica* (2002).

Adam David Morton was formerly an Economic and Social Research Council (ESRC) Postdoctoral Fellow at the University of Wales, Aberystwyth and is now Lecturer in International Relations at Lancaster University. He has published in various journals, most recently the *Review of International Political Economy*, and co-edited *Social Forces in the Making of the New Europe: The Restructuring of European Social Relations in the Global Political Economy* (2001).

James Petras is Professor Emeritus in Sociology at Binghamton University, New York. He is the author of numerous works, including *Globaloney: el lenguaje imperial, los intelectuales y la izquierda* (2000), *Hegemonia dos Estados Unidos no Nova Milênio* (2001); and, with Henry Veltmeyer, *Unmasking Globalization: The New Face of Imperialism* (2001).

George W. Schuyler is Professor of History, University of Arkansas, Little Rock, Arkansas. A specialist on issues of land reform he is author of numerous studies on developments in Latin America, including *Hunger in a Land of Plenty* (1980) and *Canada and Cuba: A New Policy for the 1990s* (1994).

John Saxe-Fernández is Professor of Political Science at Universidad Nacional Autónoma de México (UNAM) in Mexico City. He coordinates 'El Mundo Actual,' Research/Publication Program of the Interdisciplinary Research Centre (CEIICH) and is the author of innumerable studies on international relations and Latin American development, including *La Compra-Venta de México* (2002).

Henry Veltmeyer is Professor of International Development Studies at St. Mary's University (Halifax) and Adjunct Professor of Development at Universidad Autónoma de Zacatecas (UAZ), Mexico. He is author, inter alia, of *Transcending Neoliberalism: Community Based Development in Latin America* (2001).

Acknowledgements

The editor and authors gratefully acknowledge the financial aid provided by the International Development Research Centre (IDRC) of Canada and the Social Science Humanities and Research Council (SSHRC) of Canada. This support allowed a number of the contributors to this volume to complete their research as well as come together at several workshops and international conferences to discuss their findings and ideas.

The editor also acknowledges the encouragement and support given to this project by his life partner, Annette Wright.

Introduction

The book examines the macrodynamics of globalization and antiglobalization in the world economy, with particular reference to developments in Latin America and Asia. The context of this examination is provided by an epoch-defining shift in social and economic organization associated with what has become known as 'globalization'—the process of integrating societies across the world, and their economies and cultures, into one system. There are serious questions as to whether the term 'globalization' describes at all the major dynamics of change and development in the world. In fact, one of the authors in this book, James Petras, argues that the term 'imperialism' provides a better short-hand description of what is going on in the world and thus a better explanation of its major dynamics. The contributors to this book generally agree with this judgement and are disposed to accept 'imperialism' as a more useful framework for their analysis, a framework that is outlined by Petras in Chapter 1. Nevertheless, there are practical reasons for continuing to make use of 'globalization' and 'antiglobalization' as shorthand reference to the complex dynamics of world developments. For one thing, these terms dominate the theoretical discourse in the field. For another, both terms do make reference to, and allow for a description of, several important dimensions of analysis both in regard to structural change and the forces of resistance against this change—against the forces that drive the system forward. In these terms, globalization has the appearance of a process that is irresistible, inevitable and inescapable—all countries and people having to adjust to it the best way they can, to insert themselves into the process under the most favourable conditions or to make the best deal possible.

This book explores some of the macrodynamics of this process as well as some strategic and political responses to these dynamics. Appearances and arguments to the contrary, globalization is neither inevitable nor immutable. Diverse groups of people in an increasingly organized, albeit divided and fragmented, global civil society are coming together to mobilize the forces of resistance into an antiglobalization movement. This book deals with the political dynamics of this movement as they are played out on the world stage in Latin America and Asia.

Alternative Understandings: Development, Globalization and Imperialism?

In the post World War II period it is possible to identify diverse permutations of three alternative ways of understanding the fundamental dynamics of change in the world—*development, globalization and imperialism* (McMichael, 1996) Each of these terms can be constructed as a descriptive or analytical category, a tool for decoding what is happening in the world and providing a theoretical discourse for explaining it. In each case, reference is made there to a geopolitical or geoeconomic 'project' that is pursued as a means of advancing the interests of a particular social class or organized groupings of people—interests with which the agent of the project tends to identify. In these terms we can speak of these projects as *ideologies*—ideas used to mobilize action in a direction desired by the agent group. However, more often than not, these 'projects' (development, globalization, imperialism) have the appearance not of ideology but of a process driven forth by forces generated by the structure of the system. It is in these terms that social scientists of various disciplinary orientations enter the fray, providing alternative theoretical representations of the world—models for understanding the world and advancing change.

The Development Project

According to Wolfgang Sachs and his associates in the theory of postdevelopment (Sachs, 1992; Esteva and Prakash, 1998), the idea of 'development' was invented in the immediate post World War II context as a means of directing the future of those societies involved in the process of liberating themselves from the yoke of European colonialism. The aim, not to put too fine a point on it, was to prevent these societies from falling prey to the lure of communism. To this end, the capitalist powers at the time, at a summit meeting held at Bretton Woods, designed a world economic order that would promote the free movement of capital and tradeable goods in a global economy; and, to facilitate participation in this system, they instituted a programme of 'foreign aid'—providing thereby both development finance and technical assistance (see Chapter 2 below).

Over the next five decades the development process was advanced on the basis of diverse models designed to bring about the modernization and development of societies in the capitalist world. Generally speaking, in these models the major agency for this development was the private sector, which is to say, the capitalist corporations that dominated the world economy. However, in the Third World—the 'developing' countries on the South of a major (and growing) global divide in income and wealth—because of the relative weakness or absence of a capitalist class able to exercise this role the state (or rather, the government) was assigned the role of development agent. This role was facilitated with a policy regime of nationalization (of the means of social production), protection for domestic enterprises unable to withstand the competitive pressures of the world economy, access to public credit and subsidies, regulation of private economic activity and the international movement of capital, and the promotion of domestic industry via a policy of import substitution.

This model was functional in both theory and practice for close to three decades—from the late 1940s to the early 1970s when the world capitalist system underwent the conditions of a major crisis that exposed cracks that went to its very foundation. In the context of this crisis there emerged pressures, from the Left, for revolutionary change (directed by an alternative socialist project), and, from the Right, to abandon the development enterprise in favour of another—globalization.

Reeling from these political blows on the Left and the Right, the theoreticians and practitioners of international development went in a different direction—liberal reform of the system. In this direction, they launched the search for an alternative form of capitalist development—another paradigm—initiated not from above and the outside but from below and the inside—development that is participatory, more socially inclusive and equitable, and sustainable in terms of both the environment and livelihoods. By 1990 this search for 'an other development' had grown into a worldwide movement that was advanced with the participation of a myriad of nongovernmental organizations in partnership with those governments and international organizations that stayed with the development project.

The Globalization Project

The idea of 'development' was predicated on identifiable improvements in the socioeconomic conditions lived by a larger part of the world's population and the corresponding changes in the structure of institutionalized practices needed to bring about these improvements. However, the threat of a major economic crisis in the process of capital accumulation gave rise to an alternative project to activate the accumulation and economic growth process. The project was designed to facilitate the renovation of the Bretton Woods world economic order on the basis of a programme of structural adjustments in the macroeconomic policies pursued by the governments in the world capitalist system.

The 'new economic model' (neoliberal capitalist development) was designed to create a global economy in which both the major factors of production—capital, technology (not labour)—and the social product liberated from the constraints and regulatory apparatus of the state, creating, in the process, an economy of free trade and the free movement of capital. The free market, rather than the state, was conceived of as the motor of this globalization process and the private sector was its driving force.

Under the aegis of the new economic model government after government was encouraged or induced to adopt a programme of macroeconomic policies designed to arrest and reverse the development process under way. In this programme the policy of nationalizing the strategic industries and setting up strategic state enterprises was replaced with a policy of privatization—turning over or selling state enterprises to the private sector in the local or global economy. The state in this process was downsized in favour of an expanded private sector and a retreating state was replaced with a strengthened 'civil society.' The regulation of private enterprise and economic activity was replaced with a policy of deregulation and the movement of both investment capital and trade was liberalized, undoing the protectionist measures adopted under the old economic model. The end product of this process, in theory, was the reactivation of the global accumulation process and conditions of economic growth. Those countries able to participate in the process—to integrate into the global economy, to participate in the process of productive transformation and technological conversion—would share in the anticipated prosperity.

   The economic globalization project also has a political dimension. At the structural level, the process entails a weakening of the nation-state and the search for new forms of international governance—and political control of the forces of resistance unleashed in the globalization process. The political dynamics involved in this process are explored in some detail by various authors below, particularly in Part III. At the root of these dynamics is a widespread and growing disaffection from the neoliberal form of globalization by different groups and classes within an emerging global civil society (see Chapter 8 below). One of the few generalizations that has stood the test of time since the structural adjustment program (SAP) was instituted is that globalization has few beneficiaries and many victims. Globalization has resulted in the growth of islands of prosperity within a growing sea of immiseration—the sprouting of super-rich billionaires at one social pole and the ravages of growing poverty on the other. Under these conditions, the globalization process has given rise to an antiglobalization movement of growing proportions. This movement has been organized to mobilize the forces of resistance—forces based on a growing disenchantment with the negative social, economic impacts of globalization. Chapters 9 to 11 explore the political dynamics involved.

Neoimperialism in Theory and Practice

Globalization, as the authors of this volume, conceive of it, is a project designed to serve the economic interests of what has been termed the 'transnational capitalist class' (Sklair, 2001). The precondition for this process, for advancing these interests, is a structural adjustment of the economy—structural reforms in the macroeconomic policies pursued by governments in the so-called Third World. These reforms, as it turns out, are designed to open up these economies to the forces of the 'free market' and the competitive pressures of the global economy. To the degree that the end result of this process is the domination of these economies by the forces wielded by the transnational capitalist class some radical political economists have written of 'neoimperialism.' The 'old imperialism' in this context had two centres of reference—one economic, the other military and political. One was a system of international exchange or 'trade' based on the exchange of raw materials and commodities, produced on the margins or periphery of the world capitalist system, for goods manufactured in the centre of this system. The other is a system of direct political domination based on military occupation and direct control of the state apparatus in the dominated societies by political and military forces of the imperial state. This form of imperialism has had a long and inglorious history but after World War II it was substantially replaced by imperialism in economic form—the domination of the subjugated economies in the Third World by the agents of economic power such as the transnational corporations (TNCs), the International Monetary Fund (IMF) and other 'international financial institutions' (IFIs).

   In the context of this 'development' a number of analysts have turned away from a theoretical discourse on imperialism and started to write of the emergence of a 'post-imperialist' period or even of an 'empire without imperialism' (Hardt and Negri, 2000). However, in the same context, other analysts have drawn attention to a growing trend towards the resurgence of a new form of what once was the 'old imperialism'—the projection of military force and political power by the imperial state. Chapters 1 and 3 elaborate on the political dynamics of this projection of political and military power in the context of what could well be (and is) termed 'the new imperialism.'

The Dynamics of Globalization and Antiglobalization

Chapter 1 provides an introduction to the *discourse* on 'globalization'—alternative ways of writing about the term and associated forms of thought and practice. Various analytical and ideological (theoretical and political) uses and misuses of globalization, understood alternatively as a geopolitical megaproject or as the ideology of corporate capital, are discussed. Several lines of discussion are brought into focus and pursued. One surrounds the claim that 'globalization' is a new phenomenon; another is that the state has become an anachronism; and a third is that the technological revolution is the main impetus behind globalization. We argue, to the contrary, that the concept of globalization obscures more than it reveals; that the macrodynamics of the world economy can best be understood through an analysis of the active role of the imperial state and the opening up of overseas opportunities via the projection of power, economic, political and military; and that developments associated with the new information technology are subordinate to more important developments. These are better grasped with the concept of imperialism.

Chapter 2 explores the dynamics of development and globalization associated with overseas development assistance (ODA) or, in more common parlance, foreign aid. At issue here are bilateral or multilateral transfers of technical assistance and development finance as well as resource transfers administered by organizations such as the World Bank. This chapter focuses on the leading role of the World Bank in this regard. The role of the World Bank, it is argued, is not so much to transfer these resources, providing sources of development finance, as it is to secure the ideological and political conditions for a process of renewed capital accumulation on a global scale.

James Petras, in Chapter 3, provides an alternative perspective on the issue of globalization, viewing it as an ideology and a political project designed to advance the interests of economic and political power—of what he terms the 'new American empire.' In this context, he advances an analysis of developments that have succeeded the events of September 11, 2001. As Petras sees it, the critical issue here is the strategy designed by officials in the administration of George Bush, Jr, to offset the decline in economic and political power of the US and to re-establish its hegemony over the world economic system. Key features of this strategy are a unilateral approach to international actions and an increasing reliance on aggressive military force—a strategy of open-ended war that makes maximum use of the events of September 11 and the targeting of 'international terrorism' as pretexts for the projection of imperial power. The contradictory features of this strategy are exposed by Petras, as are the challenges and opportunities that it provides for the antiglobalization movement.

Part II of the book is organized as a series of case studies into the macrodynamics of globalization and imperialism. The opening chapter 4 by John Saxe-Fernández and Gian Carlo Delgado-Ramos brings a historical perspective to the structural adjustment programme, which, it is argued, is designed to facilitate the globalization process. The authors examine in some detail the regional dynamics of this process in the case of Mexico, once a favoured 'model' of how to implement the structural adjustment programme. Focusing on Mexico's oil industry Saxe-Fernández and Delgado-Ramos analyse the workings of the World Bank both in regard to shaping economic policy in Mexico—constituting, in effect, a species of co-government—and the pillaging of the country's productive resources, particularly in the strategically important oil industry.

Like chapters 2 and 4, chapter 5 highlights the role of the World Bank but it does so in regards to its ten-year plus campaign for labour reform to facilitate thereby the adjustment of workers across the world to the idea and reality of globalization—having them accept it as a necessary evil if not a social good. Globalization, in this context, serves as an *ideology*, a set of beliefs designed to mobilize action towards a desired goal in the interest of a specific and definable social group—an emerging 'transnational capitalist class,' to use the terminology of Leslie Sklair (1997). Both this ideology and the process of labour reforms associated with it are examined critically in the Latin American context.

George Schuyler, in Chapter 6, traces out the divergent development paths pursued by the governments of Cuba and Venezuela in the context of globalization. The diverse outcomes of the alternative strategies pursued in this process are examined with specific reference to policies and social conditions in the health sector. Specifically, Schuyler explores the impact of neoliberal reforms on the health of Venezuelans and Cubans during the 1980s and 1990s. Through the lens of health care, he shows how global economic forces influence development processes at the national level and people's lives. Both countries struggled with severe economic crises during the 1980s and 1990s and their health systems suffered. The Cuban state, however, was able to preserve a greater degree of control over its adjustment process and thus has maintained a relatively good health care system. Venezuela, on the other hand, embraced neoliberal policies prescribed by the World Bank, the IMF and other international financial institutions. In this circumstance it failed to adequately protect its health care system and lost its autonomy under similar conditions to those analysed by Saxe-Fernández and Delgado-Ramos in Chapter 4.

Paul Bowles, in Chapter 7 elaborates on the response of several governments to the forces of globalization in a specific regional context—that of East Asia and China. He argues that the regional dynamics of these developments provide paradigmatic options open to governments both in Asia and elsewhere. These options are briefly but critically reviewed.

In Part III the analytic focus of the book shifts away from the dynamics of national development to the politics of antiglobalization—the forces of opposition and resistance mobilized by diverse forms of civil society organizations. The central issue here is 'antiglobalization'—to be precise, a new, more humane, form of globalization? There are a number of unresolved theoretical and political issues at play. What is the character and strength of the social forces of opposition and resistance to globalization? What is the social base of the movement involved? In what direction are the available forces of resistance and opposition mobilized? And by what type of organization and with what consequences and outcomes? What is the scope of changes involved—reform of the existing worldwide system (and the associated process of capital accumulation) or social transformation—a radical overhaul of this system? What are the political dynamics of this process?

Noam Chomsky, in Chapter 8, reflects on the political dynamics of power and ideology associated with the globalization project. He examines these dynamics in the context of events that have unfolded over the past year since 9/11, with particular reference to the concentration and projection of power in the United States, both state and private. In these reflections he also discusses the implications of this projected power for both the prospect of a new general world war and the possibilities for opposition and dissent.

Adam David Morton, in Chapter 9, explores the political dynamics of the antiglobalization Movement from a Gramscian perspective. From this perspective, he grapples with some of the crucial facets of neoliberal globalization and the recent politics of resistance. He does so by metaphorically presenting two questionable views of globalization. First, should globalization be regarded as a *juggernaut*—a vehicle on an inexorable path toward consolidating particular social, political and economic priorities? Or secondly, can it be better understood as a *jalopy*—subject to breakdown or being hijacked and thus more open to contestation. Undermining the presumption of inexorability may help to demystify globalization and reveal the jalopy behind the juggernaut. This is, in effect, what he sets out to do. Hence, after briefly sketching the understanding of globalization that underpins his argument in this regard, he questions the strategy and tactics of recent resistances to neoliberal globalization and draws several tentative conclusions from this activism. He also addresses several questions about the broader implications for the study and practice of resistance to globalization. In his approach to these questions Morton locates the dilemmas of political agency within a historical context and emphasizes a normative agenda for the search of alternative futures to the present world order.

In the concluding chapter it is argued that the antiglobalization movement is by no means monolithic. In fact it is divided at the fundamental level of an envisioned alternative and in terms of the strategy and tactics of struggle. The prospects for unifying the highly diverse social forces of opposition and resistance are not clear but they do not appear to be good. For one thing, the agents of globalization operate in different ways in diverse contexts. The international financial (and Bretton Woods) institutions, such as the World Bank and the World Trade Organization (WTO), may share a strategic interest with both the multi- or trans-national corporations that dominate the world economy and the organizations that repres ent the club of rich and powerful nation-states, but the dynamic effects of their 'operations' are different and should not be lumped together. Likewise, the social base of the antiglobalization movement is composed of diverse groups and classes, whose strategic interests intersect on some issues but diverge on others. The antiglobalization movement is also divided as to strategic direction, ultimate goal and the appropriate forms of struggle. In this connection, the actions associated with the urban-centred, middle class based antiglobalization protest movement in the North cannot be equated with the struggles of the indigenous communities and peasant producers in the South, nor even with the anti-IMF/structural adjustment/globalization protest movements in the urban centres of Latin America and elsewhere in the South. The large and growing global divide in incomes and productive resources is not easily overcome with the formation of a global antiglobalization movement. Many issues arise and need to be resolved but, first of all, the dynamics of both globalization and antiglobalization need to be more clearly understood. It is to this purpose that this book is written and put together. Although no definitive conclusions are reached, the critical issues involved are brought into analytical focus and theoretical perspective.

In short, the collection of essays that make up the book provides critical reflections on the epoch-defining changes that are sweeping the world today—the dynamics of globalization and antiglobalization. It is hoped that these essays will help dispel the fog of confusion brought in by the sweeping winds of 'globalization.' What is in a word—globalization? In this book, it is argued, it is both nothing and everything.

PART I

THE THEORY AND PRACTICE OF GLOBALIZATION

PART I

THE THEORY AND PRACTICE OF
GLOBALIZATION

Chapter One

World Development: Globalization or Imperialism?

James Petras and Henry Veltmeyer

Many writers have argued that we have entered a new era characterized by globalization, the driving force of epoch-defining changes in the nature of societies and economies across the world, resulting in the creation of an interdependent system. This notion of globalization has become a part of the everyday discourse in academia and among policymakers. It serves as a point of reference and a framework of ideas for the analysis of macro and micro socioeconomic developments and of the process that gave rise to them. The notion of 'globalization' spans the ideological spectrum and crosses academic disciplines. Even trenchant critics of the dominant discourse have been constrained to adopt the term and, in the process, tacitly accept its presuppositions.

The very pervasiveness of the notion of globalization points towards a problem. Not only does it reflect the presence of a fundamental paradigm, a worldview that structures the thinking and practice of most scholars in the field, it also suggests the working of an ideology that obfuscates reality. Although globalization is presented as an *economic* process, a paradigm for describing and explaining worldwide trends, it is better viewed as a *political* project, a desired outcome that reflects the interplay of specific socio-economic interests. We argue that 'globalization' provides an inadequate description and understanding of worldwide trends and developments. More useful in this regard are the concept of imperialism, a notion that is currently a minority view, but one that is beginning to gain attention from scholars, including some former supporters of the Vietnam War (Chalmers, 2000).

In the process of critically analysing the notion of globalization, and supporting the greater intellectual relevance of the concept of imperialism, we proceed first by critically discussing the presuppositions and claims of globalization theorists. Then we will proceed towards a systematic critique of globalization theory. This is followed by an argument in support of an alternative way of understanding worldwide trends and developments based on the concept of 'imperialism.'

The Origin and Rise of Globalization Theory

What is globalization? The term has been used in a multiplicity of senses. For some writers it refers to an increasing number of events and developments taking place simultaneously in more than one country—in an increasing number and range of countries worldwide (Stalker, 2000). For others globalization implies something beyond similarity. They argue that these trends and developments are connected and that there is a steady multiplication and intensification of links and flows among discrete national entities—a higher level of organization and integration into one system. For a few writers, the term tends to be used loosely to refer to a broad range and great variety of processes and trends, some of which, such as privatization and liberalization, are increasingly escaping control by the nation-state, reflecting a new level of capitalist development in a new set of supranational institutions which have replaced the nation-state (Griffin and Rahman Khan, 1992; Burbach and Robinson, 1999).

The notion of globalization contains a description and explanation of processes and trends that hitherto unfolded at the national level but that over the past few decades have spilled beyond the boundaries of the nation-state. In its most general sense 'globalization' refers to the upsurge in direct investment and the liberalization and deregulation in cross-border flows of capital, technology and services, as well as the creation of a global production system—a new global economy. It is in this sense that the term was apparently coined in 1986, in the context of the eighth Round of GATT negotiations (Ostry, 1990). For the theorists of this process and its many advocates these flows, both in scope and depth, together with the resulting economic integration and social transformation, have created a new world order with its own institutions and configurations of power that have replaced the previous structures associated with the nation-state, and that have created new conditions of people's lives all over the world, including a greater interconnectedness (Giddens, 1990; Holm and Sørensen, 1995; Rosenau, 1990; Therborn, 2000).

Globalization as a New Phenomenon?

There are several points of dispute about this process, particularly as to whether it represents something 'new,' a qualitatively different phase in the evolution and development of capitalism, a new epoch, or simply the latest and not necessarily most significant phase in a long historical process.

This issue has both a conceptual and empirical dimension. On the one side it is argued that the trends and developments associated with globalization cannot be equated with the evidence of the internationalization of economic intercourse and the flow of goods, capital and labour during the late 19th century. Several studies have documented that the flows capital, goods and labour were higher in the period leading up to the First World War than during the last half of the 20th century (Dicken, 1992). However, advocates of globalization argue that the earlier forms of this internationalization were not accompanied by anywhere near the same degree of economic integration and that it did not result in the creation of an integrated global production system.

As for the new global economy formed over recent decades the driving forces were different. The entire process of change, globalization theorists argue, has been underpinned by accelerated technological progress, mediated by the growing role of transnational corporations and facilitated by the deregulation and liberalization of markets all over the world (Griffin and Rahman Khan, 1992: 59-66). The difference between the past and the present, these theorists assert, is in the technological conditions of this globalization (a revolution in communications technology); its relevant institutional and policy framework (free market reforms, structural adjustment measures); and the degree of systemic integration. The neoliberal programme of structural adjustments and policy reforms of the post world war period were designed, and have served, to liberalize the international flow of capital, goods and services, technology and information. In addition, they have worked to deregulate the associated economic environments and markets.

The Myth of the Third Technological-Industrial Revolution

If indeed we were living in a new global economy based on the new information technologies, we would expect the introduction of those technologies to have a significant impact on productivity growth. In the past, during the first and second industrial revolutions, when steam power, electricity, and the internal combustion engine were introduced, productivity showed a marked increase. To speak of the information revolution means that the innovations have had a profound effect in stimulating new productive investments, more productive utilization of capital and new ways of stimulating output per capital investment. A comparison of productivity growth in the United States over the past half-century fails to support the argument of the proponents of a Third Scientific Industrial Revolution (TSIR). Between 1953 and 1973 productivity grew on an average of 2.6 percent; between 1972-1995 productivity grew a mere 1.1 percent (Wolfe, 1999: 10).

The 'information revolution' clearly did not revolutionize production. In fact, it failed to even sustain the previous levels of productivity and was not able to counteract the tendencies to capitalist stagnation that have been operative since the 1970s. Some advocates of the TSIR argue that the real 'take off,' of the information revolution should be dated from the mid-1990s, citing the productivity growth of 2.2 percent between the last quarter of 1995 and the first quarter of 1999. While this figure is substantially greater than the rate of productivity between 1992 and 1995 it is still below the growth data for the 1953-1973 period. Moreover, it is very questionable whether the increase in productivity can be attributed to the technological revolution. A recent article by Robert Gordon, which analyses an increase in productivity between 1995 and 1999, raises serious doubts about the TSIR claims (Gordon, 1999). He argues that almost 70 percent of the improvement in productivity can be accounted for by improved measurements of inflation (lower estimates of inflation necessarily mean higher growth of real output, thus productivity) and the response of productivity to the exceptionally rapid output growth over the three-year period. Thus, only one third of the 1 percent gain in productivity made during the 1995-99 period can be attributed to computerization or the so-called 'information revolution'—hardly a revolution (Gordon, 1999).

Even more devastating for the advocates of the TSIR, Gordon provides a convincing argument that most of the increase in productivity attributed to computerization is in the manufacturing of computers! The dramatic improvements in productivity claimed by the TSIR apologists are largely in the production of computers, with little effect on the rest of the economy. According to Gordon's study, productivity growth in the production of computers has increased from 18 percent a year between 1972 and 1995 to 42 percent a year as of 1995. As Gordon sees it, this accounts for all the improvements in productivity growth in durable goods. In other words, the computer has brought about a 'revolution' in the production of computers, having an insignificant effect on the rest of the economy. The basic reason is that computers have simply substituted for other forms of capital. According to a recent study, growth in computer inputs exceeded those in other inputs by a factor of 10 in the 1990-96 period (Jorgenson and Stiroh, 1999). The substitution of one form of capital for another need not raise productivity in the economy as a whole. The basic measure of a technological revolution is what the authors call 'multi-factor productivity,' the increase in output per unit of all outputs.

The basic question posed by TSIR theorists is not over whether computers have revolutionized the production of computers but how the so-called 'information revolution' has affected the other 99 percent of the economy. According to Gordon's longitudinal study of technical progress covering the period between 1887 and 1996, the period of maximum technical progress as manifested in annual multi-factor productivity growth was in the period from 1950 to 1964, when it reached approximately 1.8 percent. The period of lowest multifactor productivity growth in this century was from 1988 to 1996—approximately 0.5 percent growth! (Gordon, 1999).

Clearly the innovations in the early and middle 20th century were far more significant sources of economy-wide productivity improvement than the electronic, computerized information systems of late.

Computer manufacturers account for 1.2 percent of the US economy and only 2.0 percent of capital stock (Wolfe, 1999: 10). While corporations spend substantial amounts on computers it is largely to replace old ones. There is no evidence to back up the claims of the advocates of TSIR. There has been no such thing as the Third Scientific Industrial Revolution—at least by any empirical measure of increased productivity in the US economy. Despite the vast increase in the use of computers, the productivity performance of the US economy remains far below the levels achieved in the pre-computer age of 1950 to 1972. In fact, annual multifactor productivity growth (AMPG) between 1988 and 1996 is the lowest of the last 50 years (Gordon, 1999). Even more significantly, according to Gordon, the rate of growth between 1950 and 1996 has been steadily declining: from 1950 to 1964 AMPG grew approximately 1.8 percent; from 1964 to 1972 it grew 1.4 percent; from 1972 to 1979 it grew 1.1 percent; from 1979 to 1988 it grew 0.7 percent and from 1988 to 1996, 0.6 percent.

The claim of the NSIRs related to a new capitalist era has no basis in any purported third scientific information revolution. On the contrary, one could argue that the new information systems might have a negative effect on productivity insofar as they draw a disproportionate amount of capital away from more productive activities and feed into and reinforce 'service' activities, such as financial speculative investments, that hinder productivity growth. At a minimum one could argue that the new information systems are not likely to counteract the long-term systemic propensity towards crisis. We can also argue that rather than being the wellspring of productivity, or the determinant of capitalist growth, the new information systems are subordinate elements of a larger configuration of capitalist institutions—particularly financial—that influence their use and application.

The myth of the new Revolutionary Information Age of capitalism, however, has served several political uses. First, it is an attempt to put an intellectual 'technological' gloss on the imperial expansion of Euro-American capitalism. The driving force of what is dubbed 'globalization' is imputed to the 'revolutionary' consequences of electronic information systems that operate across national boundaries. The information systems approach renders the old Marxist categories of capitalist expansion-imperialism obsolete. The dominance of the new international information systems, according to TSIR, creates a 'global economy'—a new global phase of capitalist development. Since we have argued that no such 'technological revolution' has in fact taken place, at least as it affects the growth of the productive forces, what can we make of the arguments for a 'global economy' and 'global corporations'—ambiguous terms that mask the relations of power in the world economy.

At issue in the overseas expansion of Euro-American capital was the need to counteract, and undo, institutional arrangements that were formed in the post-war context of an east-west cold war; movements of national liberation and the desalinization of a large part of the so-called 'Third World;' and a labour and capital accord (social contract), supported by the institutions and policies of a Keynesian state in the North and a developmentalist state in the South (Arrighi, 1994: Marglin and Schor, 1990). Under conditions of an economic and fiscal crisis that beset the system as a whole in the late 1960s and early 1970s, the sweeping reforms of the New Economic Model (Bulmer-Thomas, 1996) brought about a counter-revolution in theory and practice, and with it the subversion of the post war world order—and the new Euro-American empire dubbed by then President Bush the New World Order (NWO).

The Inevitability of Globalization?

Globalization, according to its advocates, has ushered in a new era of late or post-capitalist development, the economic and political dynamics of which have become focal points of a broad range of studies from diverse perspectives (Kenen, 1994). So entrenched has this notion of globalization become that even its many critics have succumbed to the suggestion, or claim, that the process is inevitable and thus inescapable in its effects. Accepting this claim some critics argue that the best and only 'realistic option'—as Casteñeda (1993) has put it—is to enter into the globalization process under the most favourable conditions available and to adjust to its requirements as needed or possible. This position is most clearly articulated in the World Bank's 1995 *World Development Report*. Among others Keith Griffin, by no means an uncritical globalist, allows for no possible alternative to an adjustment to what cannot be avoided or changed (Bienefeld, 1995; Griffin, 1995). Against clear evidence to the contrary presented by the United Nations Development Programme (UNDP) with which he is himself associated, Griffin sees a trend towards convergence, which is creating opportunities for some developing countries to participate in the fruits of development engendered by globalization. In this connection, Griffin adopts a view held not only by the economists at the World Bank but by most sceptics and critics of globalization.[1]

Globalization and the Nation-State

The claim of globalization theory about the growing irrelevance of nation-state has also been widely accepted, even by critics. They see globalization as tending to displace the role of the state as the institution creating the conditions of capital accumulation as well as the regulation of capital. Scholars as diverse as Stalker (2000), who provides an ILO perspective on globalization, and Drucker, articulate the widely held mainstream view that globalization has ushered in a new post-capitalist form of development. They argue that the nation-state has retreated from the development process and been replaced by what Robinson conceptualizes as the 'internationalized state' (Robinson, 1996: 363-80). Some scholars in this connection more plausibly argue for a new system of global governance, a set of institutions that can secure the regulatory conditions of political stability for a global capital accumulation process.[2]

However, not everyone has accepted this notion of a powerless state, unable to resist the erosion of its economic role. Some 'realist' analysts of the political dimension of the 'globalization' process continue to see the nation-state as a major actor in international relations and its substantive conditions (Holm and Sorenson, 1995). Similarly, the notion of a powerless state, whose role and weight in the economy has been diminished by forces of globalization, has been seriously challenged (Weiss, 1998). Nevertheless, the prevailing view in academia is that the regulatory powers of the nation-state, and its capacity to make policy, have been seriously compromised and are giving way to a new set of supra-national institutions for managing the process or for securing 'good governance' (Boyer and Drache, 1996).

Globalization in Theory: an Epoch-Defining Shift or Capitalism as Usual?

Supporters of the neoliberal order and the associated Washington Consensus (Williamson, 1990) come in two varieties, as do its critics. Among the globalists there remain hard-line voices in favour of an entrenched neoliberal form of free market capitalism such as Shepard (1997: 38-40) and the World Bank (1992). However, the dominant approach is to take the pillars of the neoliberal order, its institutional framework and enabling policy framework, as a given but to recognize the need for a social dimension and to give the development process a 'human face.' The ILO,[3] the UN's Economic Commission for Latin America and the Caribbean (ECLAC) and associates of the Washington based Institute for International Economics typify this approach. However even the IMF has softened its views proposing reforms to the neoliberal model and redesigning the Structural Adjustment Program (Salop, 1992).

Critics of the NWO can also be put into two camps. First, there are those concerned with the social dimensions of the globalization process. They tend to focus their criticisms on the uneven distribution of its socioeconomic benefits— and at times its underlying agenda of corporate capitalism. Amongst these reformist critics can be found intellectuals such as Korten (1995) and other participants in the PCD-Forum, a consortium of international NGOs that have constituted themselves as a watchdog of the World Bank, the WTO and other guardians of the New World order. Also ranged within this spectrum of liberal reformers are the diverse participants in the antiglobalization Alternative Forum (Griffin and Khan, 1992), associated with the UNDP and its concept of 'human development'; Ghai and others with UNRISD (1994) and its concern with the social dimensions of the adjustment process; and Marshall Wolfe (1996), a voice for the Economic Commission for Latin America and the Caribbean (ECLAC).

The reformist critique of the NWO and the process involved in bringing it about—globalization—focus on the fundamental inequalities and inequities in the distribution of society's productive resources and fruits of development as a major problem. Most recognize as does Sengenberger, Director of the ILO's Employment Strategy Department that it is the workers who as a class bear a disproportionate share of the social costs of adjustment. To redress this fundamental market-generated inequity, reformist critics of the NWO, for the most part, turn to a Keynesian state-led form of capitalist development, based on a selectively interventionist and socially reformist state.

These reformers argue for a social dimension to development—to alleviate the worst effects of an inevitable process and to protect the poor and other vulnerable groups. They propose a turn towards social liberalism, a reformed neoliberalism, and appeal to the institutions of global capital to reform themselves. In this context, critics also appeal to an emergent 'global civil society' coalescing around a global network of international Nongovernmental Organizations (NGOs).

While this school of thought introduces a reformist agenda, it still embraces the idea that there is no alternative to capitalism, the NWO, and the globalization process. Having accepted the idea that there is no alternative, the issue becomes how best to adapt and to insert economies and societies into the process. The issue becomes: what are the most favourable conditions available in order to strike the best deal possible through direct pressure and negotiated concessions? The solution is what Griffin and Khan, Casteñeda and others see as the only 'realistic option.'

A second group of critics share a Marxist understanding of the nature and macro-dynamics of the international capitalist system, although 'Marxism' here takes diverse forms.

These critics work from very different theories of the macro-dynamics of post war capitalism and its propensity towards crisis. The general view is that there *is* an alternative to the existing order and the globalization process and that it should be sought in political terms.

The writers associated with *Monthly Review* (MacEwan, 1999; Magdoff, 1992; Sivadandan and Meiksins Wood, 1997; Sweezy, 1997; Tabb, 1997) view globalization as an obfuscating myth, an analysis of an imperialist centred international economy. Another group of left scholars (Du Boff, 1997) view globalization as the latest phase in a long historical process, representing an epochal shift in the nature of capitalism, and as such a systemic (or political) response to the crisis that beset world capitalism in the late 1960s and early 1970s (Amin, 1994; Brenner, 2000; Laibman, 1997; Welder and Rigby, 1996).

In this connection, we propose the concept of imperialism as an alternative explanatory framework of international capitalist expansion and the growing inequalities, and for describing and explaining the process—the concentration of power, property and income in the international system.

Globalization or Imperialism?

The term 'globalization' not only serves as description and explanation of what is going on. It refers even more so to a prescription—that certain developments, particularly 'the liberalization of national and global markets,' will produce 'the best outcome for growth and human welfare' and that they are in everybody's interest (World Bank, 1995). In this connection, the notion of globalization is clearly based not on science but on ideology, a manifesto, as it were, of advanced capitalism in which it serves as a shorthand reference to developments and outcomes that are deemed to be highly desirable.

In this connection, the problem is how to generate the requisite support and the 'political will' needed to implement the required reforms and policies. The World Bank, in particular, has assumed responsibility in this area, arrogating to itself the task of ensuring that governments all over the world adjust to the requirements of Euro-American multinational corporations and their states.[4]

Another issue in this connection is how to differentiate between reality and appearance. In appearance, there is an unfolding of trends that are leading towards increased integration into one world system. In the process, the nation-state is weakened, hollowed out, forced to retreat from the process of national development and surrender its decision-making power to a new set of international institutions The reality, however, is otherwise. The state in the Third World actively intervenes to subsidize and attract capital, reduce the role of organized labour, etc. The imperial state bails out banks, investors and speculators and provides political pressure to open markets, sends military expeditions to eliminate alternatives.

Within the frameworks of both concepts, that of globalization and imperialism, repeated reference is made to the dramatic increase of the international flow of capital, particularly in the form of FDI; an associated process of mergers and acquisitions; and the restructuring of capital, viz. its shift towards developing countries, particularly Latin America.[5] However, the economic restructuring associated with the so-called 'globalization' process not only has shifted the conditions of a systemic crisis from the North to the South, with a resulting deterioration of economic conditions all across the South and an economic recovery in the North, but has led to a greater concentration of ownership of the world's productive resources. In this connection, Fortune's top 100 Transnational Corporations (TNCs), 80 percent of which are based in the United States or Western Europe have dramatically increased their control of the world economy (Petras and Veltmeyer, 1999). The bulk of technological innovations and direct investments, as well as international trade, are under the direct control of these multinationals, the principal units of Euro-American imperialism. In addition, the 1990s saw a dramatic increase in the take-over, and recolonization, of the strategic sectors of many economies, particularly in Latin America, which, over the course of the decade, took over from East Asia the position of major destination for the growing international flow of productive and speculative capital in the Third World. The growth of direct and equity investment flows is only one, albeit a central, part of the mechanisms of a new resurgent imperialism, a means of securing US hegemony (Petras and Veltmeyer, 2000). Also involved are the dynamics and growing integration of world capital markets and the transnationalization of trade.

A recent empirical comparative study by Doremus, Kelley, Pauly and Reich of US, German and Japanese TNCs found that on the vital issues of investment, research and development the great majority of decisions were taken in the national headquarters of the TNCs (Doremus, et al., 1998: Ch. 5). With regard to research and development (R&D) of US-based TNCs they show that 88 percent of the total R&D expenditures are made in the 'home' country, and only 12 percent of majority owned affiliates overseas. Technology development remains centralized in the national headquarters of the TNCs. In the other key area of TNC strategy, direct investment decisions and intra-firm trade, the authors find that the priorities of nation headquarters predominate. The authors' findings and conclusions refute the myth of the 'global' multi- or transnational corporations demonstrating their ties to the nation-state and their centralized nation-centred decision-making structure. While the TNCs locate production in many countries and divide up operations and production in multiple sites, control and profits are centralized within nation-states. Expansion and control by TNCs has not changed their enduring links to nation-states; nor have their international operations transformed their centralized empire building character. The process of international political and economic expansion and its associated trends and developments has more to do with the dynamics of political and economic power than the transformative effects of new technology. If there is a driving force to the process it relates to the political and military victories of overseas expansionary social classes and political leaders over their nationalist and collectivist adversaries.

An Alternative Perspective

Globalism as a perspective is deficient at a number of levels and with regards to a number of critical issues. First, as we have seen it is clearly mistaken to view globalization in terms of linear progress based on the introduction of revolutionary technologies and, in these terms to visualize a new form and phase of capitalist development. The process involved is cyclical rather than linear and, notwithstanding the caveats of globalists on this score, not particularly different or new. More to the point, the globalist perspective misreads or ignores the major macro-dynamics of the long-term capitalist development process. Whether viewed as a process or alternatively as a project, recent trends and developments can be better grasped in terms of an imperialist perspective.

In these terms, the resurgent international flow of capital, technology and trade in commodities and services that globalists make so much of is indicative of a process in which US and European capital has not only recovered from the crisis that beset it but that provided the mechanisms of a renewed hegemony. The trend-defining facts related to this process are not in dispute. The issue is how best to interpret them. In the 1990s, the dominant trend was for FDI and other forms of capital to relocate to areas of the world where the spoils are greater—the developing countries of East Asia and, vis-à-vis the United States, Latin America.

The privately owned capitalist corporations that dominate the process are far from being stateless. On the contrary, their headquarters are located either in the United States or in Western Europe. Further, these TNCs have not escaped the regulatory powers of the nation state. They are supported and led by states that not only pave the way for their international operations but that continue to regulate their operations, working closely together with the TNCs to ensure their success in providing increased returns on invested capital. In this connection, the network of international institutions is an adjunct to the power exercised by the imperial state. The top officials of the World Bank and the IMF are always appointees of the United States for the former and Europe for the latter. Policies are always cleared with their home countries. In this context it is a serious mistake to view the state as obsolete, a hollowed out shadow of its former self, drastically reduced in its role and capacity. Rather, the state has been restructured in the interests of each country's TNCs and its neoimperialist agenda.

Retreat of the State or Resurgence of the Imperial State?

One of the myths of globalization, consumed by scholars across the ideological spectrum, is that it has led to the retreat of the state and a displacement of its former power vis-à-vis capital to an emerging set of supranational institutions at the service of capital. As Tabb (1997) constructs it, the idea of a powerless state vis-à-vis the globalization process is a powerful tool in the service of the status quo. In both intellectual and ideological terms, it gives support to the argument that the officials or occupants of the nation-state have lost control over the instruments of fundamental economic policy and that perforce they are unable to resist liberalizing pressures to open the national economy to the requirements of the imperial centres. The political implications of this position are momentous, dictating as it does the form of national politics and policy-making.

In practical or political terms, the idea of a powerless state not only ignores the continued capacity of the state to regulate capital but it totally ignores the role of the state as a major agency for imperialist expansion and the imperial as well as class character of the state at the centre of the system. The international circuits of capital and commodity flows are controlled by TNCs whose headquarters are based in the United States or Europe. Moreover globalization theorists tend to ignore or play down the political dynamics involved in opening markets, overthrowing recalcitrant nationalist regimes and invading countries.

The historical fact is that the countries in Africa, Asia and Latin America have had a long history of several centuries based on imperial ties and relations of exploitation with markets, exchanges and investments dominated by one imperial power or another. Both the current and earlier forms of internationalization in the flow of capital, technology, and trade in goods and services must be understood, and analysed, in this context.

Of late there has emerged a line of analysis that is not structural in approach. Indeed it is anti- or post-structural.[6] Through the optics of these studies the macro-dynamics of the capitalist system are not at issue. The issue *is* the subjective experience and actions of diverse agents—diverse ways of socially constructing, seeing and being in the world—and interpreting its microdynamics. The context for this form of interpretation is constituted in the search for a community-based and localized form of participatory development that is at once 'socially empowering' and 'transformative.' Advocates of this approach tend to either ignore external structures and processes or minimize their workings and impacts.

A major lacunae in this and other forms of discourse on globalization is in the area of class—an inability to understand (or deliberate avoidance of) the class character of the forces and institutions involved in what is taken as 'globalization.' One reason for this is the exaggerated focus on impersonal economic institutions. Today, class-based structures and relations operate on a world scale and in such a way that their 'objective effects' are clearly visible and recognized even by the defenders of the current world order (Shepard, 1997; World Bank, 1992). What we find today are the actions of a state-centred system in which the state, that of the US in particular, which in concert with the states of Western Europe, everywhere projects its political power in support of US capital and its project—the strategic take-over and recolonization of the of world economy and the national states tied to it. This project was advanced in the 1990s with dramatic results. By the end of the decade the United States emerged as a hegemonic force, the only super-power in political and military terms, and with strategic control of the major operating agencies of the imperialist system, the bearers of capital and technology and majority membership in the club of transnational corporations and financial institutions.

A survey published by the *Financial Times* (January 27, 1999) of the world's biggest companies based on their market capitalization shows that among the 500 biggest companies in the world, the United States accounts for 244, Japan 46, and Germany 23. Even if we aggregate all of Europe, the total number of dominant companies is 173, far fewer than those owned and controlled by the United States. Thus it is clear that European, not Japanese, capitalism remains as the only competitor to the United States for dominance in the world market. The acceleration of US economic power and the decline of Japan in the 1990s is manifest in the increasing number of US firms among the top 500, up from 222 to 244 and the precipitous decline of Japanese firms from 71 to 46 over the decade. This tendency will be accentuated over the next few years because US-based TNCs are buying out large numbers of Japanese enterprises as well as Korean, Thai, and other firms.

Looking at the largest 25 firms, those whose capitalization exceeds $86 billion, the concentration of US economic power is even greater: over 70 percent are American, 26 percent are European and four percent are Japanese. As for the top 100 companies, 61 percent are American, 33 percent are European and only two percent are Japanese. To the degree that the TNCs control the world economy, it is largely the United States, which has emerged as the overwhelmingly dominant power. Insofar as the very largest companies are the leading forces in buying out smaller companies through mergers and the fusion of capital we can expect the US-based TNCs to play a major role in the process of concentration and centralization of capital.

Conclusions

An important issue involved in academic debates focuses on how to view recent trends and developments in the world economy. As an *economic* process, impelled by dynamics of a system, or as a *political* project, the intentional outcome of a consciously pursued strategy (Aulakh and Schecter, 2000). In this connection, it has been said, globalization is not a 'monolithic, unstoppable juggernaut, but a complex web of interrelated processes,' some of which, as Stalker (2000: 10) notes, 'are subject to greater control than others.' In the same connection, international expansion of Euroamerican capital is not as so many see it: a process without a subject and as such irresistible in its logic and inescapable in its effects. To the extent that the international flows of capital, and commodities involves a process it has both a conscious direction and a political agenda: to promote the worldwide interests of a new class of transnational capitalists anchored in the US and Europe. This can best be understood as a form of empire building—imperialism.

The advocates of globalization theory argue for the inter-dependence of nations, the shared nature of their economies, the mutuality of their interests, the shared benefits of their exchanges (Keohane and Nye, 2000). Imperialism emphasizes the domination and exploitation by imperial states and their multinational corporations and banks of less developed states and labouring classes as well as international competition and cooperation among the rival imperial states and enterprises. In today's world it is clear that the imperial countries are hardly dependent on most of the Third World countries they trade with. They have diverse suppliers; the economic units operating are owned and operated in large part by stockholders in the imperial countries; and the profits, royalties, interest payments flow upward and outward in an asymmetrical fashion. Within the international financial institutions (IFIs) and other world bodies, the imperial countries wield disproportionate or decisive influence. On the other hand, the dominated countries are low wage areas, interest and profit exporters, virtual captives of the IFIs and highly dependent on limited overseas markets. Hence the imperial concept fits the realities much better than the assumptions that underlie the notion of globalization.

The concept of globalization relies heavily on diffuse notions of technological change accompanied by information flows and the abstract notion of 'market forces.' In contrast, the concept of imperialism sees the transnational corporations and banks, and the imperial states, as the driving force behind the international flows of capital and tradable commodities. A survey of the major events, world trade treaties, and regional integration themes quickly dispels any technological determinant explanations: it is the heads of the imperial states that establish the framework for global exchanges. Within that political shell the major transaction and organizational forms of capital movements are found in the TNCs, supported by the IFIs, whose personnel is appointed by the imperial states. Technological innovations operate within the parameters that further this configuration of power. The concept of imperialism thus gives us a more precise idea of the social agencies of worldwide movements of capital than the notion of globalization.

According to most advocates of 'globalization' theory we are entering a new epoch of interdependency in which stateless corporations transcend national frontiers, spurred by the third technological revolution and facilitated by the new information systems. According to this view the nation-state is an anachronism, the movements of capital are unstoppable and inevitable and the world market is the determinant of the macro-micro political economy.

The result, according to globalization theorists is a progressive, dynamic, modernizing world of prosperous nations. But the contrast between the premises and promises of globalization theorists and contemporary realities could not be starker. Instead of interdependent nations we have dramatic contrasts between creditor and debtor nations; multi-billion dollar corporations appropriating enterprises, interests royalties and trade surpluses while billions of workers and peasants reap poverty and miserable existences. Structurally we find that over 80 percent of the major TNCs control their investment, research and technology decisions out of their home offices in the United States, Germany and Japan. TNCs are based on worldwide operations but their control is centralized.

Notwithstanding the resistance of the globalists, their basic premises, viz. the claim of inevitability and the notion that it represents a novel development driven by technological change, are suspect. And the same can be said in regards to the denial of possible systemic alternatives to the dominant NWO. In this and other regards we can point to a clear divergence between the grand claims and meagre explanatory power of globalism as theory. In this context the notion of imperialism is a more useful tool for grasping the dynamics of the process.

Notes

1 These critics range from scholars of international relations or economic development such as Bello, Korten, Rosenau and participants in a series of anti-globalization forums and networks—the San Francisco based 'International Forum on Globalization;' the Bangkok based 'Focus on the Global South,' the 'PCD Forum,' the US-based '50 Years is Enough' network for global economic justice, the 'Third World Network,' and 'the Centre for the Study of Globalization and Rationalization' at the University of Warwick.

2 The political dynamics of this process have been the central concern of a number of studies sponsored or published by the US Council for Foreign Relations, such as Ostry, *Government and Corporations in a Shrinking World* (1990), its scholarly mouthpiece *Foreign Affairs* and the Washington based Institute for International Economics (for example, Kenen, 1994).

3 Werner Sengenberger, Director of the ILO's Employment Strategy Department and the ILO's Working Group on the Social Dimensions of Globalization and Liberalization of Trade (see Foreword to Stalker, 2000, pp. xii).

4 On the World Bank's strategy and its underlying ideology, particularly as relates to the world's workers see Veltmeyer (1997).

5 On the dynamics of this process see Petras and Veltmeyer (1999).

6 On the various permutations of this poststructuralist or postmodernist approach see Escobar (1995) and Esteva and Prakash (1998). For a critique of this approach see Veltmeyer (1997).

Chapter Two

Aid and Adjustment:
Policy Reform and Regression

James Petras and Henry Veltmeyer

From the outset the study of international economic development has been closely tied to questions about the need for, and the potential contributions of, what has become known as 'overseas development assistance' (ODA) or, in more common parlance, 'foreign aid.' Connected to the central question that has been raised in the literature about the link between development and aid are questions about the motivations behind the giving of aid, the link between aid and political power, and evaluations as to the positive and negative benefits to recipients. Within the debates that have surrounded these and other such questions, two analytical perspectives can be distinguished, each with numerous permutations, one based on what could be termed *realism*, the other *idealism*. In addition, there is a less scientific, more ideological tradition, with little or no reference made to substantive empirical findings or the need to explain the dynamics of ODA.

In this tradition the discourse on foreign aid takes the form not so much of description and explanation as policy prescription, with few references to donor motivations or the politics of aid, focusing instead on programme/project objectives and presumed benefits to recipient countries, and only loose abstracted reference to the analytical or evaluative literature and then only to seek justification for prescribed policies. It is in this tradition that we would place the 'essay' of Jan Pronk in a recent issue of *Development and Change*, although his ideas and theoretical perspective are suggestive of both idealism and structuralism.[1] In this tradition Pronk joins the countless aid bureaucrats called upon to write position papers that rehearse the all too familiar litany of World Bank (and IMF) doctrine: 'all developing countries' problems are internal; the aim of policy reform is to get the prices right and to roll back the government sector. This kind of reform, it is asserted, 'increases equity as well as efficiency' and 'conflict between stabilization and structural adjustment goals is minimal' (Mosley, et al., 1991: xvi).

ODA entails critical issues that from time to time surface in a seemingly never-settled academic and policy debate among liberals and structuralists, neoliberals and neostructuralists. To join this debate in its latest twist this chapter places aid in an alternative theoretical perspective, one based in part on a politically *realist* view of the process involved and in part on a critical perspective on the agency of bilateral and multilateral aid as well as the international flows of private capital. In this regard we reflect critically on the ideas advanced by Pronk and the community of policy makers and academics of which he is a part. In terms of these ideas, the issue is not whether aid contributes directly to the development process but its role in promoting and ensuring the adoption of neoliberal free market reforms. In this connection, we argue that if 'aid' is a catalyst of anything it is not of development but of regression. What are viewed as 'good policies' by both neoliberals and self-styled 'truly confident' social liberals (or idealists) like Paul Mosley (1991) and Jan Pronk in effect, if not by design, serve as an aid to imperialism, and they have served as such at a social cost borne primarily by people in the developing countries.

Aid as a Catalyst of Regression

The term 'foreign aid' is at best ambiguous, disguising more than it reveals. Bilateral and commercial loans, as well as loans from the international financial institutions (IFIs), require the payment of principal and interest. Even if interest rates on IFI loans are lower than those of the commercial banks, the onerous repayment conditions have had a devastating impact on policy-making in developing countries.

Jan Pronk argues that aid is not the prime mover of development but that it is a catalyst. However, the fundamental question is: a catalyst for what and for whom? For an answer to this question we turn to what could be termed a politically 'realist' approach to aid (Hayter, 1971; Magdoff, 1969). In this approach the role of aid is examined in its historical context, looking at how foreign aid is part of the arsenal of policy instruments used by aspiring hegemonic states to conquer markets and promote the interests of their capitalist classes against competitors and their nationalist and socialist opponents. The 'idealist' view, in contrast, conceives of aid as a disinterested policy, divorced from the interests of the capitalist class and guided by humanitarian concerns, democratic values and economic wellbeing. More often than not, idealists dissociate their discussion of aid from the historical-structural context in which it is embedded and argue in terms of normative values and the degree of compliance with those values by the recipient country.

There are two types of realist critics of the 'idealist' approach. Market fundamentalists like Milton Friedman (1982) condemn foreign aid because it is said to subsidize 'statism' and hinders market forces that are better able to deal with economic and social problems. Some critics, on the other hand, argue that 'aid' from hegemonic countries undermines Third World development by catalysing structural changes that undermine popular sovereignty, facilitate vast outflows of funds and undermine locally based productive units.

We adopt the *realist* perspective that foreign loans and grants are a catalyst of 'reverse aid'—designed to benefit the donor countries. In the context of widespread implementation of a neoliberal model of capitalist development, aid has contributed towards what could be termed 'bad governance' (neoauthoritarianism, large-scale chronic corruption and external subordination), extending and deepening social inequalities, and generating conditions of global poverty as well as economic stagnation and volatility in the international flows of capital.

Historical-Structural Context of Aid

In the colonial era, following the initial period of bloody conquest and pillage, the 'authorities' set about to combine 'normal' capitalist exploitation with foreign aid to educate and train a class of indigenous clients in the lower levels of the colonial administration and armed forces. The purpose was to maximize the extraction of surplus while reducing the level of conflict and the costs of empire. While the colonial state incurred these costs, private investors reaped the profits. The point is that 'aid' can only be understood in the context of pillage and exploitation—of extractive colonies and industrializing empires, of underdevelopment and development (Hayter, 1971; Magdoff, 1969). Aid, in this context, served as a catalyst for stabilizing imperial rule and facilitating the transfer of riches, with the overall result of what we call 'reverse aid'—net gain for the imperial country or centre at a cost borne by the colonies.[2]

The targets of aid were usually not the peons in the plantations and mines but local collaborators. The beneficiaries of aid were usually not some undifferentiated 'colony' or 'nation' but village chieftains, tribal leaders, landlords and, more recently, trained military officials. This colonial experience of conquest and aid raises several theoretical issues of continuing relevance. First, 'aid' subsumes commercial transactions beneficial to the 'donor' (or, more precisely, the colonial power). Secondly, the 'benefits' of aid to the recipient (colonized) countries are not equitably distributed among the different classes, social strata, gender-based or ethnic groups; most of it accrues to collaborators of the elite. Thirdly, the asymmetrical political and economic linkages between 'donors' and 'recipients' lead to long-term, large-scale transfers of wealth, property and power that favours donors, while the transfer of any benefits to recipient regimes is independent of the claims and perhaps 'good intentions' involved. Under the systemic forces (unequal power and exchange) at work, the class nature of the 'donor' regimes (the dominance of multinational corporations and financial institutions), the political-economic matrix of aid (protectionism and subsidies in the 'donor' country and 'neoliberalism' in the recipient country) and the subordinate nature of the recipient or client regime (macroeconomic policy dictated by IFI technocrats), foreign aid serves as a catalyst for aid reversal—a transfer of wealth to the 'donor countries.'

Neomercantilist Imperialism, Catalyst of Regression

While academics of the Left and Right write of 'neoliberalism' or 'free markets,' interstate relations between Europe and the US, on the one side, and the Third World and ex-Communist countries on the other, is characterized by neomercantilism. Euro-US state interventionist policies generally protect, subsidize and advance the interests of 'capital' while the so-called 'developing countries' are constrained to reduce subsidies, eliminate trade barriers, privatize state enterprises and end state regulation.[3] Aid is conditioned on the compliance with this neomercantilist agenda.

Euro-US takeovers of lucrative assets and current account deficits lead to increased borrowing and spiralling overseas debt payments, with predictable social consequences. There is also abundant evidence that the elite members of the donor country's multinational banks and corporations have benefited enormously from this new imperial neomercantilist system. If we look at the relations between the US and Latin America over the last quarter of a century in terms of the political-economic matrix of aid, we find considerable evidence of 'reverse aid.' The new imperial mercantilist order is built on five pillars: large-scale, long-term interest payments on external debt; massive transfers of profits derived from direct and portfolio investments; buy-outs and takeovers of lucrative public enterprises and financially troubled national enterprises, as well as direct investments in sweatshops, energy resources and low wage manufacturing and service industries; the collection of rents from royalty payments on a wide range of products, patents (especially pharmaceuticals) and cultural commodities; and favourable current account balances based on the dominance of US corporations and banks in the region (Petras and Veltmeyer, 1999). Between 1990-98 US banks received over $329 billion in interest payments, while the total debt grew from $476 billion to $698 billion, debt payments amounting to about 30 percent of total export earnings.[4]

Foreign direct investments (FDI) during the 1990s increased 600 percent over the previous decade. Most of this FDI has been used to purchase the assets of privatized public enterprises and private firms. Together such acquisitions account for 68 to 75 percent of all FDI in the region. Conditionality[5] imposed by bilateral and multilateral lending agencies facilitated the purchase of Latin American enterprises. Aid, in other words, was the catalyst for the transfer of national public to private foreign monopolies. In a three-year period, 1995-97, over $157 billion in profits were repatriated, according to the ECLAC (Petras and Veltmeyer, 1999). Thus aid and the conditions imposed on aid recipients facilitate the takeover of lucrative enterprises and the repatriation of billions of dollars to aid the global accumulation process and the expansion of the US Empire.

Royalty payments and licence fees are another source of reverse aid. During the 1990s approximately $13 billion was transferred form Latin America to the US. Royalties are the fastest growing sector of US returns (Petras and Veltmeyer, 1999). Foreign aid is conditioned on Latin American regimes accepting the US definition of 'intellectual property rights' and supporting Washington's battle to include 'intellectual property' clauses in the GATT or the WTO.

The role of trade between the US and Latin America is of equal importance as the cumulative returns to US investors and lenders. Close to a fourth of US exports are directed towards Latin America, which is the only region in the world that provides the US with a significant current account surplus. Foreign aid or loans by the IFI influenced by the US (World Bank, the IMF, IDB) is conditioned on the lowering of trade barriers in Latin America, ending subsidies and cutting back public spending on social services. The result has been a loss of market shares by local enterprises, rising unemployment and underemployment and the reindustrialization of some countries and the proliferation of sweatshop or low wage assembly plants where the workers are denied the right to organize, access to social welfare benefits and protection of labour legislation. Thus the meagre flows of foreign aid not only fail to compensate for the outflow of wealth; they are a catalyst of reverse aid.

The cumulative benefits of profits, royalty and interest payments, favourable trade balances and takeover of public enterprises forms the matrix in which foreign aid is embedded and shapes its function and impact. The trade limitations explicit in the US neomercantilist relations to Latin America is evident in the controls and quotas imposed on the importation of beef, textiles, steel, sugar, and a host of other commodities from Latin America that compete with US producers. In contrast, US aid is tied to Latin American purchases of US products that are as much as 30 percent higher in some cases. Thus aid is a catalyst for promoting uncompetitive 'first world' enterprises and mercantilist relationships.

As for the social impact on Latin America of aid it is clear that neomercantilism, and the flow of private capital and foreign aid, have had a regressive impact on developments in Latin America. From the perspective of the recipient countries, particularly the working classes, the urban poor and peasants, ODA, like other international resource flows, has led to economic stagnation, poverty and declining income. Under the facilitating conditions of what Pronk and others regard as 'good policy' aid, in both its multilateral and bilateral forms, has led to what realistically can be termed 'pillage' and a drastic deterioration of living conditions for much of the population. This regression is evident in a whole range of indicators of socioeconomic 'development,' including a general decline and at times steep fall in the value of wages,[6] a deepening and extension of social inequalities in the distribution of wealth and income,[7] and the further spread of poverty.

With regards to the latter, not even the World Bank's efforts to reduce the incidence of poverty by statistical fiat (defining as poor only those with incomes of less than two dollars a day—one dollar for those in extreme poverty) have succeeded in disguising either the extent and scope of the problem, nor its root causes.[8] Even by the Bank's controversial and conservative new measure, poverty affects over 40 percent of the growing population in Latin America, a considerable increase in the rate of poverty in 1982 at the threshold of Latin America's turn towards the World Bank's 'new economic model.'[9]

Underlying these and other regressions in living or social conditions can be found a number of 'structural' changes associated with the shifts in government policies induced by the policy conditions of aid. Table 2.1 presents one of these changes for the first decade of neoliberal structural reforms.[10] Other changes are reflected in widespread social conditions associated with increasing disparities in the distribution of wealth and income, falling wages, deteriorating health, a rise in the rate of unemployment and the proliferation of low incomes that UNRISD (1995), among others, attributes to the social effects of globalization and structural adjustment, the policy conditionalities of 'aid' in access to 'international financial resources.' Even economists associated with the World Bank and the IMF have admitted the general failure of structural adjustment policies—and the associated 'marriage of the free market and liberal democracy' (Domínguez and Lowenthal, 1996)—in terms of economic growth, increased indebtedness and a pronounced tendency towards 'social exclusion'—the restriction of 'benefits' to a relatively small privileged part of the population (Bengoa, 2000: 44f).[11] What can be said with confidence is that the 'good policies' adopted by so many governments in Latin America and elsewhere in exchange for a condition of aid are to a large degree responsible for the evident regression in social conditions across the region.

Table 2.1   Share of Wages in National Income, Selected Countries in Latin America (Percentages)

	1970	1980	1989
Argentina	40.9	31.5	24.9
Chile	47.7	43.4	19.0
Ecuador	34.4	34.8	16.0
Mexico	37.5	39.0	28.4
Peru	40.0	32.8	25.6

Source: CEPAL, *Anuario Estadístico de América Latina y el Caribe, various years.*

Both neomercantilist and neoliberal models of capitalist development have provoked extensive and deep social inequalities, decreasing the share of labour and increasing the share of corporate wealth, especially foreign capital, in national incomes. In this context, foreign aid has served as a catalyst for hastening the introduction of the free market policies responsible for the maldistribution of income. The social component of foreign aid had little, if any, effect in compensating for the loss of income shares and for the slashing of social allocations in national budgets.

The tendency for donors to channel funds for poverty alleviation through NGOs also has had little positive effect, as an earlier study by one of the authors demonstrated in the case of Bolivia (Arellano and Petras, 1997). On the contrary, foreign aid directed toward NGOs has undermined national decision-making, given that most projects and priorities are set out by the European or US-based NGOs. In addition, NGO projects tend to co-opt local leaders and turn them into functionaries administering local projects that fail to deal with the structural problems and crises of the recipient countries. Worse yet, NGO funding has led to a proliferation of competing groups, which set communities and groups against each other, undermining existing social movements. Rather than compensating for the social damage inflicted by free market policies and conditions of debt bondage, the NGO-channelled foreign aid[12] complements the IFIs' neoliberal agenda.

Policy Improvement and Good Governance

The implementation and administration of neoliberal policies and foreign aid has provoked the protest of great masses of people. Conditionality loans from the IMF and World Bank have provoked general strikes and popular uprisings in the interior of Argentina, marches and highway blockages by peasant and Indian organizations in Ecuador and Bolivia, and numerous other forms of mobilization. In order to avoid public debate and popular consultations, which would likely reject the neoliberal package of foreign takeovers and foreign aid, regimes have frequently resorted to ruling or legislating by decree. Ex-Presidents Menem, Salinas and Mahuad of Argentina, Mexico and Ecuador, privatized thousands of public firms by decree. Most of Latin America's macroeconomic policies are designed and enforced by foreign functionaries of the IFIs. Threats and psychological intimidation accompany the implementation of harsh anti-popular, so-called 'economic reforms' and accompanying loans—foreign aid. The growth of neoauthoritarianism in which non-elected foreign functionaries and local executive officials (most of them non-elected or representing a small fraction of the electorate) govern. In short, foreign aid strengthens authoritarian tendencies in the executive branches of government, undermining popular support for the electoral process and representative government, and thus 'democracy.'

To the publicists and promoters of free markets in Europe and the US, effective government and good governance is measured by the ability of client regimes to implement 'unpopular' pro-corporate policies while limiting political protest. In this context, the basic question that needs to be raised regarding 'good governance' is: who governs and for whom? According to the technical criteria of today's 'good governance' theorists, Mussolini's success in making the trains run on time would qualify him as a 'good governor' and qualify his government for foreign aid because of the 'policy improvement' effected.

Foreign aid helps grease the wheels of corruption. For example, aid ostensibly directed to curtail the growth of coca in Bolivia, Colombia and Peru and encourage alternative crops is pocketed by corrupt military and civilian elites. Large-scale, long-term corruption has exceeded the high historical benchmarks in the past. Bribes to state officials paid by leading US and European CEOs to secure favourable terms during privatization proceedings are the norm. Foreign aid is not the cause of corruption in many cases but the catalyst. Aid is based on policy improvements and 'good governance,' essentially the implementation of the free market agenda. It is the large-scale transfer of public property that is the source of corruption. In that sense, aid serves as a catalyst for policies that have almost inevitably been accompanied by corruption (Bounds, 2001).[13]

Foreign Aid and Land Reform

Despite occasional official rhetoric, foreign aid has never financed a comprehensive land reform programme in Latin America. In fact, most loans by the IFI and bilateral financing is directed at 'modernizing' large-scale commercial landlords at the expense of landless farm workers and peasants. Brazil is a case in point. Loans from AID, the World Bank and the IDB have led, during the decade of the 1990s, to the reconcentration of land, the displacement of over one million peasant families and an increase in the unemployment of landless rural workers. Given the free market farm policies, the number of bankrupt small farmers has increased geometrically, undermining the microprojects of European funded NGOs. The major group attempting to reverse the tendency toward land concentration and promote land reform is the Rural Landless Workers Movement (MST) that receives no official aid because of its organized land occupation policy that has benefited over 250,000 landless families. In order to undercut the MST, the Brazilian government has used the stick and the carrot: on the one hand, over 50 rural landless worker activists have been assassinated by the military police under the regime of Fernando Cardoso, scores have been jailed and tortured and thousands of squatter families have been evicted; on the other hand, the World Bank has designed and financed an Agrarian Bank which lends money to peasants to facilitate their purchase of land.[14] The commercial or market driven 'land reform,' however, puts heavily indebted 'family farmers' in a disadvantageous position in relation to the flood of cheap imports resulting from the free market policies and without resources to purchase inputs to become competitive. Foreign aid here has a political purpose in undermining successful indigenous social movements.

Neostructuralism, Aid and the Contemporary Crisis in Latin America

In the early 1990s many neoliberal regimes and IFI, particularly the World Bank, recognized that market excesses led to increased social polarization and poverty and threatened to bring down the free market architecture. Policy-makers and agency heads argued that the state had a role to correct the excesses by securing financing loans to finance micro-economic projects, poverty programmes and self-help community development. This new approach, dubbed 'neostructuralism' by its practitioners, has been in place in varying degrees in all Latin American countries for a decade. Yet unemployment in Brazil and Argentina is at its highest levels since the Great Depression. The Argentine economy is on the verge of collapse. Brazil, Colombia and Mexico are into a deep recession. Underemployment and the informal sector in a number of countries ranges from 30 to 80 percent (see chapter 4) The outflows of capital accumulated by the rich are fuelled by bailouts financed by overseas funding agencies. Exorbitant interest rates to attract foreign investors to pay an unpayable foreign debt exclude any credit to small and medium size producers.

The reason for the social and economic failures of 'neostructuralism' is because it accepted the basic postulates of the free market economy and believed that loans to 'civil society' could ameliorate local conditions and spread throughout the economy. In reality, the social problems the neostructuralists addressed were not on the margins of the free market policies and, therefore, could not be corrected via microeconomic projects. Rather, the problems were found on the very free market model: the elite class configuration of the state, the monopoly economic organization of the productive system and the polarized class structure, all of which required comprehensive transformations in order to achieve the general goals of equity, good government and economics. Neostructuralists choose not to confront these deep structural conditions, seeking instead to work within the free market system and provide it a social dimension and a human face (ECLAC, 1998). The evidence to the contrary is increasing throughout the region: Latin America's living standards are declining, the economy is regressing, the debt default is pending and extra-parliamentary popular opposition to neoliberalism, neoauthoritarianism and neomercantilism is growing.

Conclusion

The World Bank in its various reports and commissioned studies provides a limited and flawed perspective on the dynamics of foreign aid. At worst, it helps obfuscate the real issues involved. Aid from the hegemonic regions has a long and inglorious history as a policy tool, from colonial times to the present, to facilitate the conquest of markets, finance compliant elites, undermine indigenous insurgence and substitute ineffectual small-scale projects for comprehensive and needed egalitarian structural changes. In the present period, loans and aid have operated as catalysts for dismantling public social welfare programmes, undermining national markets and, in Latin America, facilitating the Euro-American takeover of strategic sectors of the economy. Aid is not the 'cause' per se of crisis and regression; rather it sets in motion a series of policies that are promoted by, and benefit, the elite—policies that can only be viewed as 'good' from the perspective of these elites. In the current matrix of power and corporate economic interests, aid has been successful in promoting Euro-American expansion and the regression of living standards in Latin America and in sub-Saharan Africa. In this context, the issue is not aid or no aid, but aid under what conditions and in what sociohistorical and political context?

Notes

1 It is not at all evident in his essay but Jan Pronk's thinking likely derives from the structuralism of the early pioneers of development economics (Rosenstein-Rodan, Nurske, Hirschman) or, even more likely, Latin American structuralism reformulated by Osvaldo Sunkel (1991) and others.

2 The recent UN Conference on Racism held in Durban, South Africa in its Final Resolution indicted various forms of colonialism and imperialism, including slavery, the slave trade, and the dispossession and super-exploitation of indigenous peoples, as the original or underlying 'cause' of the racist structures and practices in place today all over the 'developing world.'

3 This bias is clearly reflected in the rules of trade set up by GATT and, since 1994, by the WTO.

4 Both these figures and the data that follow, together with their sources, are presented and analysed in Petras and Veltmeyer (1999).

5 As noted by Mosley et al. (1991: xiii) conditional aid (particularly in the form of the concessional loans provided by the World Bank) entails not just the usual conditions of repayment but rather conditions that the recipient government must perform by changing some of its previously chosen or preferred policies.

6 The fall relates to both average and minimum wage rates, which, according to the ILO (see UNRISD, 1995: 45) fell a minimum of 40 percent in one decade (from 1985 to 1995) for most countries, up (or down, rather) to 94 percent in the case of Colombia and 67 percent in Brazil.

7 On the growth of social inequalities in the distribution of income over the course, and as a result of, IMF and World Bank policies of stabilization and structural adjustment see ECLAC (1998), Khor (1995) and Morley (2000).

8 In the literature on this issue, a distinction is sometimes made between old forms of poverty rooted in structures deeply embedded in Latin America's history and new forms that are clearly associated with the stabilization and structural adjustment policy measures implemented over the past two decades. On this see Lustig (1995), Bulmer-Thomas (1996), and Veltmeyer and Petras (1997, 2000).

9 Over the entire period of structural adjustment and globalization, 1983-2000, Latin America has produced poor people at twice the rate of total population growth: 44 and 22 percent respectively. According to the UNDP (1996), those living in poverty increased from 40 percent of the total population in 1980 to 44 percent in 1986 and a staggering 62 percent in 1993, after ten years of structural adjustment and five years of a widely-declared war on poverty, viz. the 'new social policy' (NSP) targeted at the extremely poor.

10 In this context, the transfer of income from wage-earners to non-wage earners in most countries in the region has been dramatic: in 1980 wages represented almost 40 percent of the national income, 34 percent in 1990 and 32 percent by 1996 (CEPAL, *Anuario Estadistico de America Latina y el Caribe*, several years). Table 2.1 shows that in some countries the process has been particularly brutal, the share of wages in national income falling below 20 percent. This 'development' is reflected in the relative regression in living standards for the majority of working peoples in the region over the course of the past two decades of free market 'structural reform.' In this connection, by the end of the 1990s the standard of living for most of the population in virtually every country was lower than that achieved in the 1970s.

11 Most analysts here (for example, Rodrik, 1999; and Lustig, 1995) take the view that this regression of socioeconomic conditions is directly attributable to the neoliberal policies

of structural adjustment promoted by the World Bank. The solution—from the point of view of the World Bank's 'friendly critics' such as the scholars associated with UNDP and UNICEF, is a 'redesign of these policies' to reflect this 'new understanding' (see Salop, 1992) or the creation of a social investment fund, a new poverty-targeted social policy, or a social net to "protect the most vulnerable groups'—those likely to be most deeply hurt and unable to defend themselves from the inevitably negative effects of the structural adjustment process (Morales-Gómez, 1999; Tulchin and Garland, 2000). Others, such as De Soto (2000: 33), President of the Institute for Liberty and Democracy and author of *El Otro Sendero*, see the 'mystery of capital' ('what makes capitalism a private club open to only a privileged few?') not in policy terms but as Karl Marx did—as a built-in structural feature of all capitalist systems: the legal institution of formal property relations that restricts access to society's productive resources to members of one social class.

12 According to a recent OECD study (Woods, 2000: 12), in the EC up to \$7.3 billion of bilateral aid in 1993 was channelled through NGOs—some 1832 (out of an estimated total of 4436). However, the critical factor is not the volume of aid channelled in this way—at the 1994 UN World Summit for Social Development, Vice-President Al Gore announced that half of all US ODA would be so channelled within five years—but the fact remains that NGOs both in the EC and the US are the executing agents of an aid policy that is closely aligned with the World Bank. On this point see Petras and Veltmeyer (2001).

13 In addition to Bound's piece in *Financial Times* on this issue see, inter alia, a recent study on corruption and development in the Congo-Zaire by Bamuamba (2001), who takes issue with the World Bank's view (see, for example, Rose-Ackerman (1998) that the development process, particularly in sub-Sahara Africa, is vitiated by problems of mismanagement and corruption rather than, as argued by others, structural problems generated by neoliberal policies of structural adjustment.

14 On this triple offensive of the Brazilian government against the MST see Petras and Veltmeyer (2001b).

Chapter Three

Imperial Counter-Offensive: Challenges and Opportunities

James Petras

The basic argument of this chapter is that the US attack on Afghanistan is an effort to reverse the relative decline of US Empire and to re-establish its hegemony in regions of conflict. The war in Afghanistan is only part of a general imperial counter-offensive which has several components: (i) to re-establish the subordination of Europe to Washington; (ii) to reassert its total control in the mid-East and Gulf region; (iii) to deepen and extend military penetration in Latin America and Asia; (iv) to increase military warfare in Colombia and project power throughout the rest of the continent; (v) to restrict and repress protest and opposition against the TNCs and IFIs like the World Bank, the IMF and WTO by replacing democratic rights with dictatorial powers; and (vi) to use state spending on weapons and subsidies for near bankrupt TNCs (airlines, insurance, tourist agencies) and regressive tax reductions to halt a deepening recession, which would undermine public support for the empire-building project.

A second argument advanced is that the preparations for the imperial counter-offensive involved a planned three-part sequence: First, September 11 (9/11) was followed by a massive propaganda effort that magnified and distorted the nature of the attack on the World Trade Centre and the Pentagon in order to secure world political support. The anti-terrorism campaign created the appearance of a 'world consensus' in favour of Washington. Second, on October 7 the George W. Bush administration launched a massive 'defensive' military attack on Afghanistan, targeting the international terrorist network al-Qaida put together by Osama Bin Laden and supported by the Taliban regime. It was actively supported by the hard-core allies in this 'war' (England, Turkey, Pakistan, France, Italy, Japan, Spain). At the same time, political, psychological and legal barriers to the war were demolished in the United States, Japan and Germany, setting the stage for a new phase of military interventions, heightened domestic repression and increased profiteering, all under the pretext of 'permanent war' conditions. The third phase of the imperial offensive involved an extension of the Afghan offensive into a generalized military offensive against 'international terrorists' and those who would 'aid and abet' them. It was signalled by a speech on 'the axis of evil,' in which George W. Bush identified Iraq and Iran as the most immediate enemies of a US-led world alliance of the 'forces of freedom' against 'terrorist' and 'rogue' states. This phase of the imperial offensive has involved operations against real or potential adversaries and critics, using intimidation (the threat of massive bombing as in Afghanistan) and an increased military presence to both extend and deepen control in regions or countries like Colombia that are crisis prone or in crisis.

The third argument is that there are three dimensions of an unfolding international crisis: (i) *military-political*—the open-ended war declared by Washington which seeks to unilaterally restore its power, by imposing new client states; (ii) *economic*—the decline and challenge to Euro-American imperial power derived from the world recession (and possible depression) and the growing opposition movements in and out of the imperial states; and (iii) *the crisis of the Left Opposition* to the forces of globalization and imperialism. The US counter-offensive has placed a new set of issues before the popular and antiglobalization movements: more repression, increased aggressive militarization, a monolithic and massive propaganda effort and actions designed to intimidate—and to instill fear and provoke anger.

The imperial new order creates many challenges, dangers *and* opportunities for the forces of resistance and opposition if they can overcome the widespread disorientation. The multidimensional crisis, affecting both pro-empire and oppositional forces, is creating an open-ended situation that allows for several possible outcomes depending on the nature and strength of political responses to the contradictions of the system. The argument proceeds by first identifying the context for the imperial counter-offensive, namely the relative decline of US power. I then examine the imperial advantages of extended open-ended war as a way out of the crisis as well as its contradictions. Finally I look at the antiterrorist war as part of the crisis situation and its impact on popular opposition as well as the potentialities for a new resurgence of popular power.

The Need for a New Imperialism

The commonly heard expression 'After September 11 [9/11] the world has changed' has been given many different meanings. The most frequent meaning given to it by Washington and echoed by the European Union (and amplified by the mass media) is that 9/11 has ushered in a whole new era—a new 'historical period' in which a new set of priorities, alliances and political relations are given.

However, Washington's periodizing the new historical era with 9/11 involves a particular perspective that reflects its own losses and vulnerabilities in the search for hegemony. From the perspective of the Third World (and perhaps beyond) the 'new era' starts on October 7, 2001, the date of the massive US intervention and carpet-bombing of Afghanistan. October 7 is important because it signals the start of a major world wide offensive against adversaries of the United States under a very elastic and loose definitions of 'terrorism,' terrorist havens' and 'terrorist sympathizers.' It clearly marks a new military offensive against competitors and opponents of US imperial power, both abroad and within.

It is important to understand the meaning of the term 'new epoch' because much of what has transpired is not new but rather a continuation and deepening of ongoing imperial military aggression that preceded September 11 and October 7. Likewise the popular liberation struggles in many parts of the world continue unabated despite September 11 and October 7, and despite some significant changes in context.

In brief, while September 11 and October 7 are significant events, it is an open question whether the events following either of these dates mark a qualitatively new historical period. In this connection it is more useful to analyze the inter-relationship *between* events and historical processes before October 7 and *after*, in order to separate what is new and significant from what is neither. Several significant factors establish the parameters and context for this argument. The first is a relative decline in US political and economic power throughout the 1990s in key areas of the world, particularly in the mid-East/Gulf region, Latin America, Asia, and Europe—a decline that is accompanied by an increase in US influence in the less important Balkan states of Kosova, Macedonia and Serbia, and relative success in its strategic direction of political developments in Central America.

The second factor is the vast expansion of US economic interests via its transnational corporations and banks into the Third World and the gradual weakening of the client regimes that support this expansion. The international financial institutions (IFIs) like the World Bank and the IMF through their structural adjustment policies, free trade doctrines and privatization directives had so drained the wealth of local economies that the client states were weakened and rife with corruption as private sector elites and politicians pillaged the treasury. Here we need but look at Argentina but it is by no means alone as regime after regime in Latin America, in the context of implementing unpopular structural adjustment programmes and neoliberal policies, have fallen prey to forces of economic recession and political 'instability.'

The weakening of the imperial 'control structure' meant that the traditional, almost exclusive, dependence on the IFIs for surplus extraction was becoming inadequate. As noted by the journalist Martin Wolf (*Financial Times*, Oct. 10, 2001: 13) the diminution of 'indirect' imperial control over the impoverished and devastated Third World state ('the failed state') requires a 'new imperialism'— 'not pious aspirations but an honest and organized coercive force. In other words imperial wars, as in Afghanistan and Yugoslavia, must be accompanied by new imperialist conquests, a recolonization; to ensure the subordination of premodern or modern states in the third world, bombs and marines should be used to supplement the economic restructuring' policies of the IMF and World Bank functionaries. The 'new imperialism,' according to Robert Cooper, Foreign Policy Advisor to Tony Blair, on the other side of the Atlantic but on the same side, should 'revert to the rougher methods of an earlier era—force, preemptive attack, deception, whatever is necessary' (2000b: 7). Blair himself, in an address to Canada's Parliament in 2001, in this connection, spoke of the need for 'force and determination' in the 'war against international terrorism'—and protesters who 'stand in the way of rational argument.'

From the end of the Gulf War and the Bush (Senior) Presidency to October 7, 2001, the United States won military conflicts in peripheral regions (the Balkans and Central America) but suffered a serious loss of influence in more strategic regions. At the same time, the US economy experienced a miniature speculative boomlet before then entering a period of open crisis in the form of a deep recession in the manufacturing sector and a major meltdown in the financial sector. The combined effect of peripheral victories on the military front and the speculative bubble was to hide a deepening structural weakness.

The decline in US influence and military losses can be briefly summarized. In the Middle East, the US strategy of overthrowing or isolating the Iranian government and the Iraqi regime of Saddam Hussein was a total failure. The regimes not only survived but also effectively broke the US boycott. US sanctions against Iran de facto, were broken by most 'allies' of the US, including Japan, EU, the Arab states etc. Iran was accepted among the revitalized OPEC countries and signed nuclear power agreements with Russia, oil contracts with Japan. Iran signed investment and trade agreements with every major country except the United States and even there, TNCs, working through third parties, became involved in Iranian trade.

Iraq was reintegrated into OPEC, was accepted as a member at meetings of the Gulf States, at Arab summits and international Islamic conferences. Iraq sold millions of 'clandestine' barrels of oil via 'contrabandists' through Turkey and Syria, clearly with the foreknowledge of the 'transit regimes' and the Western European consumers.

The Palestinian uprising and the unanimous support it received from Arab regimes (including US clients) isolated the United States that remained closely tied to the Israeli state. In North Africa, Libya developed strong economic ties with EU and their oil companies, particularly with Italy and diplomatic relations with many NATO countries.

Thus three strategic oil producing countries labelled as prime targets of US policy, increased their influence and ties with the rest of the world, thus weakening the US stranglehold in the region immediately following the Gulf War. Clearly Bush Senior's 'New World Order' was in shambles, reduced to mini-fiefdoms, in the backward, mafia infested Albanian provinces in the Balkans.

Another major sign of declining US power was found in the massive growth of trade surpluses accumulated in Asia and the EU at US expense. In the year 2000 the United States ran up a $430 billion trade deficit. Western Europe's 350 million consumers increasingly purchased European-made goods—over two thirds of EU trade was inter-European. In Latin America, European TNCs, particularly, the Spanish outbid US competitors in buying up lucrative privatized enterprises.

Politically, especially in Latin America, the US dominance was being severely tested particularly by the formidable guerrilla movements in Colombia, by Venezuela's President Chavez and the mass movements in Ecuador, Brazil and elsewhere. The collapse of the Argentine economy, the general economic crises in the rest of the Continent and the significant loss of legitimacy of US client regimes were other indicators of a weakening of US power in its neocolonized provinces.

The massive growth of the 'antiglobalization movement,' particularly its 'anti-capitalist' sector, throughout Western Europe, North America and elsewhere challenged the power of Washington to impose imperial friendly new investment and trading rules.

Faced with its declining influence in strategic regions, a growing economic crisis at home, the end of the speculative (IT, biotech, fibreoptic) bubble, Washington decided to begin militarizing its foreign policy (via Plan Columbia) and to aggressively pursue comparative advantages via unilateral state decisions: abrogating treaty agreements (ABM missile agreement with Russia, Kyoto Agreement, the International Human Rights Court, anti-biological warfare and anti-personnel/mining agreements, etc.). Unilateral action was seen as a way of reversing the relative decline, combining regional military action and economic pressure. To counter the decline of US influence in Latin America and increase its control, Washington pushed the Latin American Free Trade Agreement (LAFTA) to limit European competition and increase US dominance. However opposition was strong in four of the five key countries in the region: Brazil, Venezuela, Colombia and Argentina.

Following the bombing of the US battleship Cole in Yemen, the attacks on the Embassies in Kenya and Tanzania and the previous attempt to bomb the World Trade Centre, September 11 was another indication of the relative decline in US power—this time of Washington's incapacity to defend the centres of financial and military power within the empire.

September 11 *is* and *is not* a significant date. It *is not* because it continued to mark the relative decline of US influence. It *is* because it becomes the turning point for a major counter-offensive to reverse the decline and reconstruct a US-centered 'New World Order.'

The Counter-Offensive of October 7

Washington's declaration of war against Afghanistan has two important phases: first, the engineering of a US dominated broad alliance based on opposition to the terrorist attack on the World Trade Centre and the Pentagon; and secondly, the conversion of this anti-terrorist front into a political instrument to support the US military intervention in Afghanistan and beyond. The clear intent of the Bush Administration was to launch a worldwide crusade against opponents of US power, and in the process reverse the decline in order to rebuild a new imperial order. From the onset, the massive bombing attacks and the invasion by hundreds of Special Forces, on kill and destroy missions, were intended to obliterate domestic objections to future ground wars and new military interventions. Equally important, the massive slaughter and displacement of millions of civilians served the explicit purpose of political intimidation directed at forcing real or imagined state adversaries to accept US dominance and control over their foreign and domestic policies, as well as to threaten social movements that the same violence could be directed against them.

In a word, the declining effectiveness of the IFI as instruments of US hegemony has led Washington to increasingly rely on raw military force and a move from low to high intensity violence. The overt threat of a series of military assaults is explicitly contained in the Administration's reference to the Afghanistan Invasion as phase one, with the clear implication that other imperial wars will follow. Most prominent here is Washington's threat to launch another full-scale military assault against Iraq and other 'safe-havens' for 'terrorists.' In mid-June 2002 Bush signalled a move towards a second phase in authorizing the CIA to use any and all methods to oust Saddam from power, including the resort to 'lethal force.'

In this transition the so-called 'anti-terrorist alliance' has been melded into a War Alliance (including all the major NATO countries). Significantly, all the major military and political decisions in this 'war,' from general strategy down to operational tactics, are taken exclusively by Washington without even the pretence of some consultation. In other words, the War Alliance is a continuation of Washington's prior unilateralism; only now the Bush administration has successfully reasserted its dominance over the EU. While Tony Blair's hyper-kinetic activity on behalf of Washington's war has elicited praise from the President and the US mass media, it has not led to any sharing of decision-making power.

At least in this phase of the US counter-offensive, Washington has reasserted its domination over Europe. Taking maximum advantage of its strongest card in the inter-state system, military power, Washington has sought to militarize political-economic realities. By making 'anti-terrorism' the dominant theme in every international and regional forum (APEC, UN, OAS) Washington hopes to undermine horizontal divisions between rich and poor countries and classes and replace it with a vertical ideological-military polarization between those who support or resist US defined 'terrorist' adversaries and military intervention.

Many regimes have already seized upon this military definition of socioeconomic realities to repress popular and left movements and liberation organizations in the Middle East, Latin America and Central Asia. The multiplication of 'anti-terrorist' purges by client regimes serves Washington's policy perfectly, as long as the newly labelled terrorist movements also oppose US policy and as long as their authoritarian clients accept the New Imperial Order.

Washington's threat of indefinite and extended wars of imperial conquest has been predictably accompanied by repressive legislation, which, in effect, confers dictatorial powers to the President. In this legislation, all constitutional guarantees are suspended and all foreign-born terrorist suspects become subject to military tribunals in the US—no matter what their particular geographical location. In this connection there is a broad consensus that the war-making powers assumed by the Executive violates the letter and intent of the Constitution and the norms of a democratic regime but this consensus has been to no avail. The argument by the defenders of authoritarianism that these clearly dictatorial measures are temporary is not convincing given the President's position that we are in for a long and extended period of warfare.

In other words, authoritarianism and engagement in aggressive imperialist wars go together, obliterating the democratic republican vision of the 'American revolution.'

History teaches us that imperial wars are always costly, the economic benefits are unequally distributed and the burdens are borne by the wage and salaried workers. The authoritarian measures serve to repress or intimidate, those who question the patriotic rhetoric: who begin to interpolate the war slogan 'United We Stand' by adding 'Divided We Benefit.'

The resurgence of empire building at a time of deepening economic recession is a problematic strategy. While the Administration slashes taxes for the rich, the war increases expenditures—putting deep strains on the budget and mass of taxpayers. However, military Keynesianism might stimulate a few sectors of the economy but it has not reversed, and will not reverse, the sharp decline in profits for the capitalist sector as a whole. Moreover, stretching the repressive apparatus of client regimes to secure their acquiescence with the global empire-building project will not expand overseas markets for US exports. In fact, overseas conflicts will shrink markets deepening the negative external accounts of the US economy.

More significantly, the current military approach to empire building in the post-Afghan period (phase 2) is designed to reassert the hegemony of the US state and capital over the system as a whole and will undoubtedly destabilize the economies of Europe, Japan and the US's mid-East states in the process. The military attack and occupation of Iraq to some extent has disrupted the flow of oil to Europe and Japan and is threatening to destabilize domestic politics in Saudi Arabia and other Gulf and Middle-Eastern countries. Fear of the destabilizing effects of this phase of empire building has already led to dissent, even among Washington's most servile European followers in England, and certainly in France and Germany. Nevertheless, given Washington's imperial vision, unilateral approach and its access to alternative sources of oil (Mexico, Venezuela, Ecuador, Alaska, Canada, etc.) a military attack on Iraq served three strategic objectives: (i) weaken European competitors in the battle of the world marketplace; (ii) eliminate Iraq as a potential regional rival; and, concomitantly, acquire strategic and operational control over the second largest reserves of oil in the world.[1] In the military conquest of Iraq the US state was quite prepared to damage the economies of the EU, alienate its two major Arab clients (Saudi Arabia and Egypt) and risk both an involution of capital markets all over the world and the consolidation of an anti-American clash of civilizations—a war between Islamic fundamentalism (and associated 'terrorism') and the non-Islamic capitalist 'West'. A secondary objective of the conquest was more symbolic than real to assert US hegemony and demonstrate its capacity and willingness to assert its power. Washington has also demonstrated that it can brush off European objections and still secure their acquiescence.

It is too early to notice the fallout but the war on Iraq and other rogue regimes such as North Korea, has created uncertainty among investors worldwide, and the weakening of Europe will have negative repercussions for the US economy at a time of negative growth. A war-induced European decline might improve the *relative* position of the US, but its economy would decline in *absolute* terms.

In focusing exclusively on pursuing a handful of supposed terrorists, President Bush strains at gnats and swallows camels. The overall damage to the economies of the EU and the US resulting from a new war far exceeds any possible losses resulting from terrorists. The imposition of the Bush Administration's military definition on the political-economic conflicts in the Third World resonates with the state terrorist policies of Israel (against the Palestinians), Algeria (against the Berbers) and Turkey (against the Kurds) in the Middle East and North Africa and no one else.

The Ariel Sharons in Washington (advocates of permanent war for empire building) have given virtually no thought to the *economic* consequences of military intervention in the Middle East. The collapse of the financial architecture and energy supplies of imperial states can bring down an empire far more quickly and with greater certainty than any real or imagined terrorist network.

The Counter-Offensive in Latin America

The imperial counter-offensive is worldwide. In the hierarchy of regions to reconquer Latin America stands out as second, after the Middle East. It is the region that has provided the United States with its only favourable trade balances. Its ruling and affluent classes have drained hundreds of billions in illegal transfers to US banks, and the US economy has received almost a trillion dollars in profits, interest payments, royalties and other transfers over the last decade. Latin America's client regimes usually follow US positions in international forums and provide nominal military forces in its interventionary forays thus providing a fig leaf for what are in effect unilateral actions.

Washington identified the Colombian peasant based guerrilla movements, especially FARC, which presents the most powerful challenge to its dominance in the hemisphere, as a 'terrorist' group. Controlling or influential in over 50 percent of the country municipalities by the mid-1990s, the advance of the FARC, together with the independent foreign policy of the Chavez regime in Venezuela, and the revolutionary government in Cuba represent an alternative pole to the servile Peon Presidents of the Continent serving the empire.

Beginning late in Clinton's Presidency and deepening during the Bush Administration, the United States declared total war on the popular insurgency. *Plan Colombia* and later the Andean Initiative, were essentially war strategies which preceded the Afghan War but served to highlight the new imperial counter-offensive. Washington allocated 1.5 billion in military aid to the Colombian military and its paramilitary surrogates. Hundreds of Special Forces were sent to direct operations in the field. US mercenary pilots were subcontracted from private firms to engage in chemical warfare in the poppy fields of Colombia. Paramilitary forces multiplied under the protection and promotion of the military command. Air space, seacoasts and river estuaries were colonized by US armed forces. Military bases were established in El Salvador, Ecuador and Peru to provide logistical support. US officials established a direct operational presence in the Defense Ministry in Bogotá.

The worldwide counter-offensive of October 7 deepened the militarization process in Colombia. Under US direction the Colombian air force violates the airspace over the demilitarized zone where the FARC and the Pastrana regime negotiate. Illegal cross border forays into the zone led to conflicts. The State Department labelling the FARC as 'terrorist' puts them on the list of targets to be assaulted by the US military machine. Under the Bush-Rumsfeld Doctrine, half of Colombia is a haven for terrorists and thus subject to total war.

The imperial war fever caused the State Department to send an official delegation to Venezuela to bludgeon the Chavez government to support the imperial offensive. According to officials in the Venezuela Foreign Ministry when Chavez condemned terrorism and the US war, the State Department threatened the government with reprisals in the best traditions of Mafia Dons.

The key dimension of Washington's empire building project in Latin America is the proposed LAFTA. This proposal will give US-based TNCs and banks unrestrained access to markets, raw materials and labour while limiting European and Japanese entry and protect US markets. This neomercantilist imperialist system is a unilateral initiative, taken in agreement with the satellite regimes in the region, without any popular consultation. Given the high levels of discontent already in the region, under the neoliberal regimes, the imposition of neomercantilist imperialism will likely lead to explosive social conditions and the re-emergence of nationalist and socialist alternatives. Washington's anti-terrorist military doctrine, with its threats of violent interventions and its active and direct military presence, serves as a useful ideological weapon to impose the neomercantilist empire.

Latin America is today half colonized: its bankers, politicians, generals and most of its bishops stand by and for the Empire. They want deeper 'integration.' The other half of Latin America, the vast majority of its workers, peasants, Indians, lower middle class public employees and above all its tens of millions of unemployed who are exploited by the empire reject and resist it. The imperial counter-offensive is directed at intervening, in order to sustain its colonial clients and to cower the other half of Latin America—that owns no property but represents the historical interests of the region.

We are entering a period of intensified warfare, constant military threats, savage bombings, wholesale massacres, and tens of millions of displaced persons. The sites of violent social conflict are no longer confined to the Third World, though that is where the people will pay the heaviest price. Will this period of war also be a period of revolutions—as in the past? Can the US economy sustain a sequence of wars, without undermining its own economy? Can it survive by destabilizing its European and Japanese competitors but also its trading and investment partners?

The Centrality of the Imperial State

There are clear indications that the economic bases of the US Empire are weakening for economic and political reasons. At the economic level, in mid year of 2002, the US manufacturing sector finally began to pull out of an 18 month long recession but there is every indication of a continuing underlying propensity towards crisis. Over the same period (and the 1995-99 speculative boom masked an underlying trend towards recession), hundreds of billions of dollars invested in information technology, fibreoptics and biotech ventures were lost. As revenues plummeted thousands of firms went—and continue to go—bankrupt. Both the 'old' and 'new' economy are having great difficulties in pulling out of a deep and prolonged crisis. The financial and speculative stock market sectors are heavily dependent on volatile political-psychological circumstances in the United States. and in the world economy. The vertical decline in the stock market following September 7, and the sharp recovery following October 7, reflected the volatility. More specifically, US stock and bond markets depend heavily on overseas investors, as well as local speculators. These wealthy investors as well as their US counterparts, tend to invest in the United States as much for political as for economic reasons: they seek safe and stable havens for their private fortunes. But 9/11 shook their confidence because it demonstrated that the very centres of economic and military power are vulnerable to attack and destruction. Hence, the massive flight of speculative and productive forms of capital and the continued vulnerability of financial markets.

However, the October 7 counter-attack, the massive worldwide counter-offensive of the Empire, and the destruction of Afghanistan, restored investor confidence and led to a significant influx of capital and the temporary recovery of the stock market. The 'total war' strategy adopted by the Pentagon was as much to restore investor confidence about the invincibility and security of imperial power as it was for any political reason or even future oil pipeline. Stock market behaviour, particularly large scale, long term foreign investors in the US stock and bond market, seem to be influenced as much by security and safety reasons as the actual performance of the US economy. Hence the paradox of the inverse relation between the stock market and the real economy: while all the economic indicators of the real economy decline, toward negative growth, the stock market temporarily recovered its pre-9/11 levels.

Nevertheless, there are limits to this political basis for investment. Prolonged negative growth and declining profits (or increasing losses) will most certainly eventually end the recovery and produce a sharp decline in the stock market.

The theoretical point is that as the economic foundations of empire weaken, the role of the imperial state increases. The empire becomes even more dependent on state intervention, revealing the close ties between the imperial state and investors, including the TNCs. Equally significant the military components of the imperial state play an increasingly dominant role in re-establishing 'investor confidence' by smashing and intimidating adversaries, buttressing faltering neocolonial regimes, imposing favourable economic accords (LAFTA) for US investors and prejudicial to Euro-Japanese competitors (by military action in the Gulf and Middle East).

The old imperialism of the 1980-90s that depended more on the IFIs (World Bank and IMF) is being supplanted and/or complemented by the new imperialism of military action: the Green Berets replace the bowtie functionaries of the Fund and the Bank.

Washington-led NATO extends its dominion from the Baltic client states to the Balkan satellites, and beyond Turkey and Israel to the Central and Southern Asian (ex-Soviet) Republics. The missing link in this imperial chain is the strategically important Gulf States: Iran and Iraq. While this imperial chain is militarily significant it is more a cost to empire than a source of revenue: it borders great riches but does not produce them, at least as yet. This is clear to the Bush Administration which is more interested in destroying regional powers than in large scale investments in building colonial states, as is seen in the meagre resources invested in the Balkans, Central Asia and is likely to be the case in Afghanistan.

The centrality of the imperial state in conquering and expanding US power has refuted the assumptions of those leading theoreticians of the anti-globalization movement like Susan George, Tony Negri, Ignacio Ramonet, David Korten, etc. who think in terms of the 'autonomy of global corporations.' Their emphasis on the central role of the world market in creating poverty, dominance and inequality is in the present context an anachronism. As the Euroamerican imperial states send troops to conquer and occupy more countries, destroy, displace and impoverish millions, there is a great need to shift from antiglobalization to anti-imperialist movements, from the false assumptions of autonomous TNC-dominated 'super-states' to the reality of the TNCs tied to imperial states.

The worldwide counteroffensive led and directed by the US imperial state has as its goal the reconstruction of the failed NWO of the post-Gulf War period. Today in the face of economic crisis and growing popular resistance, the TNCs do not have the will or resources to act 'autonomously' via market forces. The new imperialism is based on military intervention (Afghanistan/Balkans), colonization (military bases), terror (Colombia). From the wars in Iraq, the Balkans, to Afghanistan, the imperial juggernaut advances, each more horrendous human catastrophe justified by an even greater barrage of propaganda of humanitarian missions.

The imperial offensive after October 7 is based on strategic and economic imperatives and has nothing to do with the 'clash of civilizations'. The US Empire includes Muslim states (Pakistan, Saudi Arabia, Egypt, Turkey, Morocco, Bosnia, Albania, etc.), Jewish states (Israel), as well as secular, nominally Christian, regimes. What defines the US imperial offensive is not permanent allies (of one religion/civilization or another), but permanent interests. In the Balkans and earlier in Palestine and Afghanistan, Washington promoted fundamentalist Muslims and drug traffickers against secular nationalists and socialists. Yesterday's Muslim clients (Taliban) are, in some places, today's enemies. The thread that unifies these changing alliances is the need to defend imperial spheres of domination. The apparent 'hypocrisy' or 'double standard' of the imperial elites is only in the eyes of the beholder who mistakenly believe in the propaganda of the empire and now feel 'betrayed' by the switch in imperial clients.

The US military advances in Afghanistan have prepared the way for new wars. The military alliance in Afghanistan is built around rival tribal warlords, who live off contraband, drug trafficking and the pillaging of booty from local wars. Elsewhere severe structural contradictions and crisis are looming on the horizon.

Contradictions of Empire

The US imperial offensive faced two types of contradictions that were conjunctural and structural. The Afghan War polarized the Muslim states between their pro-empire leaders and the mass of sympathizers for the Afghan people and Osama Bin Laden. This polarization has not yet produced any serious organizational challenge to the client rulers, though the key Saudi monarchy is most vulnerable. The military victory of the United States and its client 'Northern Alliance' and the resultant Muslim coalition regime dissipated the purely Muslim amorphous mass opposition. The opposition of some EU and Arab states was activated when Washington unilaterally extended its war to Iraq, destabilizing Europe's oil suppliers as well as directly threatening carefully cultivated European interests in the region. However, although they have isolated the US diplomatically, particularly in regard to the United Nations and its push for multilateral actions in the international arena, these and other conjunctural contradictions have not slowed down or waylaid Washington's imperial drive.

The more profound long-term structural contradictions of the 'new imperialism' are found in the military expansion in a time of deepening economic recession, both locally and worldwide. Military Keynianism—increased war spending—has not, and will not, reverse the recession, as few sectors of the economy are affected and the industries that may receive some stimulus. The aerospace industry, for example, is hard hit by the recession in the civilian airline market.

While the military machinery of the imperial state promotes and defends the interests of American TNCs, it is not a cost-efficient service provider. The multi-billion dollar overseas expenditures far exceed the immediate benefits to the TNCs and do not reverse the declining rate of profits nor open new markets, particularly in the regions of maximum military engagement. Military intervention expands the regions of colonization without increasing the returns to capital. The net result is that imperial wars, in their current form, undermine non-speculative capitalist investment, even as it symbolically assures overseas investors.

As in Central America, the Balkans and now in Afghanistan and Colombia, the United States is more interested in destroying adversaries and establishing client regimes than in large-scale, long-term investments in 'reconstruction.' After high military spending for conquest, budget priorities shift to subsidizing US-based TNCs, and lowering taxes for the wealthy—there are no more 'Marshall

Plans.' Washington prefers to leave it to Europe and its other 'allies' to 'clean up the human wreckage' after US military victories, although post-war reconstruction in Iraq poses particular problems for the US, including the need to share the costs whole maintaining total control over what will undoubtedly be a protracted process. The military victory of the US (and the-called 'coalition forces') in the present conjuncture leaves unsettled the consolidation of a pro-imperial client regime. Just as the United States financed and armed the fundamentalist victory over the secular nationalist Afghan regime in 1990 and then withdrew, leading to the ascendancy of the anti-western Taliban regime, the US's victory and eventual withdrawal is likely to have similar results over the next decade. The gap between the high war-making capacity of the imperial state and the weakness of its capacity to revitalize the economies of the conquered nations is a major contradiction.

An even more serious contradiction is found in the aggressive effort to impose neoliberal regimes and policies especially when the export markets that they were designed to service are collapsing and external flows of capital are drying up.

The recession in the United States, Japan and the EU has severely damaged some of Washington's most loyal and subservient neoliberal client-states, particularly in Latin America. The prices of the exports that drive economic growth in the 'new' (neoliberal) global economy have collapsed: exports of coffee, petrol, metals, sugar, as well as textiles, clothes and other manufactured goods elaborated in the 'free trade zones' have suffered from sharp drops in prices and glutted markets. The imperial powers have responded by pressing for greater 'liberalism' in the South while raising protective tariffs at home and increasing subsidies for exports. Tariffs in the imperial countries on imports from the Third World are four times higher than those on imports from other imperial countries, according to the World Bank (2002). Support for agricultural TNCs in the imperial countries was $245 billion in 2000 (*Financial Times*, 21 November 2001, p. 13). As the World Bank Report points out, 'the share of subsidized exports has even increased [over the past decade] for many products of export interest to developing countries.'

The neoliberal doctrine of the 'old imperialism' is giving way to the 'neomercantilist' practice of the 'new imperialism.' State policies dictate and direct economic exchanges and limit the market's role to a subsidiary one—all to the benefit of the imperial economy.

The highly restrictive nature of neomercantilist policies in the past and in the present polarizes the economy between local producers and the imperial state backed monopolies. The decline and collapse of overseas markets prejudice 'neoliberal' export sectors. The highly visible role of the imperial state in imposing the neomercantilist system politicizes the growing army of unemployed and poorly paid workers, peasants and public employees. The collapse of overseas markets means that less foreign exchange can be earned to pay foreign debts. Fewer exports mean less capacity to import essential foodstuffs and capital goods to sustain production. In Latin America the export strategy upon which the whole imperial edifice is built is crumbling. Unable to import, Latin America will be forced to produce locally or do without. However, the definitive rupture with the export strategy and subordination to empire will not come about because of internal contradictions: it requires political intervention.

By Way of a Conclusion: Opportunities and Challenges for the Left

In the short run (the present 'conjuncture') the left faces the full thrust of Washington's imperial counter-offensive, with all that implies in terms of increased bellicosity, threats and greater subservience from ruling client elites. Nevertheless, while this new military-led imperialist effort at 'reconquest' is underway, it faces serious practical, ideological and political obstacles.

For one thing, the offensive takes place in the face of a major political resurgence of the left in various strategic countries and a serious decline in the neoliberal economies. In Colombia, Brazil, Argentina, Ecuador and Bolivia, powerful sociopolitical movements have emerged and have consolidated influence over important popular constituencies, while the incumbent client regimes are deeply discredited, in many cases with single digit popularity ratings.

This situation presents dangers and opportunities. Dangers from the increasingly militarized and repressive response pushed by Washington and echoed by its Latin client regimes, as witnessed by the Ibero-American Conference Declaration in November 23, 2001 on Terrorism (*La Jornada,* 24 November 2001). Opportunities from the fact that the resurgent left has not suffered a major defeat in this period (comparable to 1972-76) and is in a strong position to make the leap from protest to power. Neoliberal regimes have failed to find overseas markets, in order to sustain domestic production or locate new flows of capital to compensate for the vast outflows in debt payments, profit remittances, etc. The prolonged depression in Argentina is emblematic of the direction in which all of Latin America is heading.

The current crisis is systemic, in that it not only affects workers and unemployed—by increasing poverty, unemployment and inequalities—but the very mechanisms of capital accumulation. What capital is accumulated in Latin America is stored in overseas accounts as 'dead wealth.' It is evident to any but the most willfully blind academics—of which there are not a few—that neoliberalism is dead and that the new mercantilist imperial system offers no room for 'market choices.'

In this perspective, what is essential for converting these objective opportunities into substantial structural changes is political power. The social movements have mobilized millions, they have realized innumerable changes at the local level, they have created a new and promising level of social consciousness and in some cases they control or influence local governments and have secured concessions via mass pressure from the dominant classes. However there are several as yet unresolved issues before these movements can be said to pre-figure a political alternative to state power.

First, politically the movements espouse a series of programmatic demands and alternatives—that are positive and important but lack a theoretical understanding of the nature of the evolving imperial system, its contradictions and the nature of the crisis.

Secondly, there is disunity, uneven development between urban and rural movements, between the interior and the coast, and within some of the movements rivalries based on personalities, tactics, etc. The aggregate existing movements, if unified in a coherent single movement, would be significantly closer to challenging for state power.

Thirdly, many of the movements engage in militant tactics and articulate radical programmes, but in practice engage in constant negotiation to secure very limited concessions, thus reducing their movements to pressure groups within the system rather than protagonists to overthrow the regime. The challenge is how to develop a transition programme adapted to the immediate demands of the people but which put in the centre of the struggle in the construction of a socialist alternative. The growing authoritarianism of the imperial directed client regimes requires the building of mass democratic and anti-imperialist movements.

The US imperial strategy of militarization to impose a neomercantilist empire requires greater capacity for incorporating new allies and the need to prepare for diverse forms of struggle. The imperial strategists have selected Colombia as the testing ground for the new imperialism because it is Colombia where they face their greatest politico-military challenge. All the reactionary forces in the hemisphere have been mobilized against the guerrilla armies as well as the growing mass movements. All the peon presidents of the hemisphere have signed onto the anti-terrorist crusade, and the FARC is designated by the empire as terrorist. Military success in Colombia will encourage the military conquest and colonization of Latin America, just as the US-directed military coup in Brazil (1964) was followed by invasions (Dominican Republic 1965) and subsequent coups in Bolivia (1971), Uruguay (1972), Chile (1973) and Argentina (1976).

A prolonged war by the guerrillas in Colombia will provide breathing room for the rest of the Left. Thus it is essential that maximum support and solidarity be extended to the struggle. Internationalism is not only the solidarity network against the new imperial offensive but in support of the Colombian peasants and workers organized in their 'Peoples Army.'

These are dangerous and hopeful times—dangers that cut both ways: for the Empire and for the Left.

Note

1   In regard to this objective, we can go straight to the horse's mouth, as it were: 'Let's look at it simply. The most important difference between North Korea and Iraq is that economically, we just had no choice in Iraq. The country swims on a sea of oil,' Paul Wolfowitz, US Deputy Defense Secretary. At http://www.guardian.co.uk/Iraq/Story/0,2763,970331,00.html. A 'private sector' perspective on this issue is given by Larry Goldstein, President of the Petroleum Industry Research Foundation, as follows: 'If we go to war, it's not about oil,' he told the Wall Street Journal, 'But the day the war ends, it has everything to do with oil'.

PART II

THE MACRODYNAMICS OF GLOBALIZATION

Chapter Four

Denationalization of Mexico: The World Bank in Action

John Saxe-Fernández and Gian Carlo Delgado-Ramos

To reflect on the processes of economic internationalization requires a serious effort to identify the specific agents involved as well as to gauge the weight and effect of their actions. These agents or agencies include the capitalist states at both the centre and the periphery of the world capitalist system (hereinafter CCSs and PCSs), the multinational corporations (MNCs) that roam the world in search of profitmaking opportunities and the international organizations that dominate the world economy. An indispensable step in this analysis is to elaborate a 'situational frame' that allows us to delineate the relations of domination and subordination that exist at this level.

After taking this first step we proceed towards a deconstruction of the workings of the US imperial state in Mexico via the agency of the World Bank. The secular empire of the World Bank group of international financial institutions (hereinafter the WBG) is analysed in some detail with regard to efforts to exploit and gain control of one of Mexico's largest pools of strategic productive resources and wealth. The processes of privatization and denationalization involved in these efforts could be analysed in terms of the major assaults made in recent years against Mexico's agricultural production, its water resources and other areas of the country's biodiversity. In this chapter, however, we concentrate on the World Bank's imperial strategy with regards to Mexico's oil resources and associated petrochemicals industry.

The operations of the World Bank in Mexico can be categorized and periodized in two phases, the second of which roughly corresponds to the implementation of the 'new economic model' (neoliberalism) in the wake of 'the debt crisis' (1982-3). With regard to the first phase, we focus on the political dynamics of the conditionalities attached to World Bank loans—and the political leverage gained over government economic policy by these means. We first examine some paradigmatic examples of World Bank loans in the first phase of Bank operations in Mexico. We then proceed with the documentation, and analysis, of some of the World Bank's principal Mexican operations in regard to the privatization and denationalization (*extranjerización*) of resources that are of vital economic and political importance. This analysis relates to the second phase of World Bank operations. In the interest of brevity we limit our discussion here to the production of oil and the associated petrochemicals industry.

In the conclusion to this chapter we provide some final considerations on the impact of the World Bank's operations in Mexico on behalf of the US imperial state.

A Situational Frame—a Matter of Analysis

At issue in our analysis is the persistence of assymetrical relations of imperialism and colonialism that after Bretton Woods were maintained but took on a new or different form, preserving operations of economic exploitation between the centre and the periphery while the formal institutions of colonial rule were generally abandoned. Thus, with reference to the *modus operandi* of the World Bank Group of institutions[1] and associated institutional 'actors' such as the *Inter-American Development Bank* (IDB), the *Global Environmental Facility* (GEF) and the *Economic Commission for Latin America and the Caribbean* (ECLAC), we will undertake a critical analysis of the role of these institutions in inducing a process of denationalization of Mexico's strategic assets in the guise of 'privatization.' We explore this process in the geoeconomic and political context of Mexico, and with particular reference to the sociopolitical and military-strategic outcomes of this denationalization process, categorized by James Petras, an American political sociologist, as a 'cogovernment.'

Petras (1987: 28-30) distinguishes between three types of relations that exist between the World Bank group of institutions (hereinafter the WBG) and peripheral capitalist or 'Third World' States—relations of (i) subordination; (ii) convergence on the basis of unequal and coerced agreements; and (iii) negotiation and resistance.[2] This categorization corrects a number of the epistemological vices characteristic of the euphoric, abstract and deterministic discourse on 'globalization,' enabling him to reincorporate the power equation as an indispensable frame of reference in the study of economic internationalization and, at the same time, to analyze the changing correlation of changes in the correlation of internal and external forces.

This perspective can be contrasted with that of those theorists who view 'globalization' as if it unfolds in a power vacuum—as the result of the automatic, if hidden, workings of the 'free market.' A countercurrent to this conventional or mainstream approach proceeds by identifying the instruments of state and class wielded from the imperial power in the North via what Costa Rican ex-president Rodrigo Carazo terms the World Bank's *'country managers* in the South' (Saxe-Fernández, 1999: 9-68; 2001). In these terms one of the the aims of this chapter is to expose the relations of power inherent in, and the political-institutional parameters of what is widely known as 'globalization.'

In this context it makes sense to ask whether there exists any empirical basis for the widespread notion of a self-regulating world economic system that is beyond political control. Alternatively, does it make sense to speak and write of national economies across the world that have been inserted into the system by means of the automatic processes of the 'world market?' Is it possible to view markets and production systems, and the world economy overall, as essentially self-regulated? If these questions can be answered in the affirmative then the regulatory mechanisms of the state, both in the North and in the South, vis-à-vis the operations of the MNCs are increasingly obsolete or irrelevant (Saxe-Fernández, et al., 1999: 12-13; Petras, 2001: 33-85; Bellamy, 2002: 1-16). One would have, in effect, a world of weak or powerless states, dominated by the global reach and economic power of stateless corporations.

Nevertheless, both historically and in the current context, international economic transactions have always taken place within a 'cauldron of power' centred on the relationship between, on the one hand, the CCS and their instruments of hegemonic projection such as the WBG of IFIs, and, on the other, the MNCs (Magdoff, 1978; Kolko, 1972). In this context, far from being 'stateless' virtually all the MNCs operate across the world from a home base in a nation-state (Hirst and Thompson, 1996; Doremus et al., 2000; Petras and Veltmeyer, 2001).

As Harry Magdoff (1978: 183) has put it: 'it is necessary to recognize that each capitalist firm relates to the world system through, and must eventually rely on, the nation state.' At issue is an imperial state that regulates and protects its MNCs, providing them all manner of subsidies whether these be charged to the public purse or take the form of pressures exerted through diverse financial or economic, poltical or diplomatic channels—or the projection of military power. This point is made by Diaz-Polanco (2002: 59) in the following terms:

> it is not the free development of the market that determines politics, but it is politics (via the formidable weapon of the nation-state) that defines the direction and behaviour of markets. It is not . . . the impersonal forces [of the market] but powerful interest groups, with their human and contingent aims that make decisions, project and implement strategies of capital...the so-called 'globalization' is in reality a political project that is clearly designed [within the centre of power] and that allows the holders of this power to use their preeminent position in the countries at the centre and on the periphery, and its international financial institutions, to impose their policies and appropriate wealth and use of the nation-state.

The history, evolution and current behaviour of the WBG validate this perspective. It is worth noting in this regard that after World War II, the United States and its principal European allies considered it inadvisable to maintain the form of political colonialism that had hitherto characterized the international economic system. However, it was necessary to substitute for this system another that permitted the continuation of imperialist control over, and exploitation of, the natural resources and markets of capitalism's peripheral areas. To this purpose they designed a new international economic architecture that would secure the avoidance of another 'great depression,' the nodal point of the complex causality of World War II and the likely cause of another. The fundamental motivation behind US foreign policy, then as now, was to place the rest of the world under the dominion of institutionalized principles that reflect its economic and geostrategic interests. The IMF and the World Bank were designed for this purpose, as was the WTO some fifty years later. These Bretton Woods institutions were so designed, via the voting mechanism, that Washington could dominate their policies and foment programmes that would facilitate the growth of its 'private sector.' Those mechanisms were meant for the mutual protection and enhancement of their strategies. For this 'reason' membership in the IMF is a prerequisite for incorporation into the World Bank. The architects of this system, according to Joyce and Gabriel Kolko:

> designed (these institutions) not merely to implement disinterested principles but to reflect the United States control of the majority of the world's monetary gold and its ability to provide a large part or its future capital. The IBRD (BM) was tailored to give a governmentally assured framework for future private capital investment, much of which would be American (Kolko and Kolko, 1972: 16).

Although these instruments—to which GATT (now the WTO) would be added—were designed as a substitute for the pre-war colonial system and in no way was it intended to transform the system in such as a way as to deny the new hegmonic power (the US) and its allies access to the natural resources, cheap labour and markets of 'the South.' Indeed the system was so designed as to mantain for the countries 'at the centre' (North) a favourable balance in terms of international transfers of 'productive resources' and economic surplus. And, as argued by the economists at ECLAC,[3] this was particularly the case for the United States vis-à-vis Latin America and the Caribbean (González-Casanova, 1999; Saxe-Fernández and Núñez, 2001: 87-166).

The end of the *belle epoque* by the end of the Second World War, led to the weakening and collapse of colonial institutions based on the principles and institutions of British 'free trade' (the forced exchange, by the colonies, of raw materials for imperial manufactured goods), making it impossible to maintain colonialism in its traditional form and, as indicated, leading to the elaboration of new mechanisms of economic exploitation. 'The only solution,' as noted by Edward Goldsmith (1999), 'was to open our markets to the countries in the Third World, incorporating them into the industrial system within the orbit of our commerce.' This, he added, 'was the essence of the Bretton Woods conference.'

In Bretton Woods as well as subsequent summit meetings, to set in motion a worldwide process of financial reorganization, Washington characterized the resulting institutions as 'multilateral' or 'international' when in reality they were fundamentally conceived of as an important part of the *Pax Americana*, and, as such, a means of exercising a specific form of 'selective bilateralism.' In this agenda, the United States also consolidated its projection of the dollar as the major international currency and standard of exchange (Kolko and Kolko, 1972: 84).

The idea was to create a complex of 'international' institutions, whose control by the United States was guaranteed by means of an internal voting system based on the principle of 'one dollar, one vote.' The case of the IMF is illustrative. According to Section 2-c (Adjustment of Quotas), Article III (Quotas and

Subscriptions) of the *Agreements of the IMF*, 'an 85 percent majority of the total voting power shall be required for any change in quotas.' Because of the capital that it has contributed, the US can count on 17.16 percent of all the votes (Borón, 2001: 46). In contrast, China and India, with more than a third of the world population, barely have a 4.88 percent of the voting power. As a result, the United States can block any actions that it sees as contrary to its interests and, at the same time, it can count on the support of 'allies' on a 'quid pro quo' basis. Moreover, as a crucial aspect of the IMF is the formalization of impunity vis-à-vis the national and international normative system. Section 3 (Immunity from Judicial Process), Article IX (Status Immunities and Privileges) of the *Agreements of the IMF* reads as follows:

'The Fund, its properties and its assets, wherever located and by whosoever held, shall enjoy immunity from every form of judicial process except to the extent that it expressly waives its immunity for the purpose of any proceedings or by the terms of any contract.' According to Section 9 of the same Article, 'All Governors, Executive Directors, Alternates, members of the committees, representatives . . . advisors of any of the foregoing persons, officers and employees of the Fund: (i) shall be immune from legal process . . . except when the Fund waives this immunity' (www.imf.org).

In effect, we have here a 'New International Order' in which, as explained by former Secretary of the Treasurer, Henry Morgenthau, 'international trade and international investment can be carried on by businessmen on business principles' (Senate Committee on Banking and Currency, Bretton Woods Agreement cited in Kolko and Kolko, 1972). The specialists of the Department of State at the time were emphatic in their recognition that this state of affairs could only be achieved on the basis of institutions that operated with the principles 'of free trade and private enterprise, the conceptual nucleus of the foreign policy of the United States' (Kolko, 1974: 698). And, they added, 'this [foreign policy goal] was incompatible with an extensive growth of state property and with commerce in state hands.'

These principles have been maintained to this very day as evident in the IMF's webpage (http://www.imf.org/external/about.htm):

since the IMF was established in 1946, its purposes have remained unchanged but its operations—which involve surveillance, financial assistance, and technical assistance—have developed to meet the changing needs of its member countries in an evolving world economy.

The aforementioned has led to a policy of the privatization and decentralization of strategic national assets, including 'natural assets' such as biodiversity and water. It is the *International Finance Corporation* (IFC), within the World Bank system, together with the *Global Environmental Facility* (GEF), that has been the major 'actor' in this regard. As noted on the GEF (http://www.gefweb.org):

... the World Bank, in its role as a GEF implementing agency, should play the primary role in ensuring the development and management of investment projects. ... The World Bank draws upon the investment experience of its affiliate, the International Finance Corporation (IFC) . . . to promote investment opportunities and to mobilize private sector resources.

We have here the institution of the IFC, as part of the WBG, as an agent for articulating relations of cooperation among various international 'partner' institutions including the MNCs and 'host' nation-states with their governments. The IFC, in effect, has positioned itself, as of the 1980s, as the launching platform for projects not only of privatization but of the denationalization of the strategic assets of countries on the periphery. In this context, it operates in a very convoluted manner to hide the true beneficiaries of its programme. The IFC

promotes sustainable private sector development primarily by a) financing private sector projects located in the developing world b) helping private companies in the developing world mobilize financing in international financial markets c) providing advice and technical assistance to businesses and governments (www.ifc.org).

The IFC's actions are organized and implemented through diverse interconnected working 'clusters' and 'sub-clusters.' Invariably, at the end of this 'clustering' process the primary, if not exclusive, beneficiaries are selected, usually US- or EC-based, MNCs.[4]

The World Bank in Mexico

A review of the World Bank's major operations in Mexico demonstrate in concrete form the operational principles of US imperialism synthesized above. These operations can also be found in other PCS, particularly in Latin America where facilitating or enabling conditions for the penetration of US capital have been generated by close to two decades of neoliberal policies. These conditions threaten to deepen under Plan Pueblo Panama (PPP) and the proposed formation of a Free Trade Area [in] the Americas (FTAA).

It is possible to distinguish two major phases of the World Bank's operations in Mexico. The first dates from the launching of the Bank to the mid-1970s and the beginnings of the 1980s; it relates to the an import substitution model of industrial development. The second represents the neoliberal model, implemented under conditions of a widespread 'debt crisis' (in 1982), based on what has become known as the 'Washington Consensus' (Williamson, 1990).[5]

The impact of the World Bank and related institutions on the structure and intra-institutional dynamics of Mexico's economy were extended and deepened throughout the 1980s with the growth of the national debt and the servicing of this debt by the government. Undue influence on the dynamics of government policy applied particularly to the IMF at the macroeconomic level and the WB in regard to sectoral programmes. This influence was particularly strong in regards to the Secretaries of State and in the executing agencies vis-à-vis new loans.

In the first phase of Bank operations (up to the 1982 crisis) projects were managed and supervised by the Fideicomiso of the *Banco de Mexico* and later by *Banxico*; others were managed by the National Fund for Tourism (*Fondo Nacional para el Turismo*), the Secretary of Agriculture and Water Resources (Secretaría de Agricultura y Recursos Hidráulicos), the Secretary of Ports and National Railways (*Ferrocarriles Nacionales de México*), the Federal Electric Power Commission (*Comisión Federal de Electricidad*), the secretary of Budgeting (*Secretaría de Programación y Presupuesto*), *Fertilizantes de México*, the National Bank of [Public] Works (*Banco Nacional de Obras*), *Nafinsa*, the Rural Bank (Banco Rural), etc.

Loans always include commission payments, a formal and legally established procedure in international agreements. Within the framework of international law, they refer to stipulated amounts (generally a percentage negotiated on the basis of the total amount of capital borrowed) to be paid once the operation is approved—although the project in question has not been approved by either the executive or the legislature of the host country. Thus, even though approved funds have not been disbursed the 'loan' begins to incur interest and generate profits for the creditor, the cost of which is added to the total amount of the debt owed. In this way, the WBG (World Bank, IMF, IDB, etc.) receives both a commission and interest payments on top of the money borrowed, as negotiated by the Executive and invariably approved by the Legislature. We can add to this the mechanisms used by the Bank to *jinetear* ('jockey') the amount borrowed, paid out in *tramos* ('tranches'),[6] for other investments. *Tramos* are also functional for the power exercised by the Bank over the PCS because of the conditionalities and performance schedule attached to them.

In the first phase the emphasis was on construction or the improvement of communications infrastructure as part of the Bank's effort to promote North-South trade and the position of the MNCs in this trade, particularly in the US's Latin America's periphery. The hegemony of the CCS in this phase is manifest in the dominant position of their MNCs in regard to both exports and domestic markets. Unlike Asia where national firms, on the basis of domestic savings and investment strategy dominated the home market, in Latin America these markets were dominated by the MNCs (Petras and Veltmeyer, 1999).

Returning to the Mexico case, loans for infrastructural projects and for other activities in agriculture, mining, industry, services, housing, etc., tended to have a national component, generally 50 percent. But in each case the participation creditor country enterprises, principally from the United States, is part and parcel of the 'conditionalities' attached to the lines of credit extended—and facilitated—by the Bank. Thus the World Bank not only directed how and where borrowed money was to be used but it set parameters on the investment and use of public funds derived from taxes collected from the Mexican population. This is also a characteristic of developments in the second phase (see below) but with even greater intensity.

Some Pradigmatic Examples of World Bank Loans (First Period)

In May 1972 the Secretriat of the Navy sought funds of US$42 million to upgrade port facilities. The project, approved by the Bank, included the purchase of dredging equipment; storage, warehousing and communications systems; loading and fire protection equipment; and consulting services and personnel training. The Bank's participation in the funding (820 ME) was in the form of a $20 million loan. Its agreement commission, in this case, was US$429 million; the interest rate was 7.25 percent; and interest payments (up to March 1977) were US$9,650 million.

It would not be incorrect to suggest that the central concern in this and other cases was not to stimulate development in the debtor country but to strengthen various private interests in the creditor country, in this case, the United States. Although the dominant paradigm was 'import substitution industrialization' all equipment acquisitions were made through creditor country MNCs. Of the group of foreign enterprises that directly benefited in this way—including *Seadrec LTD*, *Dubigean Normandie, Sumimoto, Shoji Kcuslea, LTD*—six were American, one was English, one French, one Canadian, one Swiss and one Japanese. Collectively these MNCs received US$15,480,249 in loan funds.

As for the various railway 'projects' approved and funded by the WB in the same period they were not generally directed towards their indirect control—and the privatization of FNM—as was the case throughout the 1980s and 1990s. The aim, instead, was to ensure the modernization of the system and increased capacity vis-à-vis commerce between Mexico and the United States, that is, Mexico's exports of minerals, petroleum and other raw materials, and its importing of goods manufactured in the United States.

The World Bank's 'Second Railroad Loan' (June 1972) of US$75 million was not paid off for another 25 years but by September 1977, five years into the loan, had already generated close to US$53 million in interest payments. Into the 1990s the government was still meeting interest payments of US$125 million even though the Bank itself pushed for the dismantling, privatization and denationalization of state enterprises. As in most of the Bank's pre-privatization 'loans' funds directed towards the national railroad system were designed to privatize (and denationalize) profits and to socialize (nationalize) the costs. For a *bonus*, the Bank in this case favoured *Motorola Communication Division* (US), *Sidney Steel Corp.* (Nova Scotia), *Nippon Electric* (Japan) and la empresa maderera *Hondumex*, a forest products company registered in Honduras.

The World Bank's 'third Railroad Project' loan (11232 ME) for US$100 million was negotiated in 1976, with the last 'tranche' payment set for November 2000. The agreement commission was US$2,526,000 and interest payments were US$16,258,000. Beneficiaries included 35 US-based MNCs, six Japanese, two English, one German and a Dutch one. The World Bank doled out to these MNCs a total of US$94 million, including US$3 million for *Missouri Pacific Railroad*; US$21 million for *Nippon Electric*; US$2.3 million for *NAB International*; US$4.9 million for *Koyo International*; US$16.6 million for *Sidney Steel*; US$3.3 million for *Breuco Inc*; US$6.8 million for *Multisystems Inc*; US$6.8 million for *Fruit*

Grower. Most of the remaining funds went to scores of small or medium-sized firms, mostly American.

A paradigmatic case of World Bank loans, under the rubric of 'import substitution' in the industrial sector was 1205 ME, negotiated by *Banxico* and designed to 'finance fixed assets and feasibility studies for Mexican industrial firms that produce goods and services for exports [and thus] reduce imports [for the country].' The project, financed with US$50 million, was signed in April 1976, with a grace period of two years and ten months, and the last 'tranche' of capital between 15 February 1979 and 15 August 1992. The interest rate for the loan was 8.5 percent and interest payments were set at US$15,133,000, with another US$ 732 million in the form of an Agreement Commission. Two thirds of the firms favoured with a 'contract'—collectively worth US$37 million—were US-based MNCs. With the participation of over 300 firms the actual amounts involved per firm is not large, but everything indicates that the aim of the Bank was to inhibit development of a national sector of machine tooling and railroad stock, displacing Mexican firms in the industry with foreign ones and opening up spaces for MNCs in the domestic market. The World Bank programme, in effect if not by design, served to promote US and European Community exports and to create conditions for the concentration of capital and the virtual dismantling of the national industry in machine tools and metallurgy. Under NAFTA, initiated in 1 January 1994, the same day on which the Zapatistas exploded onto the national—and world—scene, this 'development' would be accelerated.

Another interesting case involved FERTIMEX, a *paraestatal* or state enterprise in the agricultural sector, whose privatization was brought about with the considerable 'aid' of the WB. The loan (1112-ME) for *FERTIMEX I* was for US$50 million. It was negotiated and signed in May 1975 with a grace period of three years and eight months and a final 'tranche' payment in July 1989. It was directed towards the construction of diverse plants to produce the basic ingredients for fertilizers. For example, the Urea plant in Coatzacoalcos, Veracruz, with a capacity of half a million metric tonnes annually. Another is in Salamanca, Guanajuato, with an annual production capacity of 330,000 metric tonnes.

A central notion behind *FERTIMEX I* and most infrastructure loans, as shown above, is not only to stimulate MNC operations but also to promote small and medium firms in creditor countries. In this case, 100 percent of equipment and materials, valued at an estimated US$33 million, together with all engineering and consulting services, as emphasized in the document, were 'imported' from 'outside the country.' In this case the beneficiaries (of US$30 million in contracts) included 111 US firms; seven others were Italian, three of them German, three Japanese, one from Israel and one was French.[7]

The given examples not only provide indications of the role played by the World Bank in the *sui generis* 'import substitution' model in this period. They also point towards the role played by the Mexican state in the context of the drive towards 'globalization' (to insert Mexico into the process) and, as noted by Fernando Jajnzylber (1983), 'the absence of an effective leadership [within the Mexican capitalist or political class] in the construction of a potential endogenous industry capable of adapting, innovation and competing internationally in a broad range of production sectors.'

The 'development option' for the great part of Mexico's 'political class,' members of which historically have shown themselves all too keen to exploit any opportunities for personal enrichment, has been relegated to denationalized programmes and economic strategies based on external debt financing and indebtedness), FDI, bank loans (*los empréstitos*) and the so-called 'forces of the market.' In this context no country in the region, not even Chile, currently the darling of the free marketeers, in its *modus operandi* (clientelistic relation with foreign capital and CCS) has managed to produce overall positive results.

These 'developments' in Mexico and Latin America contrast markedly with similar developments in Japan, South Korea and other 'rapidly growing countries' in South East Asia. In these countries high levels of economic growth and 'development' were achieved on the basis of a highly interactive relationship between the 'private sector' and the state, with strategic planning generally undertaken by the latter and imposed on the former or implemented under conditions of shared interests (Saxe-Fernández, 1998: 120-138). From this we should not infer the absence of corruption, personal enrichment, speculation, and profoundly inequitable owner-worker relations in these countries. The relevance of the comparison between countries in Asia and Latin America consists in the fact that in the case of the Asian elite we have an 'establishment' of national capital with chartacteristic vices and advantages, As to Mexico's elite we have a new oligarchy whose reference group and psycho-social indentification is with the Anglo-American 'way of life.'

As Carlos Monsivais, the well-known writer and political commentator of Mexican affairs, observed, the behaviour of this oligarchy can be characterized as one of 'willing subservience' and thus intregally 'antinational.' Large elements of this elite have responded to the siren of American 'culture' (opportunities for personal enrichment—for 'making it') by a willingness to appropriate any crumbs (migajas) left by Americans in their economic 'operations' in Mexico and, in this context, to be content with even a marginal participation in the 'wealth' or economic surplus generated in the process of capitalist development of the country's 'productive resources.' The result? In addition to the huge transfers of wealth outside of the country, the concentration of the remaining 'wealth' in the hands, pockets and banks of the country's elite—and poverty for the immense majority of the population. According to the National Statistics Agency (*Instituto Nacional de Estadística, Geografía e Informática*) and the Bank of Mexico (1994), in 1984 the poorest decile of households received only 1.7 percent of national income (the GNP), a share that was reduced to 1.6 percent by 1989 and 1.5 in 1992 (Saxe-Fernández, 1994: 333). At the same time, the share in national income of the richest decile of families rose from 32.8 percent in 1984 to 37.9 percent in 1989 and 38.2 in 1992.

In this context World Bank loans reinforced tendencies within Mexico's elite—and those in the rest of Latin America—to accept a subordinate position within the structure of North-South relations. In the same context diverse proposals for intra-regional economic integration and the construction and consolidation of regional trading blocs have not fared well.

The failure of schemes for regional integration can be attributed to various factors, including an inversion of priorities vis-à-vis commerce and the currency. The general weakness of national monetary and financial instruments, and the absence of regional ones, a situation that in part has been encouraged by the World Bank and the IMF, and in part by Latin America's indigenous 'oligarchy,' have not allowed for any effective endogenous regional development plannning or institutions. In the face of this situation, and with the growing power of the euro, the WBG has promoted the replacement of national currencies with the US dollar (as in Panama, El Salvador and Ecuador). This 'situation' and 'development' both anticipates and makes more likely the eventual adoption of a Latin American Free Trade Area (LAFTA), which most observers see as an arrangement designed to benefit, above all, the US economy. In fact, some see it as a new form of colonialism, based as it is on a structure (relations of dependency) that favours the MNCs.

Mexico's path towards industrial nationalism staked out by the State as of the late 1930s under the rubric of 'the [Mexican] Revolution' was synthesized by Lombardo Toledano in the slogan *'to nationalize is to decolonize.'* The influence exerted by the World Bank in its Mexican 'operations' over the past two decades can be seen in the modification in this slogan made by José Angel Conchello, former Partido Acción Nacional (PAN) senator: *'to privatize is to recolonize.'* This formula expresses succinctly developments in the next phase of the Bank's Mexican operations.

The Period After 1982: Co-government with the World Bank

The installation of a regime dominated to an astonishing degree by international creditors, in the context and as a result of negotiations arising out of Mexico's debt crisis in 1982 involved a frontal attack against the as yet fragile pivots of Latin American nationalism, and, as have noted, a major campaign to provide private (and foreign) interests greater access to the country's productive resources.

With the added newly acquired leverage of debt renegotiation mechanisms, and of the associated 'conditionalities,' the World Bank campaigned for greater influence over the levers and deployment of state power vis-à-vis the economy. The result: a form of co-government formed between state officials and the WBG, who installed their own functionaries in the design of 'national' development plans, and in preparation of the national budget, accounting procedures and management of the economy. In relatively short order, the World Bank, the IMF and other international organizations such as the BID, extended their intervention from trade policies to those involving mining, biodiversity and water, the 'restructuring' of the energy sector (oil, natural gas, electric power), transportation (railways, airports and highways), heavy industry, agriculture and fertilizers, financial deregulation, employment retraining and 'human resource development,' housing construction, social assistance and the vaunted 'war against poverty' (World Bank, May 1989).

In each of these areas the Bank intervened with its 'loans' and thus with its missions of technical evaluation, control and supervision. Between 1982 and 1990 the Bank's sectoral loans were increased to US$11,500,000 and each Department of State (*Secretaria*), each state enterprise—and private ones—formed an ongoing relationship with the Bank, whether this relation be direct or indirect, or one of evaluation and supervision—or control. This relationship, in its diverse permutations, seen by the Bank as one of 'partnership,' persists to this day.

At issue is the denationalization (*extranjerización*) of the decision-making process, with profoundly negative implications—economic, sociopolitical, constitutional, and with regards to national sovereignty and national security. Also at issue is the *de facto* or virtual co-government formed in the process of a 'double conditionality.' We refer here to a twofold synergizing process involved in the institution of NAFTA in 1994 and subsequent (and on-going) efforts to extend 'free trade' to the entire hemisphere. On the one hand, there is the cross-fertilization that exists between the conditionalities (stabilization measures) imposed by the IMF on the government's macroeconomic policy and the conditionalities (structural adjustment reforms) applied by the World Bank to different economic sectors. This could be viewed as an 'external synergy.' Then we have the same structure reproduced within each organization in the context of its programme operations. A matter of internal synergy.

The dynamics of this process are clearly illustrated in the regime and administration of de la Madrid (1982-1988), which took Mexico's economy on a neoliberal path. First, there was the declaration by the Mexican government in 1982 that it would not be able meet its debt repayment obligations. It was this declaration and the underlying situation, conditions of which were also present elsewhere in the region, particularly in Argentina and Brazil, that provoked the 'debt crisis' and led the IMF and the World Bank to concert their policies vis-à-vis the requirement for both macroeconomic stabilization and structural adjustments to the economy. Second, the loans arranged by the Bank and the Fund were conditioned on the acceptance by the government of a new set of economic policies—and an agenda set by the country's creditors. Specifically, the *Trade Policy Loans* arranged by the Bank, on condition that the government meet the requirements set out in the Letter of Intent signed with the IMF, was designed so as to open up the Mexican economy and to liberalize trade—and integration into the US economy. This 'development' was induced by means of the following operations: TPL 1 (Loan 2745 ME) and TPL-2 (Loan 2882 ME) as well as two export loans. In 1989, the President of the World Bank (1989) talked of the instrumental effects of these loans in the following terms: 'most promising . . . import barriers have been dramatically reduced for agricultural inputs such as machinery, pesticides and other high technology products.'

The loans in question, totalling a million dollars, were very 'persuasive' in causing the government to adjust its trade policy to the requirements of the United States and the agenda of the creditors. For example it has allowed the highly subsidized surplus production of US grains (wheat, corn) and other agricultural products to be shipped to Mexico, with drastically negative effects on Mexico's agriculture. In 1988, 4,900 tariffs on US exports as well as the need for export licences were entirely eliminated. In this regard, the President of the World Bank (1989) pointed out that

> the Mexican government fulfilled its obligations and commitments according to the operations stipulatd in both loans. It liberalized over three quarters of its internal production and licensing. Less than a quarter is left under state control, in some agricultural and food products, petroleum and its derivitatives, automobiles, some electronic products, pharmaceuticals and a few others.

He added:

> [T]he trade policy loan was a major breaking point. By this means the World Bank managed to finance the introduction of the process of trade reform. The second loan was oriented towards maintaining this opening within the parameters established by the first and it had a series of objectives, that the Mexican government must meet for funds in the second phase to be freed.

By means of just a few millions of dollars this 'breaking point' changed the internal dynamics of the Mexican government as well as the 'correlation of forces' involved in the relationship that had existed between two very unequal economic and political systems. It also established a very different trading relationship, a commercial opening without reciprocity, based on what could well be viewed as a new form of imperialism, a system dominated by the United States.

In this regard, consider that in 2000 the World Bank (2001) estimated Mexico's GNP as US$574.5 billion, while the GNP of the United States was US$9.9 trillion. Mexico's annual per capita income, measured in terms of a seriously overvalued *peso*, was in the order of US$5,070 while in the United States it was US$34,260. These figures indicate a ratio of 17 to one between the size of the two economies but on a per capita basis this ratio is reduced to 6.5. But this statistical procedure does not reflect the actual or real dimensions of the assymetry between the two economies. This would require a different perspective, based on a comparison of the two countries' stock of accumulated wealth (assigning value to all manner of assets—natural, physical, financial—including highways, railroads, industries, real estate, automobiles, etc. By this measure it is estimated that the ratio of difference between the United States and Mexico rises to an order of 250 to 300. With an assymetry of this magnitude it is not possible to have a type of relationship that would permit serious negotiations leading to a mutuality of national interest, particularly if one party to these negotiations (the United States) has at its disposal such a disporportionately large arsenal of weapons, instruments and agents, including the World Bank and the IMF. At issue is a power structure with its inevitable relations of domination and subordination, (neo)imperialism and (neo)colonialism, between two sets of economic interests.

Mexico's Oil in the Bank's Crosshairs

With the exhaustion of reserves of petroleum, natural gas, coal and other sources of energy in the United States, and a concomitant and growing dependency on external sources of supply, the interest of both Washington and the World Bank in the western hemisphere's hydrocarbon reserves and associated industries has intensified, particularly over the last two decades. Consider that in 1958 the American geologist King Hubbert elaborated a statistical methodology that permitted him to predict a serious shortfall in domestic reserves and supply of oil in 1970. A more refined form of this methodology has been applied by other geologists for other areas of the world (Deffeyes, 2001). The results indicate reserves of anywhere from 1.8 to 2.1 billion barrels, which suggests that the wave of world production of conventional (cheap) sources of crude oil would crest either in 2001 or 2003/4, with a persistent decline thereafter in production levels—and a dramatic repercussion on the world capitalist economy geared to the production and consumption of oil (Deffeyes, 2001: 4).

In the context of this problem the reserves and supply of oil in the region, particularly in Venezuela and Mexico, have increased in strategic importance to the United States, which, as a result, has pursued a series of strategies designed to improve and secure access of its MNCs to these hemispheric reserves. The Bank's campaign for Mexico and other countries in the region to structurally adjust their economies—to liberalize trade and the movement of investment capital; to deregulate private economic activity; and, above all, to privatize ownership of productive resources and enterprises—has also been brought to bear on the problem. As of the 1980s, the parastal Petróleos Mexicanos (Pemex) has been targeted by the WB for privatization. Using the argument or excuse of the need for 'efficiency,' the World Bank in its *Strategy Papers* (1995: 110) instructed the Mexican government as to the need to increase 'the participation of private initiatives in the hydrocarbon sector as much to allow companies [the MNCs] to compete against Pemex as the sale of Pemex's assets, which promise to bring enormous advances in efficiency.'

Although the World Bank over the course of little more than a ten-year campaign has achieved substantial 'advances' in regard to its privatization strategy—under the Presidency of Carlos Salinas de Gortari the privatization of up to 1200 state enterprises, including *de facto* privatization of some of Pemex's important activities—it does not consider the 'end result' to be satisfactory. Its 'objective' is to secure the privatization and denationalization of Pemex, particular its most profitable sectors such as petrochemicals.

Without a doubt the United States's agenda includes the privatization (and de-nationalization) of Mexico's oil industry. The aim of the United States government vis-à-vis securing the privatization of Mexico's oil industry is manifest, inter alia, in the World Bank's privatization agenda and in the effective *in situ* control by US-based enterprises of Pemex operations. The Bank's strategy revolves around five measures conceived by its technocracy and outlined in the Bank's 'Hydrocarbon Strategy Paper' (1995: 98-113) as a 'roadmap' that the Mexican government should follow. This roadmap includes the following steps:

- Allow risk contracts for oil exploration and development.
- Allow a majority interest of foreign investment in petrochemicals.
- Break up Pemex into separate enterprises and under competition.
- Subject Pemex to both domestic and foreign competition.
- Privatization of Pemex.

Three of these steps have been incorporated into an argument made by the Bank in favour of privatization in diverse documents and published by the Heritage Foundation in terms of the following justifications:

- That Pemex does not invest sufficiently in either explorarion, in development or petrochemicals.
- That Pemex should be dismembered, broken up into separate and independent entities, each operating independently and with proft criteria, permitting domestic and foreign competition, and resulting in greater efficiency.
- That privatizing Pemex totally would allow Mexico to pay both its external and domestic debt.

These three justifications are fallacious. First, because the Mexican government imposes irrationally high taxes, representing 95 percent of profits, that are directed towards debt service and other nonproductive expenditures, so that there is scarcely enough left to maintain the immense infrastructure of Pemex, which covers the whole national territory. During López Portillo's six-year term as President direct taxes paid by Pemex were equivalent to 61 percent of its total exports. Under de la Madrid they were pushed to 84 percent and during Salinas's term (or reign) taxes charged to Pemex rose to an irresponsible 158 percent of its export earnings (Manzo, 1996: 51).

Secondly, under the auspices of the World Bank Salinas, Gortari and Zedillo implemented a process dubbed by the United States as a 'divestiture' that, in effect, constituted a partial dismemberment of Pemex. The big oil companies, however, at the same time went in a different direction (Tanzer, 1983; Gachúz Maya, 2000: 64-114). They pursued a strategy of vertical integration to increase their capacity to coordinate decisions on the production, refining and marketing of oil. The 'divestiture' of Pemex was designed to create small and inefficient companies that would be vulnerable and easily dominated by the stronger MNCs that would at some point 'reintegrate' them within their vertical structure. This was the apparent and largely successful aim of the Bank.

As for the Bank's third 'argument,' it is worthwhile remembering that Michael Tanzer has demonstrated that if Pemex were privatized, say for US$150 billion as proposed by the *Heritage Foundation* the investment would necessarily be foreign: DuPont, Exxon-Mobil, Shell, Amoco, etc. Since the profit expectation of these corporations is at a minimum 20 percent the Mexican economy would likely yield an annual 'export' of $30 billion in the form of capital (Tanzer, 1983). Such a privatization would have a devastating effect on the Mexican economy and the national treasury, constituting as it does the principal source of financing of the federal budget as well as an important source of 'unconditioned' profits. The future contributions of the oil industry to the country and its people would not remotely compare to the value (US$30 billion) of the resources lost each year to the new owners of these resources. If the privatization were fully achieved it would undoubtedly generate conditions of a crisis, both political and social, that would compare with the crisis that has engulfed Argentina under similar conditions (having pioneered the policy of privatization and, in the 1990s advancing further in this direction than any other country in the region, Argentina has been portrayed as the model of privatization). The privatization of Pemex would entail enormous social, economic and political costs for the Mexican population, with few benefits; most of the benefits would be siphoned out of the country into the accounts of the MNCs and their investors, managers and directors.

Returning to the recipe synthesized in the Bank's *roadmap* for the privatization of Pemex, the Bank is very clear as to the parameters under which Pemex should operate as a parastatal enterprise. First, Pemex should

> extend [to the private sector] competitive contracts for exploration and development of each oil field so that the biggest would yield higher rates of profit (ground rents) because the extraction of the resource would be cheaper . . . For Pemex, these contracts would commit the firm to pay the same earnings and taxes as the private firms, and to offer, in addition, incentives for risks taken (World Bank, 1995: 102).

At present the Vicente Fox government is proceeding with this guideline or directive in terms of the Multipler Service Contracts (MSCs) prepared by the Bank for its predecessor but modified in the search for legislative approval. Formally a MSC implies the implementation of a project and tasks set by Pemex although financed by the 'private sector,' both 'national and foreign,' in different areas, including the exploitation of oil deposits under the responsibility of *Pemex Exploración y Perforación*, one of the operating subunits created in Pemex's 'divestiture.'

To a considerable extent MSCs are oriented toward the promotion of 'integration' into the monopoly sector. In the words of Senator Cantón Zetina:

> given their size, the technical requirements and economic capacity of the enterprises participating in the bidding are oriented towards foreign capital, contravening various articles of the Constitution and Mexican laws . . . it violates art. 134 . . . given that these contracts raise the final cost of the work and services and, thus there is no taking advantage of the lowest cost available. Also, our country will not benefit from the wealth generated given that this ends up in the country of origin of the [invested] capital (cited in Rocha, 2002: 1,10).

In the Preliminary Version of the Terms and Conditions of the Project elaborated by Pemex's consultants, all of whom are American, the 'rights' of those party to the contract, mostly MSCs, include:

- Free access to the contract zone and exisiting hydrocarbon installations and duty free use of these installations.
- Use of any sand, grava, suelo and water in the public domain.
- The right to employ workers and personnel, both national and foreign.
- Import any needed goods, services and equipment.
- Freely buy or contract any national service or equipment.
- Finance operations in any way decided on, always and when the contractor [Pemex] will place no duties on reserves and hydrocarbon production.
- Use the hydrocarbons produced in the contract zone for use as energy in the field in conformity with permitted operations.

The concession granted of 20 years differs from the norm of five years, leading deputy (member of Congress) Rosario Tapia to argue that

> The contractee is practically given a piece of national territory to do whatever up to the extraction of gas and the construction of treatment plants. . . . It entails a massive surrender of resources. We are returning to the risk contracts of a century ago that had provoked the oil expropriation [by the state]; they are riskless risk contracts because they [the wells] are perfectly located (cited in Carriles, 2001: 43).

In the case of the basic petrochemicals industry—the second point on the Bank's *roadmap*—its 'deregulation' was effected according to the directions, timetable and needs of foreign interests. The Program, initiated in 1986, had as one of its principal objectives the participation of private enterprise (including foreign) in the sector, which is constitutionally reserved for the State. According to Bank documents the Program was designed to:

- Limit the role of Pemex as the sole producer of basic petrochemicals (de la Madrid and Salinas complied to the letter of this condition with a strategy elaborated by the Bank to have basic petrochemicals reclassified and placed on a 'secondary' list. Also, the Bank insisted on the 'flexibilization' of pricing policy in regards to basic petrochemicals).
- Permit the private sector to import basic petrochemicals and provide fiscal incentives.

Pemex is considered a 'serious impediment'—strategic, political, commercial and entrepreneurial—by the World Bank and the oil and gas industry in the United States. In unpublished World Bank documents it is viewed as 'an obstacle to the development of the petrochemicals industry,' and, therefore, according to the Bank's President, the Mexican government should face swiftly the problem that affects the dominant position of the parastatal in the industry . . . [even worse] the private international firms *cannot achieve vertical integration* because of Pemex's control over basic chemicals . . . [while] Pemex's plans for expansion results in possible foreign investors viewing Mexico as a market of short duration (World Bank, 1995: 102. Emphasis added).

The Bank also notes that in 1989 the Mexican government finally agreed to apply

in this sector a Plan of Action that would include the following fundamental measures: (i) limit the exclusive right of the parastatal [Pemex] to produce a maximum of 25 basic chemicals and to define an initial list of 'secondary' petrochemicals open to private sector participation; and (ii) foment a program of cooperative agreements between the private sector and Pemex.

The plan to privatize the petrochemicals sector has accelerated as a result of the chronic underfinancing and decapitalization to which it has been subjected, this to the point that many of the petrochemical complexes are in ruins or 'chatarra' (steel garbage). The fact is that Pemex's petrochemicals infrastructure has been taken to what the Bank terms the 'selling point.' In addition, the reclassification of basic petrochemicals as secondary has been extended to include oil fields, as President Fox is fond of saying, 'the table has been set.'

It is worth remembering that with the alienation of the petrochemicals sector, the country has lost control and usufruct rights over the sector with the greatest capacity to add value to the country's natural resources. According to calculations made by engineer Rafael Decelis, for a barrel of oil to undergo the various steps in the process of transformation not only adds considerable value to the product—up to US$700 barrel—but it involves a similar increase in employment generation. Considering the growing unemployment and widespread poverty, surrendering these fruits of development is irrational.

In regard to the third ingredient in the Bank's recipe for change—Pemex's administrative reorganization—its goal has been the eventual dissolution of the parastatal, subjecting it to a process of *divestiture*—dismantling it as if it were a 'monopoly' operating in the normative context of anti-monopoly legislation in the United States. In this case, and without regard for the Constitution which places the oil industry under the exclusive control of Pemex, the Bank's *roadmap* proposes to pave the road for the privatization of Pemex by breaking it up 'into competitive units, each of which would be of the size of a big private transnational firm' (World Bank, 1995: iv, 109-110).

Following this signpost, the government of Salinas Gortari 'reorganized' Pemex into four 'decentralized' units (i) Pemex-Exploration and Production; (ii) Pemex-Refining; (iii) Pemex Gas and Basic Petrochemicals; and (iv) Pemex-Petrochemicals, with a coordinating holding (non-operating) company named *Pemex Corporativo* that, according to one of the 'options' presented to the government by the Bank, will eventually disappear in a process of further *devestiture*: 'each subsidiary enterprise will be divided, perhaps, into four independent enterprises. . . . The Corporation Pemex will cease to exist' (World Bank, 1995: 109).

With the view of Pemex's eventual disappearance, the Bank has proposed the establishment of an institutional apparatus similar to what exists in the United States vis-à-vis the hydrocarbon sector, an entity that is, and would be, subject to the power and influence of the industry in the country. According to the World Bank, the Mexican government should proceed with the establishment of a bureacratic apparatus that would be in charge of the administration of hydrocarbon resources—a Federal Hydrocarbon Agency ('authority') that would be independent from Pemex. Such an agency would be responsible for exploration and production, negotiate and sign exploration and production in all existing and future sites; supervise the implementation of investment commitments contracted by Pemex and subsidiary private enterprises, and serve as a depository of information—as is the case, for example, with the *Land Commission* in Oklahoma and the *Texas Railroad Commission* (World Bank, 1995: 109).

The World Bank, Pemex and Workers

During Salinas' Presidency, the Bank, by means of a Hydrocarbon Sector Loan, fomented a programme of 'administrative modernization,' a key element of which was the 'flexibilization' of the Collective Contract signed between the Oil Workers Union (*Sindicato de Trabajadores Petroleros*) and the government as well as a massive downsizing of the labourforce. The Bank had induced a similar development in the Railway sector as part of a region-wide campaign for labour reform (see Chapter 5 below). In 1989 Pemex had a workforce of 280,000; by 1998 this force was reduced to 121,000. However, the 'restructuring' of 150,000 jobs in the areas of drilling, construction, maintenance and general service did not, as announced, result in 'greater organizational, functional and productive efficiency.' On the contrary. The Bank 'prepared' (softened) Pemex so that the international oil companies would take over precisely those areas most affected by the downsizing of both the technical personnel and workers. For example, drilling operations were given over to the private international companies without establishing for them minimal requirements such as the use of Mexican inputs, services and labour. Not only were the adopted measures in flagrant contradiction with the Bank's rhetoric in this regard, but union sources indicate that it was inevitable that the restructuring would not result in any reduction of management or in any unit labour power costs (Gachúz, 2000: 17-118).

As a result of 'decentralization' into four separate units, the number of adminstrative and management personnel grew disproportionately as the production and technical workers were let go. For example, in 1982, when Pemex produced 1.4 billion barrels a year it had a management staff of 203. In 1995, with a lower production level by 117 million barrels, the number of management positions grew to 1,255; that is, the *divestiture* arranged by the Bank resulted in the addition of 1,055 new managers, vice-managers, subdirectors and executive

Directors, with a corresponding layer of supervisors, Heads of Department, Heads of Section and support staff (STPRM, document cited by Gachúz, 2000).

Another major objective of the Bank has been to stimulate exploration and the drilling of wells with the aim of increasing the export of crude oil to the United States, and not withstanding evidence of serious over-production vis-à-vis refining capacity and the overexploitation of reserves, which has caused irreversible damage to the wells. According to Walter Friedeberg, former Pemex Manager:

> the data indicate that the damage to wells caused by immoderate exploitation. In Tabasco-Chiapas average production per well from 1995 to 1998 dropped [significantly]. The decline has been even more dramatic inoffshore fields in Campeche. There average production per well fell to below one half former levels. The average per well of light crude in the region declined by two thirds (cited in Shields, 1996: 32. See also Gachúz, 2000: 120-121).

According to the Bank, however, the over-exploitation of wells does not exist or is not a factor. At the beginning of Zedillo's government in the early 1990s the Bank, with criteria diametrically opposed to those used in available technical reports, but consonant with the interest of the United States in the increase of exports from Mexico, proposed the extension of private investment 'risk contracts' to the end of expanding production for exports (World Bank, 1995: 99).

With the government of Vicente Fox and with Muñoz Leos, former *Dupont CEO* at the Head of Pemex, the exploitation of crude and exports were increased in the context of what the Company Union, the *Unión Nacional de Trabajadores* termed 'the silent privatization' of Pemex (Rocha, 2002). According to this source, each month an average of 179 workers, 'de confianza' and unionized, are fired; exploration and drilling contracts are awarded by Pemex to foreign companies; and management positions are occupied by private sector executives. It is anticipated that 4,000 professionals and technicians, and over 30,000 workers, will be let go, leaving Pemex 'without a cadre of professional and experienced personnel.' As for management personnel they come from firms such as *Dupont, Negromex, ICA, Resistol* (Rocha, 2002: 1,10).

It appears that the new senior management personnel are also remunerated with exhorbitant salaries and benefit packages. To pay the salary of a new manager without experience in the industry Pemex fires four experienced workers. Pemex pays a private foreign consultant, whose function precisely is to help move Pemex towards disintegration, US$1,500 a day. Alberto Rocha, in this regard, notes that 'in the obtained document'

> it is made clear that the firing and pension programmes are a complemenary part of the project that Pemex's project for the participation of big foreign capital in the oil industry via the *Pidiregas* and Multiple Service Contracts (MSCs). . . . The participación of foreign firms . . . is headed by *Degoller McNaughton,* the *Scotia Group, Dowel Schlumberger, Halliburton, Drilling Fluids de México* and *Zapata Internacional*—all TNCs. They are given all the facilities to do their 'work' and charge millions of dollars even though to date there have been no [concrete] results.

With the help and means of the *Public Enterprise Reform Loans* the correlation of forces within the Federal Government and the parastatals, of which Pemex is the biggest, has been changed in favour of the 'reformers' or 'privatizers' (World Bank, without date). In the case of Pemex, this is reflected in the acceptance of its *divestiture*, something that would have been impossible in an earlier more nationalistic and populist political climate.

The administrative dismemberment of the strategic state enterprises (*Pemex, Ferrocarriles Nacionales* and the *Comisión Federal de Electricidad*), as emphasized above, has been promoted by the Bank, in its *roadmap* as a step towards privatization—and denationalization. Although they have occasioned little debate there are immediate and ultimate consequences of this surrender to outside interests of the country's major productive resources. They will require a lot of further study—and collective action.

Final Considerations

The World Bank's intervention in Mexico's economy can be traced back to the mid-1970s. The presence of the Bank, via the power derived from its loan conditionalities and synergies, was a determinant factor in the privatization of the railroads and, as we have shown, in the *de facto* privatization of the petrochemical sector in Mexico's oil industry, which, together with electric power, is reserved by the Constitution for the state. The actual role of the Bank in this regard can be observed in the equally disturbing way in which Mexico's geographic and territorial spaces have been managed and its usufruct given up; the sacking of strategic resources of immense strategic importance such as water and biodiversity; and the exploitation of the knowledge and labour power of the population—all in the interests of the MNCs, which are protected and promoted by the WB functioning as an instrument for the projection of the imperial power of the United States and its 'European allies.'

The documents cited and analysed in this chapter show that the Bank has virtually served as an American political party, that works from both inside and outside the country to influence and direct the actions and policies of the Mexican government, in the process constituting itself as a virtual 'cogovernment.'

This 'cogovernment' involving the WBG is a matter that remains, for the most part, outside the realm of public awareness and debate. The problem is that it has been instituted under conditions of what has been described as 'stealth imperialism' (Johnson, 2000), the power of which resides precisely in it being undetected and unable to be located. This situation, highly functional for the Bank's privatization-denationalization scheme, is well understood by Bank officials. For example, in the Bank's 1995 *Mexico Strategy Papers*, the reader can easily follow the foot-and thumb-prints of the WBG in the corridors of state power from one *sexenio* (presidential regime) to another, in this case from Salinas to Zedillo. In the *Office Memorandum* that accompanies the document, classified as 'confidential' and 'for official use only,' there appears the following request:

Please take note that much of the material in these documents is highly sensitive for the Mexican government. The Bank agreed with the stipulation that as a condition of [preparing this document] that the texts would be kept confidential and would not be processsed by the Bank beyond its actual informal state. We ask for the [reader's] consideration in helping us keep to this agreement. In this spirit, we also ask that any external enquiries in regard to these documents be directed towards this División (World Bank, 1995).

The documents in question are 'unclassified' and 'sensitive' precisely because they outlined the role of the Bank in delineating the heuristic principles and parameters of Mexico's 'national agenda,' particularly with regards to the design and implementation of the federal budget. For one thing, they clearly raise the question of who is the 'the power behind the power'—who makes policy in the context of a peripheral client state. In this context, the Bank has assiduously worked to create in Mexico a cadre of local *country managers* who are disposed, if not compelled, not to act in the national interest but to advance the interests of the imperial power in the North, particularly as regards the design and execution of the federal budget. It is clear that we have here a case of the 'power behind the throne' in regards to major policy issues, which is only possible with the control over the instruments of state power and with the acquiescence of a key part of the ruling circle. This acquiescence is secured by the spoils left by the foreign actors and given to their local 'country managers' as a reward for facilitating the 'Mexico Purchase,' an old colonial practice (Saxe-Fernández, 2002).

We hope that the data and analysis presented in this chapter will stimulate and contribute towards an urgent political debate in other countries, especially in terms of the urgent need to review similar tendencies and reflections of the Mexico model in Canada and the United States. For this we hope to have opened up in public, legislative and judicial spheres, and for political parties, discussion of the mechanisms that have to be established in order to render accounts with the sacking of the country's wealth and productive resources, and of the profoundly negative impacts of the measures involved on large sectors of society.

In Mexico, the Bank's policies of pillage and denationalization, implemented by the Bank and its *country managers*, constitute a veritable 'class war' whose campaigns have not been limited to any particular arena but ranges from the economic and political to the diplomatic-military and the ecological-social. Nevertheless, we are not in the face of a monolithic power that allows for no alernatives. The process involved, full of cracks and contradictions, has generated, among other things, an enormous reservoir of social discontent within sectors most affected by the policies of empire. This discontent, and associated forces of opposition and protest, is manifest in, and has been moblized by social movements, both those advocating peaceful methods and armed force, that have surfaced all across the country.

In this political context, the forces of protest and opposition threaten to destabilize the cogovernment regime. For its part, the Mexican 'oligarchy' has reponded to this threat by pouring oil on troubled waters—an explosive mix that blew up in Chiapas on the first of January in 1994. This is the World Bank in action—a predicament not shared by NAFTA's other partners (the United States and Canada).

In the Zapatista uprising we see a population, deeply aggrieved, reacting against the loss of hope and desperation. But their ongoing struggle is not just to live with dignity, for social and cultural identity, to establish their right to the land and manage their own resources in the collective interest of their population and communities. The struggle today is to ensure that these *rights* are given to and enjoyed by following generations. This struggle began within various nuclei of the most aggrieved indigenous communities and peasants (for example, the *Ejército Zapatista de Liberación Nacional*) but it has been joined by a growing number of diverse social groups and organizations (the *Frente Zapatista de Liberación Nacional*). Such a social construction of oppositional forces—for alternative development—within the popular movement will eventually have to take state-power, to assume control over the instruments that will allow these social subjects to design an alternative project for the long term.

If we do not join this struggle and commit ourselves to this project, and from within our own space—according to our capacities and condition—to help consolidate the participation of all affected social classes, to construct a consciousness that will permit and lead to actions that might revert the situation lived by so many in Mexico and Latin America, the possibility of a peaceful way out of this situation is greatly reduced.

In the case of NAFTA what is needed is a renegotiation of the agreement that, in addition to securing the national interest in each of the three countries, also includes mechanisms for correcting the asymmetry of relations that exists between Mexico and the other two countries—an asymmetry conceded by the Mexican government under conditions that need to be changed. At the same time, it is of critical importance to the Mexican people that the expropriation of their productive resources via privatization be reverted.

To this end, freedom of access to relevant information and studies such as this are critical factors in the formation of a class consciousness that might mobilize the population at large and provoke discussions as to the direction that the country (Mexico) should take—a direction geared to the public interest rather than in pursuit of the geostrategic interests of an imperial state or the personal enrichment of the oligarchy. NAFTA, like the other projections of US imperial power in the pursuit of hegemony—*Plan Colombia*, *Plan Puebla Panama* (and its 'green' version, the Mesoamerican Biological Corridor) and the Free Trade Area of the Americas (FTAA)—can be viewed as acts of 'brutal aggression' and concessions made on the backs of the Mexican people.

Notes

1   The World Bank Group is organized by region (East Asia and the Pacific, South Asia, Sub-Saharan Africa, Middle East and North Africa, Europe and Central Asia, Latin America and the Caribbean) and is composed of the World Bank itself (the International

Bank for Reconstruction and Development), the International Development Association (IDA), the International Finance Corporation (IFC), the Multilateral Investment Guarantee Agency (MIGA) and the International Centre for Settlement of Investment Disputes (www.worldbank.org).

2 See also Saxe-Fernández (April 18 1989: 7ª - 8ª).

3 Variations on this argument formed the crux of the theory constructed by exponents of what came to be known as 'Latin American structuralism'—a school of thought initiated by, and still associated with, ECLAC.

4 For example, the BPD-Water & Sanitation cluster includes MNCs such as Vivendi, Ondeo (Suez) and Thames Water. In the BPD-Natural Resources cluster we have Conservations International, USAID, IDB, UNEP, UNDP, GEF, WTO, BPD Global Road Safety Partnership—3M, Daimler-Chrysler, Ford Motor Co., Royal Dutch/Shell Group. In the 'Best practices in dealing with the social impacts of oil and gas operations' cluster are: BP Amoco, Chevron, Conoco, Exxon Mobil, Shell, Conservational International, World Wildlife Fund.

5 In both periods the economic and financial characteristics of World Bank supported projects indicate systematic efforts to promote the interests of the CCS, particularly the US state. The Executive Briefs on government loans and debts elaborated by the *Nacional Financiera* focused on the 1970s but the analysis and conclusions are compatible with the first phase of World Bank operations in Latin America. Contrary to the experience in Asia it relates to the import substitution model based on, inter alia, a high level of dependence on FDI, private bank loans and, consequently, the WBG and MNCs in the design of national policy.

6 By 'a jinetear' (jockeying) we refer to the speculative or productive use of funds no erogados de un préstamo dado. Thus, while the Bank charges interest on the total amount owed, the debtor actually disposes of only a part of the funds.

7 Principal beneficiaries include: General Electric, Krupp Industrie, PHB Forder Technic, Petro Valves, Nuovo Pignone, Snamprogerry, Foster Wheeler Energy Co, F. Peroni, FMB, V. Machinefabreci Lewes Refrigeration.

Chapter Five

Restructuring Latin American Labour and the World Bank

Henry Veltmeyer

In recent years the World Bank (1993, 1995), the OECD (1994), and the ILO (1996), among other international organizations, policy-makers and academics have identified the perceived need for labour to adjust to the requirements of the new global economic order by becoming more flexible.[1] The rationale presented for this agenda is that labour either adjusts to these requirements—participates in the process of 'globalization'—or it must confront a worsening of the problems that afflict it: unemployment, economic insecurity, bad jobs and low income, among others. In this context these and other organizations have taken up the banner of labour reform—of a mandated restructuring and deregulation of 'industrial relations,' associated labour markets, and the position of labour in the organization of production.

In this chapter it is argued that this entire labour reform programme, together with the political process of convincing the workers of the world to go along with it—to adjust to globalization—is part of a protracted offensive waged by capital against labour. However, labour cannot resist this offensive without understanding what is at issue. To this purpose—to provide a few elements of such an understanding—the chapter is organized as follows. First, I reconstruct some critical elements of the globalization process that provides the context for the labour reform agenda. Then this agenda is deconstructed in terms of conditions confronted by workers not only in Latin America but also in other areas of the world. Key dimensions of these conditions are discussed below as they relate to the changing position of labour in the process of production and associated labour markets. My focus here is on the issue of wages and their connection to productivity gains made in the organization of production and the process of capital accumulation. I also address the issue of productive investment as it relates to a process of productive transformation and technological conversion underway. In the conclusion I draw together the threads of this analysis, providing a brief theoretical discourse on problems of Latin American labour.

Globalization and Adjustment

In the late 1960s the Golden Age of Capitalism or what French historians have termed 'the thirty glorious years'—a period characterized by continuous and unprecedented rates of rapid growth in world output of marketed social production—came to an end (Marglin and Schor, 1990). Behind (or rather underneath) this denouement was a crisis in what Aglietta (1979, 1982); Boyer (1989); Lipietz (1982, 1987) and other proponents of Regulation Theory, have termed 'global Fordism,' a mode of labour regulation that corresponds to a regime of accumulation instituted in the 1920s.[2] In the short period from 1968 to 1973 the initial cracks in the global system of capital accumulation widened and deepened, exposing a system-wide tendency towards declining rate of growth and subjecting capital to a 'profit crunch'—a fall in the average rate of return on invested capital under conditions of sluggish productivity growth and increased demands by labour for higher wages and improved benefits (Glynn, et al., 1990; Marglin and Schor, 1990).

After 1974 can be viewed as a protracted period of structural and strategic responses to this crisis in the capital accumulation process. Five such responses and efforts are of particular relevance to our argument.

One is the time-honoured and well-tried practice of technological conversion, the incorporation of new production techniques that increase output per units of invested capital and deployed labour. Although its specific and overall contribution has yet to be determined, there is no question that the internal restructuring process engendered by the incorporation of information (computer-based) technologies, constituting a supposed 'technological revolution,' has contributed towards a solution to the crisis of capital (Boom and Mercado, 1990; Herrera, 1995). Among other things it has dramatically shortened and transformed the communication and transportation circuits of capitalist production, creating the preconditions for a new more flexible form of production based on a new regime of accumulation and corresponding mode of regulation. A critical feature of this new postfordist form of production is increased flexibility in the organization and disposition of the factors of production, particularly labour.

A second form of restructuring has involved the relocation of industry from the centre of the global economic system to countries that have been able to provide capital the possibility of lowering the costs of labour in the production process. There are diverse dimensions to this process, resulting in what has been conceptualized as a 'new international division of labour,' the formation of a new industrial divide, with the emergence (primarily in East Asia) of various tiers of newly industrializing countries, and, to some extent, a process of reindustrialization at the centre of the system (Fröbel, et al., 1980: Piore and Sabel, 1984).

A third response to the crisis relates to political actions taken by capital, with the support of the state, in reaction to the offensive launched in 1968 by labour in the struggle for higher wages and better conditions (Davis, 1984). The resulting counter-offensive, launched by capital around 1974, has assumed changing forms—from an abrogation of the post war accord with labour on wages (to adjust them to productivity gains) and the state guarantee of full-employment, a campaign to blame high inflation on labour (high wages, excessive union power), a direct attack on unions and their capacity to negotiate collective agreements, an indirect attack on the social wage and its political institution (the welfare state), to the offering of non-standard or contingent forms of employment (part-time, temporary, subcontracted, etc.) and, more recently, in the context of a widely implemented privatization policy, a direct attack on labour in the form of wage rollbacks and the cutback of jobs. These forms of labour restructuring have been well documented and analysed in numerous national contexts, although their global and systemic effects have not been fully gauged and require further study and comparative analysis. However, it is evident that the counter-offensive of capital against labour, waged for the past twenty or so years, has contributed to the relative capacity of capitalists to offset a systemic propensity towards crisis and falling profits.

Another part of the solution to the crisis of capital has been the restructuring of macroeconomic policy under conditions of structural adjustment—a package of stabilization and structural reform measures instituted in the form of conditionalities attached to international development assistance and efforts to access funds to restructure existing debts and finance new projects. This policy reform programme, designed by economists at the World Bank and its sister institutions, has entailed the adjustment of national economies to changes that have been engineered in the world economy, exposing them to the forces of the 'free market' and obliging them to 'adjust' their economies and politics—to liberalize trade and the flow of capital; privatize the means of social production (state enterprises); deregulate markets and economic activity in the private sector; downsize and modernize the state—to decentralize government and democratize its relation to civil society; and, most importantly, changing the structure of the capital-labour relation, reducing the share of labour in national income and, concomitantly, to convert a larger part of national income into capital — money available for productive investment. This, and the previously mentioned forms of labour restructuring, I argue, is a crucial dimension of the so-called globalization process, the major mechanism of internal adjustment to an emerging new world economic order.

Latin American Labour in a Global Context

According to the World Bank, about 99 percent of the workers projected to join the world's labour market over the next 30 years will live and work in what it terms the 'low- and middle-income' countries of Africa, Asia, the Caribbean and Latin America—the latter accounting for about 8.4 percent of the world's economically active population; 6.1 percent of total output; and 3.9 percent of exports and 3.2 percent of imports, down from 12 and 10.1 percent in 1950

(UNCTAD, 1992). As the Bank sees, on the basis of a globally concerted programme of structural adjustment policies, it is possible to identify a global trend towards increasing integration into, and the interdependence of countries, within a global economy but at the same time there is no discernible trend towards convergence—equality in the form and conditions of such integration among countries or between the small number of the rich, the larger number of relatively well-off workers, and the much larger number of poor workers across the world.[3] Indeed, the Bank has argued that there are serious 'risks that the workers in [the] poorer countries will fall further behind' and that some national groups of workers, most particularly in Sub-Saharan Africa but also in Latin America, could become increasingly marginalized within 'the general prosperity in countries that are enjoying growth' (World Bank, *Policy Research Bulletin*, Vol. 6, No. 4, 1995: 6).

The only preventative remedy for avoiding this trend—for participating in this projected dynamic of rising incomes, better working conditions and enhanced job security—is for all countries to systematically pursue the right domestic policies, sound labour policies that promote demanding-demanding growth, and 'good governance.' Such policies, the Bank notes, fundamentally involve 'the use of markets to create opportunities,' and specifically include legislation designed to create more flexible forms of labour and unregulated (free) labour markets. Conditions of such flexibility include, on the part of workers, greater mobility—the capacity to relocate if necessary—and a willingness to accept whatever jobs are on offer, with possibly lower levels of remuneration; and, on the part of employers, increased capacity to participate in the production process, able to hire, fire, locate, and deploy workers as required—and to pay them on the basis of market conditions.

With explicit reference to this idea—of a labour market in which the forces of supply and demand reach equilibrium and provide an optimum allocation of resources—World Bank officials have stalked the corridors of state power all over Latin America in the search of policy-makers with the political will, and the institutional capacity, to introduce a programme of legislative (and, if necessary, constitutional) labour reforms. Associated with this idea is the notion that wages in general are too high,[4] the result not only of government interference with the labour market (particularly in the legislation of minimum wages) but of the excessive monopoly power of the unions.[5] As the Bank sees it—and it is argued (or rather, asserted) vociferously with as much technical support and data it can muster (and interpret on the basis of the formulae constructed for this purpose)—the high wage rates, excessive benefits accorded workers in the social programmes introduced by statist or populist governments, and the general inflexibility of workers, have led private sector entrepreneurs to withdraw their capital from the production process, thus contributing towards the problems of high unemployment, in formalization, and poverty. Tables 5.3 and 5.6 provide glimpses into the scope and depth of these problems.[6]

How have Latin American policy-makers responded to such advice and to the associated pressures to adopt it? First, many if not most countries in the region in the 1980s implemented a programme of structural reforms that created the preconditions and an institutional framework for the proposed new labour policy, the material conditions of which were formed on the basis of an on-going process of technological conversion and productive transformation—without the 'equity' that ECLAC (1990) has called for in its model. Those governments that had not done so in the 1980s have all come around, including Argentina, Peru and Venezuela, and even Brazil whose belated participation in the adjustment process awaited the advent to state power of Henrique Fernando Cardoso, an erstwhile important (if social democratic or reformist) exponent of a Marxist-oriented variant of dependency theory (Petras and Veltmeyer, 2001a). On the basis of this structural adjustment and its associated reforms, the entrepreneurs and employers of labour everywhere (or, at least, in many cases) have joined the financiers—and the World Bank—in demanding labour legislative reforms, and where required (as in Brazil) the constitutional amendments required to allow and secure greater flexibility of labour markets. In some cases, as in Mexico and El Salvador, the new labour regime has been established within the export enclave of an expanding maquilladora industry (Arrida Palomares, 1995; Brown and Domínguez, 1989; Ominami, 1986).

In other cases, as in Chile, the new labour regime was introduced on a national scale as a critical component of a process of industrial conversion and productive transformation (Agacino and Gonzalo Rivas, 1995; Herrera, 1995; Leiva and Agacino, 1995).

In Argentina, efforts of the Menem regime to legislate the labour reforms demanded by the World Bank created a significant mobilization within a weakened labour movement and an electoral backlash that brought to power the *Frente Amplio* (Broad Front) opposition. In each and every other case, the process of structural adjustment and productive transformation has been accompanied by a political struggle to introduce via legislative reform, administrative fiat, or, increasingly, by executive decree, a more flexible form of production and a corresponding labour regime.

Labour Market Reform: A New Regime of Accumulation

The basic idea, initially floated in the World Bank's 1995 *World Development Report* but since then widely diffused in various publications and numerous conferences staged and sponsored by the Bank and its sister institutions, is that the solution to the region's problems, particularly unemployment, requires a new and more flexible mode of organizing production, as well as legislative (and perhaps constitutional) reform leading to the increased flexibility of labour. In Latin America as elsewhere, the Bank argues, government regulation of labour was designed primarily as an instrument of social policy—above all to secure and protect the right to full employment, adequate and minimum wages, and secure tenure. In practice, such legislation, particularly as relates to minimum wages, rather than serving as a means of achieving a more equitable if not efficient allocation of productive resources, has produced a most inefficient and inflexible labour market in which the demand for labour has not been able to keep up with its supply, resulting in, among other things, an unmanageable and costly problem (in economic and social—as well as political—terms) of high unemployment and the increasing informalization of work arrangements and conditions.

Reflecting its concern that 'at the world level [as well as in the region] there exists a serious [problem] with unemployment and informality,' and without reference to the underlying process of industrial conversion and productive transformation, the response of the Bank is that governments need to reform their labour codes, to ensure a greater flexibility—and thereby the reduction of labour costs in production and the generation of more and better forms and conditions of employment.

The problem, as the Bank sees it, is twofold. On the one hand, minimum wage legislation tends to distort the proper functioning of the labour market, leading to the withdrawal of capital from the production process and thus unemployment, poverty and informality. On the other hand, it is necessary to suppress the monopolistic bargaining power acquired by labour through its sector-wide 'representative unions' so that 'entrepreneurs' and workers can arrive at and arrange independent agreements in accord with market conditions and requirements.' And one of the key requirements, the Bank makes clear, is the lowering of excessively high wages in the productive (and public) sectors of the economy, and of the associated benefits legislated by government that effectively inhibit the participation of investors and entrepreneurs in the production process.

The effective response to these requirements—and the solution to the underlying and associated problems—is labour market reform designed for greater flexibility. Since 1989, such reform has been placed on the political agenda of most countries in the region, together with (i) a programme of *technological conversion and productive transformation*; (ii) a *new social policy* designed by the World Bank to soften the blow of SAPs on the poor; (iii) the *decentralization* of government (to create a more participatory form of community-based development); and (iv) *modernization* of the state apparatus (to create a more efficient and democratic system of public service and administration—good governance).

The Capital-Labour Relation in the Production Process

The change in the capital-labour relation wrought by the processes of structural adjustment in the 1980s and globalization in the 1990s can be traced out on both structural and political levels. In structural terms, the change relates to (i) the organization of labour within a process of technological conversion and what ECLAC (1990) has termed 'productive transformation with equity;' (ii) the contribution of labour to productivity growth; (iii) the rate of exploitation (extraction of surplus value) as measured by the return to capital and labour of their respective contributions to production—the share of profit and wages in national income and in value added; and (iv) the evolution of real wages relative to growth in GNP or national income.

Productive Transformation

With respect to productive transformation, determined essentially by the rate of investment and the pace of technological conversion, significant advances have been made in key production sectors and industries in a number of countries, particularly Argentina, Brazil, Chile, Colombia and Mexico (Boom and Mercado, 1990; Morales, 1992).

The pace of advance in this transformation has been both conditioned and limited by the generally low levels of productive investment that are reflected in Table 5.1. In this respect, Chile is the only country in the region that has had in recent years what would appear to be an adequate level of productive investment compared to levels found in the expanding economies of East and South-East Asia. Another critical factor in the regional process of productive transformation is the relative contribution of capital and labour and the impact of what is termed in the modern theory of growth as 'total factor productivity.'

Table 5.1   Levels of Productive Investment and Capital Formation, 1980-94, Selected Countries

	1980/81	1984/85	1990	1994/99
Argentina	25.3	17.6	14.0	19.9
Brazil	23.3	19.7	21.9	24.5
Bolivia	14.2	7.0	13.2	15.5
Chile	16.6	12.3	23.3	29.3
Mexico	27.2	21.2	21.9	24.5
Peru	29.0	18.4	15.5	22.2
Latin America	**24.8**	**19.2**	**19.7**	**19.6**
Developing Countries	25.7	23.4	24.7	25.8
Least Developed Countries	17.3	14.6	16.1	15.5
East Asian NICs	34.4	26.2	31.3	32.1
South Korea	32.0	29.6	36.9	38.4
China	30.1	38.6	33.2	42.6

Source: UN (1996): 143, 156. 193, 196, 305; World Bank (1995, 1996).

With regard to this factor, it would appear that the relative contributions to production of both capital and labour (the increase in output per units of capital and labour employed) has been and remains relatively low and less than the increase in 'total factor productivity.' Although this point needs a closer look and more detailed and systematic analysis, it is possible to adduce that to some extent the relative increase in productivity can be associated with a change in the organization of production, viz. increased flexibility, as well as the incorporation of the new information-rich technology and an increased orientation towards export markets, which has had the additional impact of a greater realization of the surplus value embodied in the social product.

Table 5.2   Factor Contributions to Economic Growth (Percentages)

		GNP	Capital	Labour	TFP
Chile	1986-90	6.58	2.85	0.08	3.92
	1991-93	8.12	4.08	0.07	3.98
Colombia	1986-90	4.63	1.94	0.10	2.59
	1991-93	3.77	2.41	0.09	1.27
Peru	1986-90	-1.70	0.95	0.11	-2.80
	1991-93	2.26	0.69	0.11	1.46
Brazil	1986-90	1.94	1.60	0.08	0.26
	1991-93	1.48	0.84	0.08	0.56
Mexico	1986-90	1.38	1.47	0.13	-0.20
	1991-93	2.35	2.28	0.12	0.00

Source: World Bank, *World Development Report*, various years.

Income Shares of Capital and Labour

As for the distribution of the social product or national income between capital and labour, governments in the region generally have not established any specific policy. The operating theory behind this do-nothing policy is the same as that used to justify the proposed policy of labour flexibility and the elimination of minimum-wage legislation: that the free market is the most efficient mechanism for allocating resources on the basis of equitable returns to 'factors of production.'[8]

In these terms the World Bank has pushed for the elimination of minimum-wage legislation as an obstacle to the proper functioning of the labour market and indirectly to an efficient and equitable distribution of the social product (national income) or the economic surplus. On the same basis, the World Bank designed plans for economic and social development that did not include an explicit wages policy, it being understood that the advocated liberalization of prices, together with the proposed labour market reforms, by itself would lead to an optimum level of wages and employment; and that, therefore, any minimum wages, like that of wages in general, should be negotiated directly by the parties involved under market conditions. Thus has the Bank put into motion its proposal to abolish minimum wage legislation, supported with the argument (or assertion, rather) that such legislation causes unemployment and interferes with the working of the market forces of supply and demand.

Another proposition of the theory underlying the. *Plan for Economic and Social Development* that has been widely implemented in the region is that when the labour market is liberalized (freed from government interference), it would automatically regulate the level of wages according to the marginal productivity of labour, at which point the supply of labour would be equal to its demand. So, what in fact has been the dynamic of this relationship between wages and the marginal productivity of labour?

In terms of the 'research' conducted by and reported on by the Bank at its Second Annual Conference on Latin American and Caribbean Development in Bogotá, the experience of Chile, Colombia, and Peru with labour market reform (flexibilization) has been demonstrably positive: a decrease in the official rate of open unemployment and an adjustment of wage levels towards the marginal productivity of labour. As for the employment issue there would appear to be a factual basis to the Bank's assertion, although serious questions about its explanation.

However, on the issue of the marginal productivity of labour there is no basis in fact. If the Bank were correct in its assertion one would expect to find a long-term empirical trend towards the growth of average productivity at a rate below that of real wages, which, in turn, would have tended to reduce the participation of capital in the production process. Is there any evidence of such a trend? First, it is clear enough that real wages have generally declined, a trend that can be traced out in every country in the region since at least 1982. On average, real wages have dropped from 15 to 25 percent since 1985, but in a number of cases they have dropped by as much as 50 to 86 percent (Table 5.3). In the case of Argentina, Peru, and Venezuela real wages in 1995 had not yet recovered levels achieved in 1970, while in Mexico, according to the Bank of Mexico, they had lost 71.4 percent of their 1976 value, reaching their lowest point in thirty years (*La Jornada*, 5 November, 1996: 39; 15 March, 1977: 48). Given this trend, coupled with a tendency for an actual decrease in the number of workers in the formal sector, it is difficult to imagine that the rate of growth in labour productivity could have been negative as supposed by the Bank. Given the lack of data and comparative systematic analysis it is, in fact, not so easy to calculate the precise connection between wage levels and productivity, but the studies that have been done suggest a tendency towards a decline and then sluggish growth in total and industrial output throughout the 1980s as well as a gradual but persistent increase in productivity.

Table 5.3   Dimensions of Underdevelopment: Labour Conditions in Latin America, Selected Indicators and Countries

		Real Min. Wages (% +/-.)	Real Wages (% +/-)	Min Per Capita Income (% +/-)	Urban Poverty Rate (% pop.)
Argentina	1980-86	7	47	-23	7
	1986-90	-22	-64	-15	
	1990-91	-7	39	5	15
Brazil	1979-87	19	-27	3	30
	1987-90	-29	-26	-6	39
Chile	1980-87	-5		-3	32
	1987-90	11	27	18	34
Mexico	1970-84	-15	-20	31	
	1981-84	-30	-32	-12	
	1984-87	-16	-17		30
	1987-89	-2	-16	2	34

Sources: Alimir (1994: 7-32); Rosenbluth (1994: 170, 175); FUSADES (1996: 5).

Given the apparently low levels of participation of both capital and labour in the production process, this increase in productivity can be explained in terms of other factors such as the reorganization of production along the lines of greater flexibility. At one level, the decline in real wages could reflect a reduced level of labour productivity associated with the destruction of productive capacity brought about by the cut in social programmes and an investment in 'human capital' (the education and health of workers). But given the divergence between rates of productivity growth and wage rates,[9] it is clear enough that real wages, both on average and at minimum levels, are not adjusted to and determined by the marginal productivity of labour. More generally, the brutal compression of wages can better be connected to (and explained in terms of) structurally or politically determined conditions of unemployment and inflation as well as the direct repression of working class organizations. In any case, over the long term real wages in the region have tended to evolve to levels well below the marginal productivity of labour, in the process creating an essential requirement and condition for a process of renewed capital accumulation: the extraction of surplus value from its direct producer, the working class.

In structural terms, the contribution of labour to a process of capital accumulation (the extraction of surplus value) is reflected in the share of wages in the income derived from the social product—and in its share of the value added in the process. In each and every case, these ratios have tended to decrease over the course of ten to fifteen years of neoliberal reforms, in some cases dramatically—by as much as 25 percent (Tables 5.4 and 5.5). And, by the same token, the share of capital in national income and the value added increased correspondingly, anywhere from around 60 to 75 percent. However, the significant increase in the rate of exploitation (estimated by Montesino and Gochez to be in the order of 190 percent in the case of El Salvador), and in the transfer of income from labour to capital, did not translate into a process of renewed and sustained capital accumulation, raising a number of critical questions.

Table 5.4   Share of Wages in GNP, Selected Latin American Countries

	1970	1980	1985	1988	1990
Argentina	40.9	31.5	31.9	24.9	-
Bolivia	36.8	39.6	26.9	-	-
Brazil	34.2	35.1	36.3	-	-
Chile	47.7	43.4	37.8	-	-
Ecuador	34.4	34.8	23.6	16.0	15.8
Mexico	37.5	39.0	31.6	28.4	27.3
Peru	40.0	32,8	30.5	25.5	16.8
Uruguay	52.9	35.7	36.3	39.7	-
Venezuela	40.3	42.7	37.6	34.6	31.1

Source: CEPAL, several years.

First, it would seem that (i) the sharp compression of wages and reduction in the share of wages in national income has been used in a major way as a mechanism of internal adjustment, but that (ii) the extraordinarily high social costs of this adjustment, borne largely by workers, cannot even be justified in terms of the imperative of renewed accumulation and sustaining the process of national capitalist development. Productive investments in the region have been and remain at levels well below the level of surplus value extracted and the income transferred from labour. Only in Chile has a substantial part of the income transferred from labour been converted into capital, generating a comparatively high level of productive investment in physical and social capital.[10] In most other countries, it would seem, a substantial part of the economic surplus generated by, and extracted from, the workers and the direct producers has been dedicated to the servicing of the external debt, unproductive or speculative 'investments,' the purchase of the shares of privatized companies (which accounts for 50 percent of the wave of new investments in the 1990s), and consumption of the wealth and income generated in the process.

Table 5.5   Employee Earnings as a Percentage of Value Added in Manufacturing

	1967	1971	1975	1979	1983	1987	1989	1992
Brazil	17.3	23.6	18.9	20.7	19.7	15.1	15.0	23
Chile	25.1	22.8	12.3	18.2	17.1	16.8	16.6	18
Mexico	44.0	42.7	39.1	34.7	23.8	19.8	19.8	22
Venezuela	30.1	30.0	27.3	28.5	31.6	26.8	24.2	19
Colombia	28.2	24.0	20.6	19.7	20.9	18.9	16.1	15

Source: World Bank, *World Development Reports,* Various years.

Forms of Exploitation in the Production Process

At issue in the World Bank's approach to labour market reform in Latin America are the policies required to reduce the high levels of un- and under-employment in the region as well as the trend towards informalization and its associated conditions of low productivity and income. Table 5.6 provides a brief glimpse into the actual distribution of some of these conditions.[11] The evident tendency for an extension of these conditions, and a deepening of their social effects, underscores the seriousness of the issue—of confronting the World Bank's conception of the problem and its remedy of labour market reform which, we have argued, is at best designed to address and solve quite a different problem (to create the conditions for a renewed and sustained process of capital accumulation). And, as we see it, the Bank's proposed remedy does not correctly identify the structural sources of the problem—as experienced by labour or as perceived by capital.

Table 5.6   Dimensions of Underdevelopment in Latin America, 1993/4
(% Distributions)

	Un-Empl.[12]	Informal Sector	Rural Pop.	Agric. Production	Rural Poverty
Argentina	17.5	45.4	13	6.5	20
Bolivia	4.6	48.1	41	16.4	97
Brazil	5.1	48.8	29	10.5	73
Chile	7.4	37.6	16	9.1	56
Colombia	8.5	-	28	14.9	45
Mexico	6.3	41.0	26	7.6	51
Peru	8.8	-	29	6.9	75

Sources: (1) CEPAL, 1996; 14; (3) CEPAL, 1995: 179, (4-5) World Bank, 1995; (6).

Thus it might be useful to review some points of our analysis and to briefly identify the key dimensions of the problem as we see it, to contribute thereby towards a better understanding of it as well as a more appropriate political response.

The World Bank's approach to labour market reform in Latin America as elsewhere is to promote the restructuring of the relation of capital to labour in the production process. And it is well understood by the Bank and other agents and apologists of capitalism that the essence of this capital-labour relation is the extraction of surplus value from its direct producer, the worker, in the form of the wage, which represents the value of the labour expended in the process. The facts and nature of this productive relationship are well known, although it fell upon Marx over a hundred years ago to unveil its then hidden secret in a very different context. As Marx emphasized, the key to a sustainable process of capital accumulation is the extraction of relative surplus value on the basis of an exchange of equivalents, wages for power-power, the value of which, as with every other commodity, is determined by the socially necessary time-time needed to produce it. The production of relative surplus value is, as Marx argued, the truly revolutionary path towards capitalist development, as opposed to the production of absolute surplus value—increasing the productivity of labour on the basis of technological conversion as opposed to the lengthening of the work day or, as we argue, reducing wages without a change in the technological and social conditions of production. The production and extraction of relative surplus is predicated on the substitution of capital for labour, the incorporation of new technology that will raise the 'organic composition of capital;' slough off labour; and increase the productivity of labour.

In this process of technological conversion and productive transformation, to use contemporary language, labour is exchanged for wages at its value, which, given that this value is determined by the latest technological advances, implies that it is has some connection to the resulting increases in productivity. In this process, the value of labour power is essentially a function of technology although, as Marx emphasized, the rate of exploitation, which is conditioned by the capacity of workers to participate in any productivity gains, is by and large determined by political conditions of the class struggle—the correlation of forces mobilized by capital and labour.

In this context, and with reference to developments in the region that have unfolded worldwide as of the mid 1970s, it would seem that the balance of class forces has turned against labour, resulting among other things in a decreased capacity of workers to participate in the productivity gains of new technology—to adjust wages to productivity. Although this development is worldwide, the situation of workers in Latin America and elsewhere on the margins of the globalized capitalist economy is worse than that of those at the centre of the system in that the conditions of relative surplus value extraction, at the heart of the accumulation process, are often and generally combined with those of absolute surplus value as well as of what has been conceptualized as 'superexploitation'—the extraction of surplus value on the basis of a reduction of wages below the value of labour-power.

The forms and conditions of this superexploitation are complex and variable but its basic mechanism is easy enough to identify: the formation and operation of what Marx viewed as an 'industrial reserve army,' a large reservoir of surplus labour—surplus to the requirements of capital. The existence of such a reservoir of surplus labour can be identified at the global level—in, for example, the large mass of unemployed workers in Europe, as well as the interstices of an emerging global labour market—but its most substantial and significant formation is found in the economies of Latin America and other countries and regions that are, as it were, in the process of development. A characteristic feature of this process is the formation of what in the urban economies of these societies has been identified as 'the informal sector' and in the rural economies a class of small producers, a subsistent and local economy of basic grain peasant producers. Table 5.6 indicates for Latin America the scope of these economic activities and their associated problems, which are the major objects of the World Bank's professed concern—the chief target of its policy programmes.

Although it applies equally well to the large and growing informal sector, the conditions of a surplus population have been documented and to some extent analysed in the context of the region's peasant economies of small grain producers. In this context, what has been emphasized has been the classic working of a surplus population as a lever of capital accumulation—allowing capitalist entrepreneurs to depress the wages of their workers and, in the process, to increase profits and maintain the competitiveness of their enterprises. However, several additional dimensions of this economic function have been identified for the subsistence and commercial operations of the small-scale producers linked to the peasant economy: as with the informal sector they provide wage goods at low prices, even at below the cost of production, as well as a source of employment and additional income for family members. In this regard they provide to some extent a subsidy to the capitalist operations in the area. Evidence of this can be found in the basic grain component of the food basket on the basis of which the Ministry of Planning and policy-makers in every Latin American country estimate the minimum income requirements and the incidence of poverty within the urban population. Generally speaking, what is found is that the cost of basic grains over time tends to rise more slowly than the other components of the food basket (*ECA* 560: 971).

Analysts also tend to agree that the small producers of these basic grains, the social base and a principal target of the Bank's ubiquitous anti-poverty programmes, often serve as a refuge (source of employment) for an over-abundant surplus population. In this regard, the small-producer sector of Latin America's rural society, like the urban informal sector, can be seen to function as a reservoir of surplus labour, holding in reserve the labour of the semiproletarianized *temporeros*, the landless producer-workers who migrate annually for wage-work on a seasonal basis in the agro-export industries that continue to dominate the rural economies of so many Latin American societies. In addition, in the border and northern and central states of Mexico, such as Zacatecas, the small producer sector provides a source of cheap surplus labour for the low wage service industries and the agricultural sector of the US economy. In both cases, the rural society of small producers underwrites some of the reproductive costs of the labour subsumed directly or indirectly by the capitalist enterprises both in the free trade zones and in the industries that have been subject to the process technological conversion and productive transformation. This can be regarded as superexploitation.

These developments and conditions can be found all across Latin America. Not only do they underlie the problems targeted by the World Bank (unemployment, informalization and poverty), but they are also connected to the identified problem of a relatively limited unsustainable process of capitalist development in the region. The major problem in this regard is the failure of the region's capitalists and policy-makers, often one and the same, to convert the surplus value extracted from the workers (and the disproportionate share of national income which they have appropriated through various means) into capital—productive investment in physical and social capital. This problem is largely a question of these capitalists pursuing and relying on a strategy of cheap labour for enterprises and industries oriented towards exports on the world market. In many cases the cost of labour in the process of production has been lowered to a level of 20 percent and lower—as low as 10 percent in the case of Mexico.[13]

On the basis of this strategy capital has little to no interest in maintaining the purchasing power of wages and dynamizing the local and regional markets on which the process of capitalist development generally has to depend. Nor does it have much interest in taking what Marx regarded as the revolutionary path towards capitalist development—productive investment and capital accumulation on the basis of relative surplus value. In this context, the World Bank's proposed labour market reforms, even when designed to facilitate the process of technological conversion and productive transformation, is condemned to failure. They will not prevent either capital or labour, which in any case will (have to) bear the social costs of adjustment, from being marginalized in the global process identified by the Bank—'the general prosperity of countries that are enjoying growth'.

Notes

1 The term 'labour market flexibility' has taken on a variety of meanings over time, prompting US Labor Secretary Robert Reich to remark at an ILO sponsored meeting on June 10, 1994 that 'rarely in international discourse has the [term] gone so directly from obscurity to meaninglessness without any intervening period of coherence' (quoted by Brodsky, 1994). What it means for the World Bank, however, as an overlooked precondition for successful structural reform is fairly clear: 'a dynamic and flexible labour market is an important part of market-oriented policies. It helps reallocate resources and allows the economy to respond rapidly to new challenges from increased competition. Moreover, freeing the labour market of distortions improves the distribution of income because it encourages employment expansion and wage increases in the poorest segments of society' (World Bank, 1993: 92).

2 In this formulation of a crisis theory members of this school substituted for Marx's concept of a mode of production the concept of a structure composed of a particular 'regime of accumulation' ('the . . . long-term stabilization of the allocation of social production between consumption and accumulation . . . within a national economic and social formation and between [it] and the outside world') and a corresponding 'mode of regulation' ('a set of internalized rules and social procedures' which ensure the unity of a given regime of accumulation and which 'guarantee that its agents conform . . . to the schema of reproduction') (Lipietz, 1987: 14).

3 Although the UNDP, UNIDO, UNRISD and most academic researchers have pointed towards the lack of such convergence—indeed a worsening of disparities in the distribution of productive resources and income, over the years of structural adjustment and globalization—whether there exists or not a trend towards convergence remains an unsettled issue. On this issue see the debate between Griffin (1995) and Bienefeld (1995).

4 The notion that wages are too high is part of a neoclassical theory that holds that when wages decline the likely outcome is a rise in employment, and, given greater production capacity, a rise in output. This theory conflicts and can be counterposed with the 'structuralist' theory which holds that a decline in wages is more likely to result in a contraction of output.

5 The advancement of these ideas has involved numerous forums and takes many forms. There is probably not a country in the region where a team of economists from the WB or one of its sister institutions (the Inter-American development Bank in the Latin American context) has not been found delivering the same message, usually covertly, with appropriate news releases as to the promise and successful performance of such policies when adopted by the government and of the need for the government to stay the course, but occasionally, as in Argentina, all too publicly.

6 Specifically, the Bank argues that minimum-wage legislation distorts factor allocation and punishes informal sector workers, high unemployment benefits reduce work incentives, job protection provisions and the high costs of dismissal make restructuring

difficult and slow, and high non-wage costs and payroll taxes act as a disincentive for entrepreneurs to expand employment and increase the international competitiveness of local firms. The Bank expands on these points in its annual (1995) Report on *Workers in an Integrating World*. However, its discourse is highly ideological, presented in the form of a manifesto, peppered with assertions, little argument, and highly constructed and dubious data (Veltmeyer, 1997b). For one thing, the Bank underestimates the scope and depth of the problems it has identified for an alternative statistical presentation of the data relating to these problems), and the source of these problems in the policies it has advocated and that have been put into practice at least ten years in most countries. On this see Veltmeyer and Petras (1997).

7 In this connection, the economists of the World Bank depart from the neoclassical vision of workers viewed not as the member of a class, acting in solidarity, and making gains in long struggle with capital, but as an individual economic agent, capacitated as a social actor in the market, seeking and able to take advantage of the opportunities it provides. To this end, converting workers into self-seeking individual economic agents, the Bank has advocated reforms designed to strip the power of union over its members, its capacity to negotiate collective agreements on a sectoral or industry basis, mandatory dues checkoffs.

8 This neoclassical theory basically holds that under free market competitive conditions each factor of production receive in return for its contribution to production a commensurate return. In other words, the invisible hand of the market—according to Michel Camdessus, one of three pillars of IMF economic policy (the other two being the visible hand of the state and 'solidarity between the poor and the rich')—has to be left alone, assuring thereby an optimum distribution of the social product.

9 In the case of El Salvador, from 1980 to 1986 productivity on average increased by 8.4 percent while wages fell by 23.4 percent. Subsequently, growth in average productivity has slowed down while real wages have recovered. But there was no systematic correlation between the two (Montesinos and Gochez, 1995: 945-962).

10 Leiva and Agacino (1995) discount the effectiveness of this investment, emphasizing its many hidden and not so hidden costs such as the weakening and disarticulation of the labour movement, the disproportionate growth of precarious and poorly paid jobs, the dramatically increased reliance on cheap female and child labour, the increase of job and economic insecurity, and an extension of inequality and poverty.

11 The low productivity of peasant small-scale agriculture is well known, being, in fact, the basis of efforts throughout the region to modernize agriculture (read do away with the peasant sector). However, the informal sector has generated similar concerns—and policy reactions. In the case of Mexico it has been estimated by INEGI, the National Institute for Statistics, that the informal sector, which encompasses 20 percent of commercial activity, and close to 50 percent of the EAP, contributes 8 percent of GNP (*La Jornada* 15/3/97: 60). Most economists, however, would estimate its contribution to be closer to a third of GNP.

12 In some countries such as Mexico the official figures on open unemployment are particularly misleading (understating reality) in that anyone who 'works,' even 'on one's own account,' for even one hour a week is listed as 'employed.' For this and other reasons estimates as to the level of under-employment provide much better indicators as to the conditions such as low income and poverty experienced by a large part of the population. A CEPAL study (Rosenbluth, 1994: 57-78) shows that the informal sector, composed essentially of workers in four sub-sectors (i) micro-enterprises in industry and construction, and in commerce and services; (ii) domestic service; and (iii) workers on their 'own account;' and (iv) unpaid family members, harbors the largest number and

proportion of the poor, but that some of the poor are found in the lower strata of formal wage-employees.

13 For example, in Mexico's manufacturing industry, the cost of labour by the mid 1990s had been reduced to 10 percent, with wages representing only 2.8 percent (*La Jornada*, April 18, 1996). On an hourly basis, minimum wages in the manufacturing sector were set at $1.23 in Mexico (versus $12.60 in the US, $20.80 in Japan, $11.93 in Canada, $8.85 in France, $6.10 in South Korea—and $2.75 in Chile. In the case of Mexico, this wage rate in real terms was lower than in 1965 and by no stretch of the imagination covered the cost of subsistence of the worker's family. In this connection, it is estimated that a family of three to four (below the Mexican average) requires the equivalent of five minimum wages to pay for the *canasta básica*—the package of goods to meet its basic physical needs (*La Jornada*, 11 May 1996: 40). According to the World Bank (1998), 60 percent of Mexican families in 1996 did not receive enough income to provide adequately for their basic needs. Into the next millennium the situation has not improved despite the World Bank's lowering of the poverty threshold—to earnings of US$2 per day.

Chapter Six

Cuba and Venezuela in an Era of Globalization

George W. Schuyler

> *Globalization appears to increase poverty and inequality . . . The costs of adjusting to greater openness are borne exclusively by the poor, regardless of how long the adjustment takes* (The World Bank, *The Simultaneous Evolution of Growth and Inequality*, 1999).

> *The world's biggest killer and the greatest cause of ill-health and suffering across the globe is listed almost at the end of the International Classification of Diseases. It is given the code Z59.5—extreme poverty* (*World Health Report*, 1995)

This chapter deals with the effects of public policy on private lives in the global system of the 1980s and 1990s. It uses health to explore human development in Venezuela and Cuba, two countries on the periphery of the global capitalist system. Both countries embarked on different development paths in the early 1960s, supported by powerful patrons, the United States and the Soviet Union. Thirty years later, both faced enormous obstacles to the elusive goal of Latin American development—improving the well-being of their citizens. My research asks why Cuba, a poor nation, was able to preserve a relatively good health care system during the 1980s and 1990s, while oil-rich Venezuela experienced a marked deterioration in health care. It seeks to illustrate how global economic forces influence similar processes at the national level (ECLAC, 2001: 14). I begin with a brief discussion of globalization and development, provide an overview of development and health, and then turn to health care in Venezuela and Cuba.

Globalization

Globalization is a process that embraces various aspects of human society: economic, social, political and cultural. But its core meaning is the worldwide integration of economies and societies through technology, markets and trade. Its underlying philosophy and its economic theory—neoliberalism—assert that individual freedom is the highest human goal and that the rational pursuit of self-interest, especially economic self-interest, will create the greatest good for the greatest number. Neoliberalism claims that there is no freedom without markets. It insists that markets are the most efficient mechanism for achieving the greatest good for the greatest number and can solve social inequality and poverty through the 'trickle-down' process (Labonte, 2000:106; Valdés Paz, 1997: 28).

Globalization is inseparable from the capitalist expansion that began at least five centuries ago. In the late twentieth century, however, capitalism entered a new phase of expansion and complexity, driven by technological innovations in communications and transportation that separate it from the past. States have less sovereignty over domestic policies and development is less nationally based; it must occur within the context of the global economy. Global forces now influence virtually every aspect of human society. Our activities are more closely linked than ever before, from what we produce, consume, or watch on television to diseases like AIDS or environmental problems like global warming that affect health and well-being. Values and ideas such as equity, human rights and social justice are gradually spreading through international agencies, the internet and people to people contact. Moreover, the 'unprecedented intensity' of global linkages have blurred distinctions 'between international and domestic, external and internal affairs' (Kiely, 2000: 182-183). US agricultural subsidies and trade adversely affect the lives of thousands of small farmers in Mexico and steel tariffs may harm Brazilian workers.

Globalization is not only a set of characteristics but also a neoliberal prescription for development (Veltmeyer, 1999). The prescription calls for the market and unregulated private decision-making to solve economic and social problems. It limits the role of government in economic affairs, social welfare and the management of international trade and financial flows. Markets, privatization, free trade and financial flows, and exports comprise the engine of economic growth. Equity and poverty have been lower priority concerns under the assumption that distribution and poverty reduction are natural outcomes of economic growth. Yet inequality is a crucial obstacle to development and poverty reduction (Londoño and Székely, 2000: 125).

For the past two decades, neoliberalism's market ideology spread relentlessly throughout the world, heavily promoted by the IMF, the World Bank, and other international financial agencies. Deeply indebted countries were forced to adopt neoliberal development policies as a condition of obtaining new loans or attracting foreign capital. From 1988 to 1993, however, the share of world income going to the poorest 10 percent of the world's population fell by over a quarter, while the share of the richest 10 percent rose by 8 percent (Wade, 2001). From 1988 to 1998 the incidence of global poverty fell by only 0.2 percent per year while high income countries—14 percent of the world's population—raked in 75 percent of world income (Watkins, 2002). Latin America and the Caribbean adopted neoliberal strategies more rapidly than any other region but per capita GDP grew by only 7 percent from 1980 to 2000 versus 75 percent from 1960 to 1980 (Weisbrot, 2002).[1] In the late 1990s, the region had an increased concentration of wealth and fifteen million more people living in extreme poverty than in 1987 (Watkins, 2002).

Globalization has both advocates and critics but for much of the past two decades neoliberal prescriptions have dominated development strategies and policies. Advocates point to gains in macroeconomic stability, solid growth and poverty reduction in countries such as South Korea and Southeast Asian nations. They argue that global integration leads to faster growth and poverty reduction in poor countries if accompanied by lowered trade barriers and market reforms (Watkins 2002). Market discipline curbs corruption, improves efficiency and competitiveness, and accelerates the transformation of technology. It helps to reduce inflation, spread wealth, skills and technology, and reduce isolation (DeLong, 2001).

Critics see globalization's development outcomes differently. In *Globalization and Its Discontents*, Nobel Prize winner Joseph Stiglitz (2002) asserts that a small group of powerful people in the rich countries established international rules that benefited them but damaged many countries on the periphery. Others call this global apartheid, in which an international minority shapes the rules and benefits disproportionately from trade expansion and openness (Booker and Minter, 2001). The *Human Development Report* (2000: 70) points out that finance ministers and officials of international financial institutions, acting behind closed doors, set economic policies that 'profoundly affect the lives of hundreds of millions of people.' Despite deteriorating health and well-being, poor countries have little say in establishing the rules of global trade and development.

Critics do not necessarily reject globalization but question the form that it has taken, enforced and implemented by a global elite and undemocratic institutions such as the IMF and the World Bank, both controlled by the US Treasury Department. Some scholars argue that national governments must play a larger role in managing policy reforms and protecting their citizens from the negative social impacts of globalization (Rodrik, 1997). But regaining greater national control over the development process is difficult to achieve for heavily indebted peripheral states vulnerable to strong pressure from international financial institutions. The IMF and World Bank pushed many developing nations to replace their country-specific development strategies with a neoliberal formula that often ignored local conditions. Consequently, governments have been less able to choose policies that respond directly to the basic needs of their citizens.[2] Together with unsatisfactory growth, this has meant poor outcomes for the reduction of inequality and poverty.

Most Latin American countries in the 1980s and 1990s embraced neoliberal development prescriptions. Neoliberalism's advocates predicted that diminished state intervention, the free market, trade expansion and fiscal discipline would bring renewed development and reduce poverty. After twenty years, however, the results were disappointing. Despite considerable success in macroeconomic stabilization, spurts of growth did not significantly diminish poverty or inequality. At the end of the 20th century, Latin America remained the most unequal region in the world with an extreme concentration of wealth and income at the top (see Table 6.1). According to ECLAC, 224 million Latin Americans—45 percent of the population—lived in poverty. The richest 20 percent of the population had average annual incomes of over $17,000; the poorest 20 percent received $930.[3] As the 21st century opened, poverty, hunger, malnutrition and disease still plagued Latin America—the most recent manifestation of what one scholar has called an 'historic [development] failure of epic proportions.' Despite ample resources to raise the people out of extreme poverty, Latin America has failed to do so (Coatsworth, 1998).

Table 6.1 Poverty in Latin America and the Caribbean, 1970-1995

	Moderate Poverty (millions of poor)	Extreme Poverty (millions of poor)
1970	117.1	51.4
1980	93.8	36.0
1990	147.9	73.1
1995	152.5	74.5

Source: Adapted from Londoño & Székely 2000: 112.

Continuing or growing levels of impoverishment after twenty years of neoliberal development in Latin America illustrate that the reduction of poverty and inequality are moral and economic necessities for development. The immorality of great wealth co-existing with great deprivation is a development issue.

A recent ECLAC report (2001: 28) argues that greater equality of opportunity is a primary goal of development. Nobel Prize winner Amartya Sen (1999) has urged development that enhances people's choices and wellbeing. Mahbub ul Haq (1994: 40-43) calls for development to enhance human life, not marginalize it. Jeffrey Sachs advocates a halt to debt service and repayment and application of those resources to health and education (Mekay, 2002). Such views reflect the fact that ethical values are involved in translating development prescriptions into action that improves the lives of people. They imply that people are the principal ends of development and that economic growth is a means toward human development (Anand and Sen, 2000, cited in Gasper 2002: 10).

Values are also inherent in the choice of development strategies and policies (Goodwin, 2001). This assertion challenges a core assumption of neoliberal economic theory: that people are economic beings and that the economic person makes only self-interested rational choices (Skirbekk and St. Clair, 2001). The benefits of growth are not necessarily distributed fairly or efficiently through unregulated markets and rational individual choice. Inequality persists partly because some individuals, institutions and nations begin with greater accumulations of wealth, power and status than others. These differences help such individuals and nations to shape social and political relations and distribution policies to their own self-interest. Poorer individuals and nations, on the other hand, face enormous obstacles in pulling themselves out of poverty.

Health and Development

Health is a cornerstone of economic growth and the reduction of poverty and inequality. It undergirds mental and physical development, learning ability and work productivity. It helps people to acquire capabilities and gives value to human life by enabling them to achieve their full potential and freedom as human beings. A recent global poll ranked good health as 'the number one desire of men and women around the world' (WHO, 2001: 21). Health is a basic human right, articulated over fifty years ago in Article 25 of the United Nations' Universal Declaration of Human Rights.

Social conditions are critical to good health. These involve adequate food, pure water, decent housing, a clean environment, safe working conditions and non-violent communities. Improving the social conditions that affect health depends upon how the income from growth is used and whether resources available for health and other basic services are distributed equitably to enhance the public good. Over a billion people in the developing countries, however, have a life expectancy of only forty years and lack access to clean water. Some 840 million people are undernourished, leaving them vulnerable to illness and disease (UNDP, 1999: 28). As Amartya Sen (1999) notes:

> premature mortality, escapable morbidity, undernourishment are all manifestations of poverty. I believe that health deprivation is really the most central aspect of poverty. . . . Health should be seen as an integral part of the development agenda.

Health is primarily an economic and social problem, not a medical one (Stillwagon, 1998: 8). It is a problem of class inequality.[4] The poor often live in unhygienic conditions. They are more susceptible to all health hazards, from infectious diseases to street violence. They are more likely to get malaria or cholera—the latter often contracted from unsafe water supplies. They are more vulnerable to new infectious diseases such as HIV/AIDS or drug resistant tuberculosis. At least 100 million Latin Americans, including over half the total rural population, are so poor that they lack essential nutrition (Coatsworth, 1998).

In Mexico of the 1980s, infant mortality stood at seventy-nine deaths per one thousand live births in rural areas, versus twenty-nine in urban areas. Just over half of Mexico's rural dwellers had access to safe water versus 79 percent of the urban population (UNDP, 1990: 31).

Class is one of the best predictors of health and life expectancy (Levins 2000: 15). Social and economic advantage correlates powerfully with health, and the affluent live longer, healthier lives. Life expectancy and health in wealthy nations are far better than in poorer nations. Great inequality is unhealthy for societies and studies suggest that unequal distribution in countries, states or cities is associated with lower life expectancies for people at all income levels (Angell, 2000: 43; Cohen and Rogers, 2000; Reuss, 2000: 11). More equal distribution of income and the gains from growth can yield better health indicators and better life expectancies even in poor countries—such as Cuba or the Indian state of Kerala demonstrate. When income and wealth are concentrated, however, poverty and health worsen.

Venezuela: Health and Development

In the 1980s, low oil prices and external debt helped push Venezuela into an economic crisis. Between 1981 and 1990 growth rates averaged –2.3 percent and per capita gross domestic product fell by 18 percent (Inter-American Development Bank (IDB) 1991: 273). Inequality rose sharply during the decade.

Table 6.2 Inequality in Venezuela 1981, 1990

	Part of national income received by the poorest 40%	Part of national income received by the richest 10%	Distance between the extremes
Venezuela 1981	20.2	21.8	1.6
Venezuela 1990	16.8	28.4	11.6

Source: CEPAL, *Panorama Social de América Latina*, 1993; cited in Filgueira and Papadópulos 1997: 384.

Earnings per employee, which had grown at an average annual rate of 3.8 percent from 1970-1980, stagnated at 0.1 percent during the decade while inflation averaged 16 percent annually (UNDP, 1992: 160, 184). Average real wages fell by 53 percent between 1982 and 1995, and labour's share of wages in the GNP dropped from 42.7 percent in 1980 to 31.1 percent in 1991. Unemployment and underemployment soared and the percentage of people living in poverty exploded by over 150 percent from its 1980 level (Márquez Mosconi and Alvarez, 1996;

Veltmeyer, 1999: 17-19). By the start of an IMF adjustment programme in 1989, over 79 percent of Venezuelans lived in abject or relative poverty (Castañeda, 1998). Some of these conditions are indicated in Table 6.3.

Advised by internationally known economist Jeffrey Sachs and the IMF, the newly installed government of President Carlos Andrés Pérez chose an orthodox package of neoliberal reforms (Drake, 1994: xxxii). The 'paquete' as it was commonly known, sought stabilization, fiscal balance, trade liberalization, a free market, government austerity and privatization. The Pérez government applied these measures as a 'shock' and they were unexpected and disliked by Venezuelans (Naim, 1993: 49). A doubling of transportation costs enraged the poor and many members of the middle class. Riots swept across urban Venezuela in late February 1989, causing extensive damage and looting over several days. The military eventually put down the rioting but at a cost of over one thousand deaths as untrained and fearful recruits sprayed the streets and slums with bullets— the largest frenzy of violence and deaths triggered by an IMF adjustment programme in Latin America (Hellinger, 1991: 3; Coronil and Skurski, 1991: 310).[5] This event angered young army officers and led to two attempts to overthrow the government in 1992.

Table 6.3   Venezuela Selected Economic Indicators

	1988	1989	1990	1991	1992	1993	1994
GDP growth (%)	5.9	-7.8	6.8	9.7	5.8	-1.2	-2.9
GDP/capita growth (%)	3.1	-10.2	4.2	7.1	3.4	-2.4	-5.1
Open unemployment (%)	7.9	9.7	10.4	10.1	8.1	6.8	8.7
Real Wage (1990=100)	145	106	100	90	99	75	-
Consumer prices gr. (%)	35.5	81.0	36.5	31.0	31.9	45.9	70.8
External debt (% GDP)	64	85	74	69	65	67	67

Source: ECLAC, *Economic Survey of Latin America and the Caribbean 1994-1995* (1996).

The social costs of neoliberal development mounted. Venezuela's social spending fell from 11.8 percent of GDP in 1980-81 to 8.5 percent in 1990-91, in absolute terms a drop from $480 to $300 per capita (CEPAL, 1994). Social spending (see Table 6.4) declined in the 1990s as a percentage of GDP.

The urban unemployment rate rose from 7.8 percent in 1992 to 14.9 percent in 1999 while nearly half of those employed worked in the informal sector, without benefits or readily available access to health care. Women's unemployment doubled and this meant fewer family resources to support nutrition and health (ECLAC, 2001).

Nutritional deficits increased during the 1990s. As Venezuelan governments privatized and slashed public expenditures and employment, they cut public subsidies that served as a form of distribution. The cost of water, natural gas and gasoline jumped while the consumption of meat and milk by low income Venezuelans dropped (Melcher, 2000: 14). At the same time, Venezuela's food self-sufficiency declined under free trade as food imports replaced much of the national production (PROVEA, 2001). Low wages and high inflation—49 percent average annually (1990-98)—meant deteriorating nutrition for hundreds of thousands of poor Venezuelans. Nutrition indicators fell at the beginning of the 1990s and remained low during the decade, with severe malnutrition cases appearing in school children (Lopez de Blanco, 1997: 510-512; PROVEA, 2001; PROVEA, 2001). Between 1997-1999, 21 percent of Venezuela's population suffered from malnutrition, putting them at risk from malnutrition-related illnesses (United Nations FAO, cited in *Latinamerica Press*, February 11, 2002: 7).

Table 6.4   Venezuela: Social Spending and Inflation 1993-1999

	1993	1994	1995	1996	1997	1998	1999
Social spending (% GDP)	9.3	10.2	9.7	8.9	8.9	8.4	7.6
Annual inflation rate	38.1	60.8	60.2	94.4	52.2	36.0	21.9

Source: *Anuario estadistico de Venezuela*, 1998, cited in PAHO 2001.

As unemployment, inflation and poverty rose, violence became a critical public health problem. Crime rates soared in Caracas where many of its three and a half million inhabitants refused to leave their homes after 8 p.m. Homicides—a major public health issue—reached 200 per month in Caracas, a 'social bomb' (Márquez, 1999: 112, 115). In 1995, 25-50 people were murdered each weekend in Caracas (*Latinamerica Press*, July 20, 1995: 7). By the mid- 1990s, an estimated 84,000 Venezuelan children lived by drug trafficking, prostitution and robbery. Another 176,000 children lived by begging and 1,210 minors were in prison for murder with a firearm (*Latinamerica Press*, July 27, 1995: 7).

In 1982, one-third of Venezuelans lived in poverty. By 1997, two-thirds lived on less than two dollars a day and more than one-third earned less than one dollar a day (CIA, 2002; Rosen and Burt, 2000: 15). Safe water and sanitation services did not reach the mountainside slums where millions of the urban poor lived in makeshift settlements that are high-risk health environments.[6] Crowded and unhealthy living conditions and nutritional deficits made the poor susceptible to diarrhoea and gastro-intestinal illnesses, particularly children. Neighbourhoods lacked primary care facilities, forcing families to forego medical aid or travel considerable distances to crowded, poorly staffed public hospitals where long waits were tantamount to a denial of service. Strikes paralysed emergency services in some public hospitals (PAHO, 1998: 538).

Venezuela's neoliberal technocrats, often educated in the United States, looked to privatization and decentralization to solve the country's social and health problems. As one observer noted, 'market discipline' was a crucial element in the 'production' of social services (Márquez, 1995: 401). The cash-strapped state, in effect, shifted part of its responsibility for health to the private sector and made individual citizens more responsible for their own health care. Private sector medicine took over services in some public hospitals. People who could pay went to the more prestigious private clinics while the poor relied on deteriorating public health services.[7] Municipal public hospitals often charged fees for services while patients also increasingly paid for medicines, immunizations, tests and other services. Hospital patients brought their own bed linen and other supplies. Falling health indicators were associated with privatization and the de-emphasis of prevention and primary care. Public expenditure on health dropped to 1.87 percent of gross domestic product in 1995, versus an international standard of 5.0 percent (PAHO, 1998: 542).

Venezuela's health system was highly fragmented and ill prepared to respond to shrinking resources and rising health needs. From 1960 to 1980 the country had developed a good network of public hospitals and outpatient clinics offering free services to people who were poor or not part of a public or private programme. The public system, however, included multiple, unintegrated institutions. During the 1980s and 1990s, economic crisis, mismanagement and corruption increasingly weakened the functioning of the system and several major reform efforts did not correct the problems (PAHO, 2001: ii). Health spending increased in the 1990s but 80 percent of such increases went to personnel costs. Service delivery remained poor and hundreds of thousands of the poor, including low paid and informal sector workers, were not covered by any of the system's programmes. Moreover, graduating doctors flocked into lucrative plastic surgery and other specialties while general practice remained badly under-subscribed (Wallerstein, 2000).

The health of Venezuelans continued to slip in the 1990s. Contagious diseases, once thought eradicated, reappeared at alarming rates. Basic sanitation services such as water and sewage deteriorated. Dengue fever—transmitted by mosquitoes—reappeared in 1989 and in 1997 there were over 17,000 cases. The reported cases of diarrhoea jumped from 275,000 in 1989 to 494,000 in 1991, and those were just the reported cases. Child diarrhoea reached the epidemic stage in the heavily populated Federal District. In 1982, there had been 4,200 cases of malaria; in the first 38 weeks of 1997 there were over 21,283 recorded cases. Tuberculosis and cholera cases soared. Measles reached epidemic proportions and diseases such as scabies and amebiasis rose sharply—both are associated with poverty, unsafe water and unsanitary living conditions (Castañeda and Ávila, 1998: 2). In a 1998 Oficina Central de Estadistica e Informatica survey of 6,898 homes, only 35 percent had access to basic services. One-third of those surveyed who had suffered an acute health problem did not see a doctor and a majority of the remainder consulted naturalist physicians. Twenty-two percent used home remedies or a remedy prescribed for another family member, with only 5 percent consulting a pharmacist (*El Universal*, 8 February 2001).

Class differences and inequality were associated with Venezuela's health outcomes. Infant mortality rose to 31.3 in 1990 and then fell to 28.1 in 1995—still high for a country with abundant resources. But states in southern and western Venezuela, with high levels of unmet basic needs, showed infant mortality as high as fifty. Life expectancy also showed dramatic class differences—70.1 years for the richest; 58 years for the poorest (Castañeda and Avila, 1998: 2; UNDP, 2000: 152-153). Venezuela's poor had triple the rate of death from contagious disease. The cost of medicines, previously subsidized by the government, rose by nearly 2,000 percent, making it more difficult than ever for the poor to obtain them. Over 93 percent of drugs sold in Venezuela are now sold in the private sector. Private health services and modern technology were located in the larger cities, catering to people with higher incomes (PAHO, 1998: 541-542). These class disparities underline the inequities inherent in Venezuela's society and health system. They also are one reason why Venezuelans lost trust in governments and democratic political institutions as their income, health and living conditions worsened during the neoliberal era. They assumed that elites and the political and economic leadership had siphoned off a huge share of the country's oil wealth that properly belonged to all Venezuelans.

Cuba: Health and Development

Like Venezuela, Cuba's crisis began in the 1980s and exploded after 1989 (see Table 6.5). In 1990, the Soviet Union halted its subsidy programme estimated at four to six billion dollars per year. Over the next three years, the Cuban economy contracted by at least 35 percent (AAWH, 1997: 10). Hard currency debt rose to some $11 billion plus a large debt to the former Soviet Union (Eckstein, 1997: 135-136). Cuba had very little capacity to borrow and the severe lack of foreign exchange meant a 75 percent drop in imports. This caused critical shortages of fuel, food, raw materials and spare parts (PAHO, 1994: Vol. II, Cuba). Inflation soared and government enterprises laid off thousands of workers (Romero Gómez, 2001: 62-64; Ferriol Muruaga, 2000; Ganuza and Taylor, 1998).

Severe economic contraction meant a steep decline in the living conditions of Cubans. They ate less after the government cut subsidies for foods and fresh products such as bread, potatoes, tomatoes, carrots, beets and bananas. Cubans lived with frequent electric power outages that disrupted family life and work and hurt production. Public transportation ground almost to a halt; daily bus trips in Havana fell from 30,000 to 6,500. People walked or rode bicycles to work resulting in a substantial decline in deaths from auto accidents but a 78 percent rise in bicycle-related deaths (Garfield and Holtz, 2000: 117). Factory closures left 125,700 workers unemployed by late 1992 (Díaz González, 1995: 19). Many simply stopped going to work. Crime rates and prostitution rose sharply although

still low by Latin American or US standards. Political tensions mounted in the
1990s along with increased questioning of Cuban socialism. Thousands of Cubans
sought to emigrate to the United States. Scattered worker protests erupted in 1991
and 1992 and larger demonstrations broke out in 1993 and 1994 (Gunn, 1992: 60;
Cuba News, November 1999). During three decades of socialist development, the
Cuban state had established a standard of living that its economy could no longer
fully meet.

Cuba adjusted to its crisis with both socialist and capitalist strategies. It
liberalized trade, encouraged direct foreign investment, reduced public
expenditures, devalued its currency and shrank the public sector. It converted
Soviet-style state farms into private cooperative production units, legalized the use
of dollars and other hard currencies, re-established farmers' markets and allowed
self-employment in some activities. By January 1996, over 208,000 Cubans had
received licences to run small businesses, restaurants, drive taxis, sell goods or
provide services such as carpentry, hairdressing and plumbing (CIA, 1998).[8] To
fortify its hard currency income, the government sought to increase tourism and
non-sugar exports, especially biomedical products.

Table 6.5   Cuba: GDP 1989-1998

Year	Growth (%)	Exports Current US$ (millions)	Imports Current US$ (millions)
1989	1.5	5400	8140
1990	-3.1	5415	7417
1991	-9.4	2980	4234
1992	-11.6	1779	2315
1993	-14.9	1137	2137
1994	0.7	1381	2353
1996	7.8	1866	3657
1998	1.2	1661	4048

Source: Adapted from Weeks (2001: 20).

Cuba, however, did not unconditionally surrender to the market and the
neoliberal formula. The state maintained a substantial degree of control over the
adjustment process and the country's re-insertion into the global economy. It
attempted to restructure its economy in ways that were consistent with preserving
its thirty year commitment to human development and social gains.

Obtaining enough food, however, became a primary concern for millions of
Cubans as the island's food imports plummeted by 50 percent between 1989 and

1993 (Garfield and Holtz, 2000: 114). Food prices rose sharply as the rural economy virtually stopped because of input shortages and machinery rusted in the fields because of a lack of spare parts (Sinclair and Thompson, 2001). In August 1994, when food supplies were lowest, hundreds of Habaneros took to the streets in protest, possibly a reason why authorities re-opened farmers' markets in October 1994, allowing the sale of farm products at unregulated prices (Eckstein 2000; Hernández-Cata, 2000: 29).

Facing great scarcity, Cuba launched an all-out effort to increase food production. The country shifted from high-input, mechanized and export-oriented agriculture, to diverse, low-input agriculture, using organic techniques and biological pest controls. Production largely moved from the state to the private sector although the state continued to own 75 percent of the land (Sinclair and Thompson, 2001). The government organized agricultural and cattle cooperatives, promoted urban gardening and mobilized agricultural work brigades. By 1998, some 210,000 urban farmers, using organic methods, produced 30,000 tons of fruits and vegetables, 7.5 million eggs, and 3,650 tons of meat (Wald, 1999: 9). Two million Havana residents get half of the fresh produce they consume from urban farms, located in vacant lots, open spaces and backyards throughout the city. This popular participation in food production helped to preserve Cuban solidarity and socialism during extreme economic distress (Sinclair and Thompson, 2001).

The government also extended the rationing system to include most consumer goods, seeking to share the burden of sacrifice equitably and protect vulnerable groups.[9] This stands in marked contrast to resource allocation in capitalist systems that tend to privilege the wealthy while the burden of sacrifice falls on the poor during hard times. Rationing, however, meant sharing scarcity more equally and, for many Cubans, rationing did not provide sufficient food (Eckstein, 2000; PAHO, 1998, Vol. II; Pastor, 1992). A visiting Canadian doctor noted that his Cuban interpreter's ration book allowed the young man '4 ounces of beef twice a year, 8 ounces of poultry 8 times a year, 8 ounces of cornmeal 6 times a year, 3 ounces of bread each day, and 2 pounds of fish and 6 pounds of sugar a month.' The interpreter ate as many meals as possible with the visiting Canadians to allow his parents and siblings to use his rations (Williams, 1997). Hungry Cubans bought additional food at higher prices in the private markets, used the black market, bartered or went without.

The economic crisis and adjustment damaged the health of Cubans. While health indicators remained high and even improved during the 1990s, scarcity worsened the living conditions that undergird health. Daily per capita caloric intake dropped from 2,908 in 1990 to 1,863 calories in 1995 while protein intake fell by 40 percent, with an estimated average weight loss of twenty pounds by 1994. (Sinclair and Thompson 2001: 10). According to FAO, 17 percent of Cubans suffered from malnutrition from 1997-1999, with a daily deficit of 210 calories (UNFAO, cited in *Latinamerica Press*, February 11, 2002: 7).

The abrupt drop in nutrition left Cubans more vulnerable to infections and gastro-intestinal illnesses, especially diarrhoea or intestinal parasites. Hepatitis A cases soared from 24.9 per 100,000 inhabitants in 1989 to 189.0 in 1996 (PAHO,

1998). Deaths from acute diarrhoeal disease rose from 2.7 per 100,000 in 1989 to 6.7 in 1994 and dysentery cases showed a marked increase (AAWH, 1997: 8). Tuberculosis cases, associated with deteriorating nutrition and poor housing and sanitary conditions, almost tripled between 1990 and 1994. The economic crisis especially hurt people 65 and older whose death rate rose sharply from tuberculosis, influenza, pneumonia, diarrhoea, heart disease and other ailments (Garfield and Santana, 1997: 16-18). In the early 1990s, an epidemic of optic neuropathy, linked centrally to nutritional and vitamin deficiencies and environmental toxins, damaged the eyesight and health of over 50,000 Cubans (AAWH, 1997: 12; Garfield and Santana, 1997: 16). Nutritional deficits among pregnant women meant a 23 percent rise in low birthweight babies, from 7.3 percent in 1989 to 9.3 percent in 1993 before dropping to 7.3 percent again in 1996.[10] Milk rations for children to age thirteen were cut back to children up to age seven.

US policy intensified the impact of the economic crisis on the health of Cubans. The Cuba Democracy Act of 1992 and Helms-Burton legislation of 1996 banned US subsidiaries in third countries from trading with Cuba, including food exports, and the United States strongly pressured other countries to follow suit. Cuba had imported over $400 million in food and medicines from US subsidiaries in 1990 but this trade was virtually halted (WOLA/Oxfam, 1997). While medicines and medical supplies could, in principle, be sold to Cuba, the cumbersome licensing process effectively limited licenses from being issued—only eight were issued to US subsidiaries between 1992 and 1995, while numerous applications were denied because the exports 'would be detrimental to US foreign policy interests.' The stated policy of the US Treasury and Commerce Departments is that 'applications for validated licenses will generally be denied' (AAWH, 1997: 6; WOLA/Oxfam America Press Release, June 26, 1997). Mergers of American and European pharmaceutical and biotechnology firms further restricted Cuba's access to medicines, medical equipment and vaccines. This near-blockade forced Cuba to spend more of its scarce foreign exchange on the transportation costs of food and medical supplies from distant countries.

The tightening of the embargo, coupled with foreign exchange shortages meant erosion of the infrastructure that supported Cuba's health system. Water quality worsened because Cuba could not import purification chemicals and US-built parts for the water system. In 1994, chemical shortages and equipment breakdowns resulted in the closing of 12 chlorination plants in Havana province and 18 in Piñar del Rio province alone. The population with access to chlorinated water dropped from 98 percent in 1989 to 26 percent in 1994 (Garfield and Holtz, 2000: 117; AAWH, 1997: 20). Backups and breakage of sewer lines occurred frequently, with overflows and the risk of drinking water contamination (PAHO, 1998: 210). Unsafe water led to rises in illness and death from water-borne diseases as well as scabies and other dermatological disorders. In 1994, contaminated water caused an outbreak of over 200 cases of the Guillain Barré syndrome in Havana (Garfield and Santana, 1997: 16-17).

Spare parts and Kodak film, recommended for breast-cancer screening, were also not available, limiting the use of certain technology and US-built x-ray machines (AAWH, 1997: 6, 11-12). In turn, this meant a decrease in mammograms as a preventive measure for breast cancers—an attack on the health of women. The number of medicines and prescription drugs available to Cuba fell from 1,297 in 1991 to 889 in 1997, largely because many of these are manufactured by US corporations or their subsidiaries.[11] Surgeries dropped from 885,790 in 1990 to 536,547 in 1995, indicating the shortage of hospital resources. Heart disease is the major cause of death in Cuba but implants dropped from over 400 per year in 1990 to 174 per year in 1995 (AAWH, 1997: 6, 8, 27). Because the United States monopolizes the production of pacemakers, these are extremely difficult for Cuba to obtain.   Jose Tereul, a PAHO official, summarized the adverse health impact of the US embargo when he noted that it probably shortened the lives of Cubans through the denial of medicines, medical equipment and supplies (Kirkpatrick and Varden, 1997: 6).

Cuba had established a strong health service from the 1960s to the 1980s but economic crisis and adjustment prompted fresh reforms in the 1990s. These were aimed at improving the quality, efficiency and management of services, greater decentralization and ensuring the sustainability of the health system—a primary source of the legitimacy of Cuba's political system (PAHO, 1999: ii). Health investment was a top priority and the share of health in public spending went from 6.6 percent in 1990 to 10.9 percent in 1997 (PAHO, 1999: 7). Table 6.6 reflects the priorities of the Cuban government related to health.

Table 6.6   Health Sector Financing and Expenditures, 1990-1997 (Millions Cuban Pesos)

Indicator	1990	1991	1992	1993	1994	1995	1996	1997
Budget	1045	1038	1039	1175	1166	1222	1310	1383
PC health expenditure	99	97	96	107	106	111	119	125
Health as % of public spending	6.6	6.3	6.6	7.4	7.5	8.0	9.6	10.9

Source: National Office of Economy and Planning, Ministry of Public Health, May 1999; cited in PAHO (1999: 7).

The purchasing power of this rising peso health budget, however, dropped sharply during the 1990s. The peso, pegged at one to the dollar in 1989, collapsed to 120 to the dollar on the black market in 1992 before recovering to 22 in 1997. This effectively shrank health investment and Cuba's ability to obtain the medicines, spare parts and other inputs necessary for quality healthcare. With inflation and resource scarcity, the real incomes of doctors dropped to about US$20 per month at a time when the Cuban state could no longer provide the level of services and subsidies that had made low professional salaries tolerable. Doctors moonlighted as taxi drivers, sold food to patients and engaged in other activities to increase their incomes (Garfield and Holtz, 2000: 123-127).[12] Health workers migrated to better paying work in other sectors of the economy and in 1998 some 4,000 participated in the visa lottery to leave Cuba (Miranda Parrondo and Tabraue, 2000: 31).

To maintain health financing, the government promoted health 'tourism' (health services for foreigners), encouraged domestic and external donations and increased the development and marketing of biomedical products. The country spent more than US$300 million from 1989 to 1992 on biotechnology and pharmaceutical research (French, 1993: A3). Over one thousand people worked at Cuba's Genetic Engineering and Biotechnology Centre and its products, marketed in some forty countries, earned about US$100 million annually (Snow and Elias 2002). But during the 1990s, hard currency spending on public health fell by almost 70 percent, with the value of health-related imports plummeting from US$227 million in 1989 to US$67 million in 1993 (*The Economist*, November 14, 1998: 40).

Prevention and primary care formed the backbone of Cuba's health system and the crisis reforms re-emphasized this approach. In the mid 1990s, over half the health budget went to primary care as opposed to one-third in the 1980s (Garfield and Holtz, 2000: 125). The number of family physicians rose from 11,195 in 1990 to 30,133 in 2000 (*Anuario Estadístico de Cuba 2000*: Table XIV.l). Based in communities, workplaces and other sites and partnered with nurses, the family physicians brought free and good quality care to Cubans. The doctor-nurse teams lived in neighbourhoods and cared for about 125 families, making home visits to monitor health progress, children's vaccinations, deal with child abuse or ensure that vulnerable groups got appropriate care. Physicians at all levels worked to conserve and control medicines and materials for priority groups, promoting health education as a way to respond to limited supplies of paper, water and soap (Barrett, 1993: 1-4). In 1997, the primary care network of family physicians, oral health clinics, maternity homes, polyclinics and other institutions ensured 100 percent coverage with the family physicians providing nearly 98 percent of the population's health care needs (*Anuario Estadístico de Cuba 2000*; PAHO, 1999).

To supplement scarce medicines, Cuba turned to alternative medicine that the Cuban military had been experimenting with during the 1980s. In the 1990s, the Cuban medical community developed herbal remedies for respiratory conditions, digestive disorders, arthritis, urinary-tract infections, insomnia and toothaches (Barrett, 1993: 3). Homeopathic remedies are now widely recommended by Cuba's medical community. Some 60 percent of Cuba's 30,000 family doctors are trained to use natural remedies that are prescribed in almost all outpatient clinics and sold in government pharmacies. Acupuncture, brought to Cuba from Vietnam and China in the 1970s, is used as an anaesthetic for about twenty kinds of operations such as neck surgery, thyroid cysts, hernias or tooth extractions. By 1998 'green medicine' accounted for about 80 percent of prescriptions and acupuncture had replaced anaesthetics for minor surgery (*Latinamerica Press*, September 4, 2000: 7; *The Economist*, November 14, 1998: 40).

Cuba achieved impressive health outcomes during the 1990s despite its devastating economic crisis. Infant mortality, under-five mortality and life expectancy remained nearly at the US level. Much of this achievement was due to the existing excellence of the Cuban health system with dedicated health workers and an ethos of delivering good health care to the entire population.

The expansion and improvement of primary care substantially reduced the number of hospital visits and length of the stays by the late 1990s. Rigorous monitoring of the decentralized, efficient delivery of services and professional commitment enabled the Cuban health care system to ride out the worst of the crisis. Medical practitioners from several countries, including Britain and the United States, have gone to Cuba to understand how Cuba was able to achieve so much with so few resources.

Table 6.7   Cuba and the United States Life Expectancy at Birth, Infant Mortality Rate and Under 5 Mortality Rate

	Cuba 1970	Cuba 1998	US 1970	US 1998
Infant mortality rate Per 1000 live births	34	7	20	7
Under 5 mortality rate Per 1000 live births	43	8	26	8
Life expectancy at birth	70.7	75.7	71.3	76.7

Source: UNDP, *Human Development Report 2000*, Table 9.

Health care has been a primary goal of the Cuban revolution, embedded in the leadership's vision of development and a vital part of the regime's commitment to equity and human welfare. Cubans take pride in their health system and it serves to legitimate Cuban socialism. Universal quality health care, together with education, helped to hold the Cuban political system together in the context of a devastating crisis. The state played a key role in distributing available health resources equitably and protecting the vulnerable. The economic crisis of the 1990s, however, and Cuba's adjustment to the global economy weakened the system. The island's socialist economy has not been able to generate sufficient surplus to sustain the living conditions that make possible favourable health outcomes in the long term. Years of deficient food intake, poorer water safety and sanitation, shortages of every kind of medical supplies and very low salaries for health workers are warning signs for future problems. Cuba's human development index ranking, which stood at 61 in 1992, fell to 79 by 1996 before rebounding to 56 in 2000 (UNDP, 1992, 1996, 2000).

As the 20th century ended, Cuba's human welfare net was tattered but still holding. The state was less able to maintain the social contract that marks Cuban development and sustains political legitimacy. Cubans relied more on individual initiative within an increasingly mixed economy to satisfy their needs and aspirations. This has implications for equality if individually oriented values begin to blend with, or replace, collective values. The health system is less equal since Cubans with dollars have a greater chance of maintaining their food intake and thus their health, than those without access to dollars. Cuba's shortage of foreign exchange and the limited capacity of its economy to generate resources posed major challenges to future health achievements. Against these difficulties stood a dedicated corps of well-trained health workers, health as a primary goal of development, political will, strong institutions and the demonstrated resilience of the Cuban people.

Conclusion

Adjustment to the global economic system damaged the health and well-being of Venezuelans and Cubans but in different ways and to different degrees. Facing extreme crisis and the powerful impact of global capitalism, the only viable choice for both countries was to adjust and restructure their economies. Both had lost part of their capacity to provide their populations with an adequate level of economic and social well-being. But adjusting internally and externally to this loss differed in important ways. History mattered. Cuba's intense nationalism and its strong commitment to equality and human development aided the government in protecting its citizens from many of the harshest social impacts of adjustment.[13] Although the Cuban state took a number of orthodox neoliberal steps in restructuring its economy, it moved more cautiously than Venezuela and maintained the principle of collective responsibility for social well-being.

By retaining much of its control over adjustment and development, the Cuban state preserved its major role in the economy and allocated resources equitably to priority areas such as health. Consequently, health achievements remained strong despite the disastrous economic crisis.

In contrast Venezuela, with a long history of involvement with global capitalism, embraced neoliberal development strategies. Heavily indebted and subject to loan conditions required by the IMF, its adjustment process reflected the neoliberal belief that the free market and a deregulated economy would produce the greatest freedom and greatest good for the greatest number. The Venezuelan state thus ceded a significant degree of control over the country's development and distributional process to private interests and the market, leading to the deterioration of health care.

Distinctive adjustment and development processes meant different health outcomes in Venezuela and Cuba. Institutions played a central role in both systems. For twenty years (1960-1980) Venezuela had maintained a relatively good system of public health care, accessible to the poor. Health care 'capital' accumulated in the form of personnel, experience, research, potable water, sanitation and a network of hospitals and clinics. With the crisis of the 1980s and 1990s, however, this capital steadily diminished and the health of the poor worsened. The country's increasingly privatized health system lacked effective regulatory mechanisms to ensure efficient delivery and equitable distribution of health services. Most Venezuelans had limited ability to pay for services and medicines. Many lived in rural areas or received poor quality treatment in run-down public hospitals and outpatient centres. The state's health system reforms assigned a relatively low priority to prevention and primary care. This meant an enormous present and future cost for Venezuela in terms of more illness, unnecessary deaths, impaired learning and lower productivity.

Cuba's accumulation of health 'capital' during the first thirty years of its revolutionary history, coupled with a strong political commitment and the country's public health ethos, helped to maintain good health care during the crisis of the 1990s. Well-trained professionals believed passionately in quality care distributed equitably throughout the country. The system suffered from inadequate financing but used limited resources with extraordinary efficiency. Whereas Venezuelan health workers went on strike and demonstrated for better pay and more resources, Cuban health workers adapted flexibly to serious resource shortages (Whiteford, 1998: 199). While some migrated to better paying activities, most stayed in their profession and sought ways to help their patients. The expansion of Cuba's primary care system brought quality health services to every Cuban neighbourhood, heading off more serious illnesses and hospital stays. Despite slippage in several areas of health care, Cuba entered the 21st century with a relatively healthy population.

Participation played a key role in the adjustment processes of both countries but again in different ways. Venezuela's democratic governance had been highly centralized with little effective grassroots participation and an economy characterized by great income inequality. As social services deteriorated and poverty increased, the health of Venezuela's poor majority suffered as access and the quality of health care diminished. Deteriorating public health strengthened the popular perception that the country's political and economic elites were using a collective resource—oil—for the privileged few. Political legitimacy and trust in democratic institutions dissolved, leading to attempted golpes and, in the late 1990s, the election of populist Hugo Chávez, a former coup leader, as president.

Cuba used participation to weather its crisis and adjustment. The government preserved legitimacy through popular consultation and equitable distribution of available resources. Urban farms relieved some of the food shortages and local consultations helped to identify and deal with the basic needs of vulnerable groups. Despite continuing economic weakness and some dissatisfaction with the shortage-plagued services, most Cubans strongly supported the public health system, an institution that epitomized socialist concern with collective wellbeing.

Venezuela's neoliberal policies steered the country away from distributional priorities under the assumption that accelerated growth would, in the long term, enhance the wellbeing of the poor. Severely impoverished Venezuelans, however, could not wait for long-term gains from growth. In contrast, the Cuban state saw social gains as the central focus of development and shaped its development strategy in ways that were largely consistent with this historical commitment. Its policy choices reflected the understanding that health and development are inextricably connected and that human wellbeing requires not only economic growth but also social transformation.

Health care in both countries, however, faces daunting challenges in the 21st century. Venezuela's democracy must find ways to regain legitimacy and trust among the country's poor majority. This will involve lessening extreme inequality and renewing the nation's constitutional commitment to health care and other collective priorities. Cuba, on the other hand, must find ways for its economy to generate more surplus and regain or improve the equality and standard of living that the country enjoyed in the 1970s and 1980s.

Peripheral countries, with few resources and substantial inequality, are unlikely to deliver good health care to their citizens within the neoliberal development model. Government intervention is necessary to smooth the jagged edges of the market and allocate resources equitably. The comparative experience of health care and crisis in Venezuela and Cuba suggests that development is a social, economic and moral issue. Great wealth and great poverty do not easily coexist in democracies. Societal peace, political stability and economic progress are inextricably mixed with social justice.

Notes

1   Weisbrot (2002) also argues that poor global economic performance in the last quarter of the 20th century also brought lowered rates of social progress, measured by indicators such as life expectancy, infant and child mortality, literacy and education.

2   For example, Ecuador recently attempted to allocate ten percent of projected revenues from a new oil pipeline to health and education. The IMF condition for a $240 million loan, however, required Ecuador to use all of the revenues to service its debt. The pipeline is being built by a consortium of transnational corporations, will jeopardize pristine areas of the Amazon region as well as water sources for Ecuadorian cities and, with the elimination of the 10 percent for social spending, foreign creditors will reap all the benefits from the pipeline (Verdezoto, 2002; Lucas, 2002).

3   Michel Camdessus, former president of the IMF who vigorously promoted neoliberal economic policies, admitted that the IMF had failed to reduce income inequality in Latin America (*Latinamerica Press*, January 22, 2001).

4   For a discussion of income inequality and health, see Kawachi, Kennedy and Wilkinson (1999).

5   It is very difficult to establish the exact number of deaths but the discovery of mass graves indicates that the government statistics are highly suspect. Moreover, after a short time, the Venezuelan government virtually stopped the process of exhumation and identification (*Latinamerica Press*, October 17, 1991). In late December 1991, Venezuelan representatives of Amnesty International (AI) told the author that AI estimates nationwide deaths related to the events of February 27 at 3,000 to 3,500.

6   From the early 1980s to the mid 1990s, the percentage of Venezuelans with access to improved (safe) water sources fell from 84 percent to 79 percent. From 1990-1996, only 58 percent of Venezuelans had access to sanitation services (World Bank, 2001: Table 7).

7   A 1991 survey found that 34 percent of the respondents went to private clinics for acute illness or injury, 54 percent went to public facilities and the remainder sought treatment in their workplaces or pharmacies. Nearly 18 percent of those who had not sought treatment cited a 'lack of money' as the reason (PAHO, 1994).

8   By December 1996, their number had dropped to 180,000, partly because of new taxes (CIA, 1998).

9   Rationing in Cuba contrasts with resource allocation in capitalist markets that tends to shift resources towards the wealthy while the burden of sacrifice falls on the poor.

10   Part of the success in limiting the health impact of malnutrition on Cuba's children may have been due to the widespread family physician services. *The Human Development Report* (1997) argues that child malnutrition may depend less on income or available food than on health care available to women and children.

11   The United States manufactured or patented 50 percent of all new world-class drugs that emerged between 1972 and 1992 and these were not available to Cuba (WOLA and Oxfam, America Press Release 1997).

12   According to Garfield and Holtz, a taxi driver could earn up to fifty times more than a doctor.

13   Unemployed Cubans could count on a minimum level of income and social welfare benefits to sustain them. When a Venezuelan working in the informal sector had a bad day or week selling goods on the street, he or she faced hunger and deprivation.

Chapter Seven

Asia's Post-Crisis Regionalism: The State In, the US Out[*]

Paul Bowles

The 1997 financial crisis has proved to be a turning point for regionalism in Asia. As Higgott astutely observed soon after the crisis, 'the political manifestations of these events [the financial crisis] will linger long after the necessary reforms have been introduced to return at least a semblance of economic normalcy to the region' (Higgott, 1998: 333). One significant political manifestation has been the emergence of a new form of regionalism in Asia as evidenced by new forms of regional monetary cooperation and proposed sub-regional trade agreements, developments that signal sharp changes in direction for the region. Chameleon-like in its qualities throughout the past century, regionalism has been transformed once more; it has again demonstrated itself to be a flexible policy tool that can be used to meet a variety of objectives, economic and political (Lawrence, 1994).

This chapter argues that regionalism in Asia after the financial crisis departs significantly from its pre-crisis incarnation. Specifically, an understanding of the post-crisis regionalism requires a state-centric approach and an analysis of power relations in the global economy. The assumptions that regionalism in Asia should be analysed primarily in terms of private actors or that it is based on a benign interdependence between countries that span the Pacific, which underlay much visioning of the 'Pacific Rim' in the 1990s, is now untenable. The contours of post-financial crisis regionalism are, by state design, aimed at restoring to Asia a greater degree of political power and autonomy vis-à-vis the rest of the world, and the United States and the international financial institutions it controls, in particular. The implications of this are profound, not only for our understanding of 'the region', but also for our analysis of the current phase of the global economy.

The analysis is presented in three parts. First, a brief description is given of the characteristics and analysis of regionalism in pre-financial crisis Asia. We then analyse in more detail the emergence of a new post-crisis regionalism and examine the reasons for its emergence. Particular attention here is paid to the motives of the two most significant powers in East Asia, China and Japan. In the concluding section we discuss the implications of this regionalism for a theoretical analysis of the global economy.

Asian Regionalism Prior to the Financial Crisis

The countries of Asia did not participate in the wave of regionalism, which proved popular with other developing countries in the 1950s and 1960s. When regionalism re-emerged as a preferred economic policy in the 1980s and 1990s, Asia again lagged behind the rest of the world in terms of the formal political institutionalization of regionalism. Indeed, a distinguishing feature of Asian regionalism for many scholars was precisely the fact that the 'region' itself was ill defined (or capable of multiple definitions) and that the 'regionalism' that was taking place was doing so through market-led, rather than government-led, integration processes. As Stubbs (1995: 786), for example, has argued

> although the state has been instrumental in nurturing business growth, regionalisation in the Asia-Pacific region—unlike the other major regions of the world—has been driven by the private sector not by governments. Hence, the boundaries of the region do not coincide neatly with state boundaries. In many ways the region's governments are still trying to come to grips with the rapid economic changes that swirl around them.

Regional integration processes therefore led to the identification by economists and policy analysts of a 'regional economy' within Asia as well as in a number of sub-regions. Throughout the region, the activities of Japanese multinationals and of overseas Chinese businesses were highlighted as operating on the basis of a series of 'networks' based on the production prerequisites of post-Fordism and the personal connections which facilitated and characterized much of the overseas Chinese Diaspora. It was these business networks, rather than the existence of supranational political institutions, which led to the identification and integration of 'regional economy.' This was also true at the sub-regional level. For example, 'Greater China' was identified as one such subregion, comprising of an international division of labour that integrated production in parts of Mainland China and companies in Taiwan and Hong Kong. Here, too, the impetus for economic integration was identified as largely business driven rather than as state driven. As Naughton (1997: v) writes, 'firms, especially small and medium-size family firms, play central roles in the story, with government policies playing secondary, reactive roles.'

This analysis tended to overstate the role of 'the market' in fostering integration in the region. They present us with something of a paradox in that most of them accept that national economies can be described as 'developmental states' where governments play key roles in 'guiding the market' but where, it seems, inter-national and inter-regional integration are played out beyond the reach of the state. Such a paradox is, in fact, a false one and is solved by a better appreciation of the role that the state played in fostering inter-regional trade and capital flows. For example, Japan's policy with regard to foreign direct investment (FDI) changed critically during the post-war decades to one favourable to, and supportive of, FDI during the 1980s. The emergence of a hierarchical division of labour in the region fostered by Japanese multinationals was not a chance occurrence but one premised in no small part on Japanese policy (Bowles and Maclean, 1996b: 293-412). Similarly, the emergence of the 'China Circle' was not entirely an accident in which states were only 'reactive.' China's initial choice of venue for its four Special Economic Zones (SEZs) in 1984 was based on exploiting cultural and geographic links between the SEZs and the overseas Chinese communities in Taiwan and Hong Kong. The subsequent growth of the four cities initially chosen as SEZs and the subsequent spread of investment into other parts of Guangdong and Fujian Provinces could not have been predicted by Chinese policy-makers but the emergence of a 'Greater China' economic zone certainly owes something to their policies. However, while the above analyses may underestimate the role of the state in promoting regional economic integration, they do have to make the valid point that Asian regionalism was based on a lower level of formal intergovernmental regional institutions and policies than were observed in other regions, most notably, in Europe and North America. In this comparative sense, the above analyses are right to stress the relatively greater role of the market and relatively less importance of the state in regional integration in Asia than elsewhere, even if there has been a tendency to push the argument too far in that direction.

At the level of formal regional economic arrangements, it is true, Asia lagged behind. While Europe was moving full speed ahead with the 'Single Market' project and the United States was abandoning its traditional sole reliance on multilateralism as a route to free trade and signing free trade agreements first with Canada and then with Canada and Mexico, Asia remained reluctant to join in. The initial response to the emergence of North American and European 'blocs' included calls, made particularly loudly by Malaysia's Prime Minister Mahathir, for an East Asian Economic Group. This idea was, however, stillborn and Asian countries settled for the different version of regionalism embodied in APEC (Higgott and Stubbs, 1994). This body is much looser in regulatory design than the other 'blocs' and operates by consensus and voluntary action (or inaction) rather than by legal stricture. APEC's formation in 1989 owed as much to the perceived political need to ensure that trade across the Pacific remained open and to prevent the emergence of three closed blocs as to any substantive trade liberalization initiatives.

As the fear of the emergence of three protectionist blocs receded, APEC in 1993 formed an Eminent Person's Group under the Chairmanship of Fred Bergsten to devise a 'Vision' for APEC that would justify its continued existence. This group came up with the idea of 'open regionalism' and the goal of establishing a free trade area in the region by 2010 for developed country members and 2020 for developing country members, a goal which was subsequently adopted at the APEC meeting held in Bogor, Indonesia in 1994.

This 'vision' represented a victory for the pro-globalist thinkers and established for the institution a framework that stressed the interdependence of economies and the mutual advantages for all in trade liberalization, and that minimized the differences between developed and developing country members (Bowles, 2000: 433-455). In establishing this framework, APEC was simply following, and contributing to, the ways in which the ideological construction of the 'Pacific Rim' was being pursued in the wider intellectual and policy community (Cumings, 1993: 29-47; Woodside, 1993: 13-26). The boundaries of the 'region', at this level, were ever-expanding.[1]

The idea of 'open regionalism'—of using regionalism to further integration into the global economy—was also central to Asia's most deliberate attempt at formal economic regionalism, the ASEAN Free Trade Area (AFTA). The formation of AFTA, proposed in 1991 and coming into effect on January 1st 1993, marked ASEAN's most ambitious attempt at regional economic cooperation since its formation in 1967 and, indeed, put ASEAN on a path which it had rejected several times in the past. The formation of AFTA came after many of the ASEAN countries had struggled with the need to boost export earnings during the 1980s in response to the debt crises of the early years of that decade. The response of the ASEAN-4 (Indonesia, Thailand, the Philippines, Malaysia), following the advice of the international financial institutions, was to engage in trade liberalization, albeit at their own pace rather than collectively, and to shift towards policies more conducive to export promotion. In addition, individual countries adopted policies more favourable to FDI in an effort to attract foreign capital needed to spur continued industrialization.

These policies were fortuitous in that Japanese firms were expanding overseas rapidly in response to the massive appreciation of the *yen* which followed the Plaza Accord in 1985. Japan's FDI grew at an annual average rate of 62 percent over the 1985-89 period. At the same time, the East Asian NICs were also investing heavily overseas with the ASEAN-4 and China being favoured destinations. As a result, FDI as a percentage of GDP quadrupled in the ASEAN-4 between 1985 and 1990. Having shifted to a strategy of FDI-sponsored export-led growth, ASEAN states were keenly aware of the need to ensure that ASEAN as an investment site remained competitive. At the end of the 1980s there appeared to be a significant threat to this in the form of competition from China, the former Soviet bloc following the dramatic events of 1989-91, the potential investment-diverting effects of greater European integration in 1992, and the NAFTA, particularly the threat of investment diversion to Mexico.

The increasing concern about possible investment diversion is clear from the joint communiqués of the ASEAN ministerial meetings with the ASEAN foreign ministers responding to the 'increasing competing demand for capital and investment resources from Eastern Europe, from the indebted countries of Asia, Latin America and Africa, as well as to meet the needs of reconstruction in the Gulf and in the Soviet Union' by supporting the call for an ASEAN free trade area in 1991. A regional economic agreement was seen therefore as the best way of maintaining ASEAN's investment appeal and of fostering its continued integration into global trade and capital flows. Thus, the formation of AFTA was in large part a response to the changing external environment, and in particular the fear of investment diversion. This is further confirmed by official pronouncements at the time. For example, Singapore's Prime Minister Goh Chok Tong commented that 'unless ASEAN can match the other regions in attractiveness both as a base for investments and as a market for their products, investments by multinational companies are likely to flow away from our part of the world to the S[ingle] E[uropean] M[arket] and NAFTA.'[2]

To summarize, regionalism in Asia in the early-mid 1990s was premised on the emergence of an economic region increasingly integrated by the activities of multinational corporations, particularly Japanese TNCs, and by the network capitalism epitomized by the Chinese Diaspora. This process was undoubtedly a more market driven process than that in evidence in other regions, although even in Asia State policies played important roles in shaping the kind of regional economic integration that took place. At the level of formal regional economic institutions, the 'region' was more spatially ambiguous with APEC acting as a loose consortium of countries notionally acting to preserve open trade across the Pacific. The most concrete form of regional economic arrangement was provided by the AFTA, an arrangement premised on the need of ASEAN countries to remain competitive in attracting investment in the changed post-Cold War international political economy. The use of trade and investment liberalization agreements to promote integration into the international economy was supplemented with the domestic liberalization of financial markets with the result that financial capital also poured into ASEAN and other Asian countries in the 1990s. However, this was to lay the seeds for the financial crisis of 1997, as the money that poured into the region equally quickly poured out, and led to a crisis which profoundly altered the economic landscape in Asia and which has changed the basis for regional economic cooperation.

Asia's Post-Financial Crisis Regionalism

The events of the Asian financial crisis are well known and will be summarized only briefly here.[3] The main focus in this section will be on the response to the crisis and the implications of this for our understanding of regionalism in Asia. The Asian crisis was triggered by the decision of the Thai central bank to float the baht on July 2, 1997. The Thai government decided that it could no longer defend the currency and announced a managed float and called upon the IMF for technical assistance. The 'contagion' spread to other countries in the region including the Philippines, Malaysia, Indonesia, South Korea, Hong Kong, and Vietnam. By the time the dust had settled, the IMF had instituted the largest bailout in its history with the US$54 billion loan to South Korea. Indonesia received US$ 40 billion, Thailand US$17.2 billion and the Philippines US$1 billion.

While the facts of the crisis are well known, the causes of the crisis remain disputed. For some, financial panic provides the most plausible explanation with the irrational behaviour of foreign investors to blame for the sudden dramatic reversal in capital flows to the region (Radelet and Sachs, 1998). For others, the weakness of domestic financial institutions, their lack of regulation, and the general malaise of 'crony capitalism' were to blame (Krugman, http://web.mit.edu). It is clear that one of the critical actors in the drama, the IMF, saw the cause of the crisis as emanating from essentially domestic factors which required the tried and trusted methods associated with the stabilization and structural adjustment programmes which the IMF and World Bank had been applying to other developing countries since the early 1980s.

As MacLean, Bowles and Croci (1999) noted, the IMF intervened in Asia both at the macroeconomic and structural levels. The policies recommended at the macroeconomic level were, by and large, the typical ones that characterized IMF interventions in the past. To stop currency depreciation and restore confidence, the IMF prescribed its traditional austerity medicine. This involved, first of all, a tight monetary policy; that is, an increase in interest rates and the adoption of strict limits on the growth of the money supply. In order to cover the carrying costs of the financial bailout, the IMF also asked for the curtailment of government budgets (achieved mainly through the reduction of social programmes, the scrapping of large public infrastructure projects and the elimination of subsidies). These fiscal measures have been criticized since none of the countries in question was particularly profligate in the spending. In fact, since 1993, only Korea had run a budget deficit—equal to 0.1 percent of GDP—and this only in 1996. Thailand and Indonesia had run average budget surpluses of 2.3 and 1.2 percent of GDP respectively.

Critics argued that the tightening of state budgets would inevitably worsen the recession brought about by the crisis and it did. The recognition that these policies were not bringing about the desired effects (exchange rates continued to slide, the outflow of capital worsened and output fell more than projected), and the perception that they might trigger social unrest, led the IMF to modify some aspects of its programme. However, the damage caused by the financial crisis and, in the view of many in Asia, exacerbated by the policies of IMF had been done as economic crisis followed the financial crisis and brought with it unprecedented output declines after a decade or more of rapid growth.

A noticeable recovery in output and the trade account has taken place since the depth of the crisis. However, the cost has been high in terms of the development objectives of the countries concerned and have been achieved almost entirely through deflation. For example, in the ASEAN-4 and South Korea the change in the current account went from a cumulative deficit of US$54 billion in 1996 to a cumulative surplus of US$69.2 billion in 1998, a total adjustment of US$123.2 billion. However, as Table 7.1 below indicates, a full US$116.6 billion of this adjustment was due to a fall in imports and only US$6.6 billion was due to increased exports.

Table 6.1 shows that the restriction of domestic demand caused by the financial crisis and the IMF imposed austerity measures was sufficiently large to cause a dramatic decrease in imports and thereby lead to a turn around in the trade balance. Thailand, for example, went from having a current account deficit equal to 8 percent of GDP in 1996 to a surplus of 12 percent of GDP just two years later—a staggering change brought about almost entirely by collapsing imports. To the short term decreases in living standards implied by the drop in imports must be added, therefore, the longer-term development costs of import reductions.

Table 7.1 External Adjustment, Asian Economies (US$ Billions)

	Current Account			Merchandise Imports		
	1996	1998	adjustment 1996-98	1996	1998	adjustment 1996-98
Thailand	-14.7	14.2	28.9	63.9	36.5	-27.4
Malaysia	-4.6	9.1	13.7	78.4	58.3	-20.1
Indonesia	-7.7	4.0	11.7	44.2	31.9	-12.3
Philippines	-4.0	1.3	5.3	31.9	29.5	-2.4
Korea	-23.0	40.6	63.6	144.9	90.5	-54.4
Total			123.2			-116.6

Source: R. Ferguson, 'Tale of Two Continents: A Comparison of Asia and Latin American Experiences during Recent Financial Turmoil,' remarks before the National Economic Association, Boston, Massachusetts, January 7, 2000.
http://www.federalreserve.gov/boarddocs/speeches/2000/20000107.htm#exhibits.

The policies undertaken by the IMF at the structural level were especially criticized in Asia. Policies under this heading can be divided into two categories: (i) those designed to reform the financial system and (ii) those aiming at open up the economies of the crisis countries. Under the first category, the IMF pushed for the closure of insolvent—and, in some cases, simply illiquid—banks, the enforcement of capital adequacy standards and the adaptation of Western accounting practices and disclosure rules. Bank closures in the midst of financial panic, however, invited even greater panic, while the hasty enforcement of capital adequacy standards, in conjunction with the general credit squeeze, contributed to recession by making it impossible for many companies to obtain even working capital.

Under the second category, the IMF encouraged the dismantling of national monopolies, the sale of state assets to the private sector, the elimination of tariffs and non-tariff barriers to trade, and the opening of the financial and insurance sectors to foreign investors. These policies of 'intrusive' or 'deep' conditionality went well beyond what could be justified by economic theory alone. For example, countries have been pressured into accepting greater foreign ownership even though this runs counter to much of the literature on 'fire sale FDI'. As Bhagwati (1998: 9) noted: 'Economists have usually advised the exact opposite in such depressed circumstances: restricting foreign access to a country's assets when its credit, but not that of others, has dried up.' In South Korea, the IMF also pushed for changes in the labour laws to make redundancies easier although it is difficult to argue that this was necessary to solve the financial crisis and was seen as having more to do with effecting a transition to Anglo-American style capitalism than with solving South Korea's crisis.

The perception that the IMF was acting to protect the interests of Western lending institutions and to open Asian markets for Western firms at the expense of Asian workers and the sovereignty of Asian countries was widely held in the region. As Walden Bello noted at the time 'never has the IMF's connection to its principal stockholder been displayed so prominently' (quoted in Higgott, 1998: 345). This view was not restricted to leftist critiques either. Prominent neoliberal Jagdish Bhagwati (1998) also argued that what he termed the 'Wall Street-Treasury complex' had got it all wrong in pushing for capital account liberalization in Asia. The Wall Street-Treasury complex was not easily convinced of the error of its ways, however, and its leading exponents added insult to Asian injury by declaring, in triumphalist mood, that the Asian crisis proved the superiority of American free market capitalism over Asia's 'managed capitalism'.[4]

In the face of these policies and perceptions, it is not surprising to find that this has led, in Higgott's words, to the 'politics of resentment' (Higgott, 1998). One manifestation of this resentment is that Asian countries have embarked on a new path of regional cooperation. The idea of establishing a US$100 billion Asian Monetary Fund, more attuned to the needs of Asian economies and less bent on imposing Anglo-American style capitalism on the region, was initially proposed by Japan at the height of the crisis. This received support from some of the countries in Southeast Asia who were shocked by the initial refusal of the United States to support Thailand in its crisis and by the spectre of IMF conditionality. The proposal was rejected, however, by the United States as potentially undermining the role of the IMF and as being potentially too lax on conditionality, by the IMF itself, and by China which continued to oppose Japan's leadership aspirations in Asia.[5]

Despite the immediate rejection of this plan, the failure of other regional institutions such as ASEAN and APEC to play any significant role in responding to the crisis and the widespread resentment at the imposition of conditions by a Washington-based, United States controlled, international institution, the IMF, laid the seeds for more concerted regional initiatives. Before proceeding to analyse these initiatives, it should first be noted that a regional response was neither guaranteed nor perhaps even probable. On the assumption that regional initiatives require a sufficiently powerful and/or respected regional leader, candidates for this position in post-crisis Asia were not conspicuously evident. Japan rather belatedly began to pump money into the region but was blamed for being partly responsible for the crisis in the first place. As Higgott (1998: 336) notes, 'Japanese capital created overcapacity in the region without fulfilling the role of a market of last resort to absorb it.' Furthermore, the willingness of the Japanese government to allow the *yen* to depreciate in the wake of the crisis led to accusations that Japan was more interested in maintaining its own competitiveness than in solving Asia's problems. Japan's capitulation in the face of US pressure over the initial proposal for an AMF did not enhance its leadership claims and neither did its continuing domestic economic malaise (Hughes, 2000: 219-253). China's 1994 devaluation of the *renmenbi* was seen as a contributing factor to the current account deficits run up by the ASEAN-4 and South Korea that played a key role in triggering currency flight in 1997. Although China pointed to its maintenance of the value of the *renmenbi* during the crisis it continued to have less than cordial relations with its ASEAN neighbours on other issues such as the Spratlys and, of course, there were continuing cross-strait tensions with Taiwan. It is quite possible therefore, perhaps even probable, that regionalism would simply become a spent force under the dual weight of the financial crisis and the tarnished images of possible regional leaders.

Interestingly, this has not happened and, after the initial rejection of the AMF, closer monetary and trade ties are now being actively fostered in the region; a new regionalism, geographically well-defined and located in East Asia, involving all of the major countries of this region, is now being forged. As Bergsten (2000) has noted, the East Asian Economic Group has held summit meetings for three consecutive years under the ASEAN+3 rubric (that is the ten ASEAN countries plus China, Japan and South Korea) and a 'Vision Group' has been formed to advise on the future role and evolution of this group. Following rejection of the initial Japanese proposal for an AMF, Japan implemented the Miyazawa Plan that made available $30 billion to stabilize financial institutions in the region. This has subsequently, in May 2000, been used as the basis for a regional network of foreign currency swaps aimed at enabling Asian countries to address any future currency crises themselves without resort to the IMF. This development, cooperation between central banks in the region, constitutes a de facto AMF, providing a mechanism to meet the aims of an AMF but avoiding the more politically difficult task of establishing a formal institution that might encounter US opposition.

This measure, adopted by the finance ministers of the ASEAN+3 countries, expands the network of bilateral regional currency deals previously agreed between Japan and Thailand and between Japan and South Korea that had provision for loans of up to $7.5 billion (*Nihon Keizai Shimbun*, April 29, 2000). While details of the expanded plan are still vague it is clear that Asia has the resources to finance such an initiative with the collective reserves of the ASEAN+3 countries being over $800 billion – over twice those of the Euro-zone countries and close to ten times those of the United States (Bergsten, 2000a and Dieter, 2000: 30). Officials from Japan's Ministry of Finance will also be stationed in Thailand and Vietnam to provide advice on international debt management, the use of yen loans and other economic issues (*Nihon Keizai Shimbun*, July 2, 2000).

At the same time as these developments in 'monetary regionalism,' there have also been initiatives to create free trade pacts in the region. These include studies being conducted in China, Japan and South Korea examining the possibility for a North East Asian regional trade agreement raising the possibility that it could eventually link up with AFTA. There have also been important bilateral trade negotiations between Japan and Singapore and Japan and South Korea. This represents a considerable departure for Japanese trade policy, and in South Korea's for that matter, as these two countries are the only members of the OECD which are not members of a regional trade agreement (if APEC is excluded from such a designation) and represents a sharp reversal of Japan's previous exclusive reliance on multilateral trade agreements.

Asia's New Monetary regionalism

In analysing the emergence of Asia's new monetary regionalism, the disenchantment with the IMF and the United States has been widely recognized and accepted. However, two important issues remain in need of further analysis. The first issue is simply a lacunae in the existing literature, namely, why did China oppose the proposal for an AMF in the immediate post-crisis period but support the currency swap arrangement some three years later, and what, if anything, do the reasons for this change of position tell us about Asian regionalism now? The second issue concerns the emergence of proposals for regional trading arrangements, proposals which analysts such as Bergsten and Noland have attributed mainly to Asian frustration at the ineffectiveness of trade liberalization through APEC and the uncertainties facing the new Millennium Round of the WTO after the debacle in Seattle (Bergsten, 2000a and Noland, 2000).

Thus, much as the United States was argued to have departed from its sole reliance on the multilateral trade track in frustration at the slow pace of the Uruguay Round in the late 1980s, now history is argued to be repeating itself with Japan showing a similar interest in regional liberalization initiatives in response to the frustrations over the slowness of the Millennium Round in Seattle a decade later. In advancing such an analysis, it is implicitly being argued that the monetary and the trade dimensions of the latest round of Asian regionalism are essentially caused by different factors and are responding to quite different external forces. This assumption needs careful examination.

Let us first consider China's position. Put simply, why should China, which initially opposed the creation of an AMF for fear of Japanese domination, and which has sufficient foreign exchange reserves (in excess of US$200 billion) and capital controls to ward off any speculative currency attacks, now back an Asian only currency swap arrangement? To understand this requires an analysis of the shifting sands of wider Sino-US and Sino-Japanese relations. Although China was not directly affected by the Asian financial crisis, indirectly the crisis posed significant challenges for China and its response to the crisis offered some opportunities. The immediate challenge was how to respond to the crisis affecting neighbouring countries. China's response was to provide financial resources to the region through the IMF and to pledge not to devalue the *renmenbi*. In both of these ways China sought to establish itself as a bulwark for stability in the region and as a responsible member of the international community, a responsibility which it hoped would be recognized and acknowledged by a strengthening of Sino-US relations. To this end, China committed US$4.5 billion to the operational budget of the IMF to support financial packages to Thailand and Indonesia.[6]

Thus, China opposed the initial proposal for a Japan-led AMF and threw in its lot with the IMF and made its first financial contributions to IMF packages since

1949. The second part of the strategy for demonstrating its international responsibility was the pledge not to devalue the *renmenbi*. This undoubtedly had some domestic advantages; China's weak banking system was sitting on deposits in excess of 500 trillion *yuan* and any devaluation that might spark a run on the banks could have potentially serious consequences for economic and social stability. Furthermore, Hong Kong had just been returned to China and the leadership in Beijing was keen to provide economic stability in the new 'Special Administrative Region'.

However, there is no doubt that the 'no devaluation' policy also had risks in that the painful process of state owned enterprise reform had been begun and, in the leadership's view, needed to be accompanied by an economic growth rate of at least 8 percent in order to alleviate a potential social backlash. The policy of maintaining the value of the *renmenbi* made such a growth target difficult to meet in the light of falling regional trade volumes and depreciating currencies in competitor economies in ASEAN and South Korea. Nevertheless, the Chinese leadership decided to maintain the exchange rate and to inject additional demand into the domestic economy through a massive infrastructure-spending programme.

The stability which China's 'no devaluation' policy brought to the crisis economies in the region, together with its support for the IMF, was expected, in the calculations of the Chinese leadership, to lead to a rehabilitation of China as a responsible member of the international community and to an enhanced regional and international role. This recognition, however, appears to have been slow in coming. For example, at the Vancouver APEC Summit in Vancouver 1997, China's role in it was, in China's eyes, undervalued. Chinese academics argued, 'in its strategy to solve the Southeast Asian financial crisis, the United States has not fully recognized the importance of China.' On 24 November last year, at a press conference in Vancouver, Clinton suggested a three-point plan to solve the crisis, but he overlooked the role of China, which had not been affected by the crisis.

China's feeling that its 'constructive strategic partnership relationship' (jianshexing zhanlue hezuo houban guanxi) with the United States ought to be reaping more rewards in terms of international recognition was given the chance for further expression and correction in June 1998. It was in this month that the Japanese yen slid to a seven year low against the dollar prompting fears of a new round of financial turmoil in Asia and was also the month when President Clinton made an official visit to China when the Chinese side at least expected some breakthrough on China's WTO accession process. The continued depreciation of the yen provided China with another opportunity to contrast its policy of responsible exchange rate management with that of Japan that was accused of failing to 'shoulder its responsibility as a major power.'[7] In the end, Japan and the United States were forced to intervene to support the yen although not before concerns were expressed about why the two countries had taken so long to undertake such intervention. Japan's non-intervention could be understood simply in terms of it wishing, in China's eyes, to offload its economic problems onto other countries. The reasons for US reluctance drew upon analysis from elsewhere in the region in arguing that the United States would gain by being able to buy up Asian enterprises with over-valued dollars.

China did nevertheless have the pleasure of drawing President Clinton on his official visit into criticism of Japan's exchange rate policy.[8] China continued to promote its own role in solving the crisis and in using the opportunity to enhance its claims for greater international recognition. As Wang Menkui, Director of the State Council's Development Research Centre, indicated:

> Through the crisis, China's image as a major power has become even more prominent. . . . In the multipolar development of one superpower and many great powers, China, as one of the great powers, is still not powerful enough. This crisis has conspicuously shown that China has taken a step forward on the path to becoming a major power in the world structure.[9]

Chinese sensitivities were assuaged at the December 1998 APEC Meeting where, in contrast to the neglect of China's role by President Clinton in Vancouver a year earlier, the Chinese press reported that the Kuala Lumpur declaration fully affirmed the *mainstay* role played by China in stabilizing the Asian economy during this financial crisis. The document used the English word 'anchor' to describe the role played by China in stabilizing the Asian financial crisis.[10]

Thus, for the year and half after the outbreak of the financial crisis China had followed a consistent policy of supporting the IMF (and its policies)[11] and of maintaining a 'no devaluation' policy for the *renmenbi*, a policy that contrasted sharply with that of Japan. China did participate in the ASEAN+3 meetings but the main focus of its diplomacy was on promoting itself both inside and outside of the region as a major power that could be trusted and which acted responsibly.[12] The expected gains from this policy were not only economic—an economic recovery in the region—but also political in terms of an enhanced role and status for China in regional and international affairs. These gains were slow in coming as China met with what it perceived as US indifference and a lack of understanding of the strains that the 'no devaluation' policy was placing on its economy while Japan and the United States moved only slowly to resolve their exchange rate imbalances.

Despite the expectations that the United States would offer some WTO concessions this did not occur and it was left to Chinese Premier Zhu Rongji to visit the United States in early 1999 to offer more concessions to kick-start the negotiations. However, the policy of seeking to strengthen the Sino-US relationship was soon to come to an end not because of economic issues but because of the US-led NATO war in Kosovo. This war, premised on the need to defend human rights in a sovereign state, deeply worried the Chinese leadership. The bombing of the Chinese Embassy in Belgrade, and the 'wrong map' explanation, led to anti-US riots in China much as there had been similar riots in South Korea, Thailand and Indonesia against IMF/US economic policy earlier. The Cox Report and the 'demonization' of China in the United States meant that China's 'responsible image' disappeared; by mid-1999 Sino-US relations had turned irrevocably for the worse. China's post-crisis policy had not reaped the political gains that it had hoped for; put simply, China had backed the wrong horse.

Faced with this changed international situation, China joined others in the region as seeing the United States as the main threat to its interests and China moved to view regional solutions as more valuable in this changed context. In reporting on the currency swap agreement, reached in May 2000, China's awakened interest in regional economic solutions was clearly shown. Thus, the *Economic Daily* (14 May 2000) reported the agreement in the following terms:

> In the past, the importance of economic co-operation was not fully realized. Compared with other parts of the world, especially North America and Europe, economic co-operation within Asia lagged in the past 10 years. Asia-Pacific Economic Cooperation, a regional organization, is only a forum; it lacks binding force. However, the financial crisis that devastated the region three years ago has made Asian countries realize the pressing need for working together. Many Asian countries may still hold bitter memories of receiving loans from the International Monetary Fund. . . . The combined foreign exchange reserves of Japan, China, Singapore and South Korea, and Hong Kong and Taiwan regions is US$ 800 billion, money that will definitely promote the economy in Asia if managed well.

China had joined ranks and become a member of the Asia-only movement, and Sino-Japanese relations began to improve to make such a movement possible.

Japan and Asian Regionalism

With respect to the second issue, namely, emergence of proposals for 'trade regionalism' in Asia, it is interesting to wonder why Japan, an initiator of many of these proposals, should embark upon such a path. Japanese policy had for years been to support the overseas investment activities of its TNCs and to fashion a regional division of labour in Asia based on the so-called flying geese model of economic integration. Such a policy had been reasonably successful and, indeed, was one the factors that many analysts had pointed to as constituting an emerging integrated regional economy led by the activities of businesses in the region. To push this integration into the realm of formal free trade arrangements was a major initiative with debatable payoffs. For example, in pursuing a bilateral trade agreement with Singapore, there was much more to be gained by the small, close to free trade, economy of Singapore by having improved to the Japanese market than vice versa. In the case of the bilateral discussions with South Korea, there is the tricky question of the agricultural sector. Should this be included with the risks that this might have of a political backlash from agricultural interests in both countries or should it be excluded at the risk, as Noland points out, of inviting WTO investigation of compliance with Article XXIV of the GATT (Noland, 2000:

7). Including China in with South Korea opens up even more problems with countries at vastly different levels of economic development and with different political systems. Clearly, there are many stumbling blocks on the road to trade agreements in the region and so Japan's decision to travel down this particular road is in need of explanation.

The answer that the explanation is to be found in Japan's, and Asia's, disappointment from the fallout of the failed Seattle WTO talks is not convincing. For one thing, the trade initiatives predate the Seattle conference. More fundamentally, while Japan has always been a central supporter of the multilateral trade liberalization process, its commitment to liberalization has always been practical and strategic rather than ideological. That is, trade liberalization has been an important policy goal of Japan but this has been conditioned by its pursuit of the developmentalist model in which free trade is not presumed to be the most desirable policy in all circumstances and, in a non-insignificant number of cases, is actually a clearly undesirable policy. In initiating regional trade liberalization, the question that must be asked is whether also this implies a rejection of this developmentalist view. That is, we need to ask whether the purpose of the new trade policy is to meet existing objectives by different means or whether it is to redefine those objectives.

A more convincing explanation for Japan's regional trade initiatives is to be found, I suggest, in (i) the benefits which regional economic arrangements might have in terms of spurring regional economic growth within the context of Japan's long standing support for a developmentalist structuring of the regional economy, and (ii) equally importantly, increasing political bargaining power at the international level.

Consider first how Japan's support for regional trade agreements may be consistent with its longer-term strategy. Commenting on reactions to the Asian financial crisis, Hughes (2000: 235-240) has noted:

> Policy makers in Japan do not seem to see the [developmental] state model as a total write-off. The key to recovery is still the basic model of the developmental state in the region and export growth on the demand side. Export growth can be restarted through economic stimulus packages in Japan and continued growth in the United States, but even more importantly through the promotion of the intra-regional exports which accounted for so much growth in the region prior to the currency crises and which could sustain growth long term.

It is this context that Japan's turn to bilateral trade agreements must be understood. As a recent MITI's Report indicates, bilateral and regional trade agreements are seen as key mechanisms for increasing intra-regional exports; it notes that this has been the outcome of existing regional agreements such as the EU, NAFTA and the MERCOSUR. The Report further argues that the Asian economies continue to be integrated with Japan supplying the capital goods for Asian industrialization (with capital goods comprising between 40 to 60 percent of East Asia's imports) and the market for Asian exports, especially those from Japanese affiliates in Asian countries whose exports back to Japan now constitute

30 percent of Japan's total imports (MITI, 2000). This pattern of regional integration, approximating the familiar 'flying geese' pattern, has helped, it is argued, to restore economic growth in both Japan and the rest of East Asia following the financial crisis. The Report notes that 'Japanese exports to East Asia recovered more quickly than exports to other regions [and] . . . as the Japanese economy has recovered, imports from Asia have recovered more rapidly than those from other regions' (MITI, 2000). The implication of this, in the view of MITI (2000), is that

> the Asian recovery set in motion a virtuous circle, boosting Japanese exports, helping to place Japan on a recovery trajectory, and consequently stimulating Asian exports to Japan. Further this stimulation of East Asian export activities has produced considerable synergy, for example pushing regional trade toward recovery due to regional specialization within East Asia. The deepening interdependence between Japan and East Asia through trade has therefore helped to accelerate recovery from the currency and economic crises.

The new interest in regional trade initiatives therefore stem from a desire to keep the momentum behind this 'virtuous circle' and to continue to forge deeper patterns of regional economic specialization. The shift towards bilateralism can be seen therefore as a change of policy mechanism but not necessarily of policy objectives; the policy of forging a regional division of labour with Japanese capital and technology at the centre of the integration process remains in consistent with Japanese policy over the past two decades although the means of achieving it have now broadened to include regional trading agreements as an important post-crisis vehicle.

With respect to (ii), the broader issue of promoting regional arrangements as a way of increasing bargaining power within the global economy, MITI's *White Paper on International Trade for 1999* (published before the Seattle meetings) gives an important clue to this. It argued for the creation of a Northeast Asian trade bloc and recommended that 'Japan should seek to deepen intra-regional exchange and understanding in Northeast Asia, the only area in the world which has shown little interest in regional cohesion or integration, applying itself with greater vigour to the development of regional cohesion and presenting a model to the world which will contribute positively to the strengthening of the multilateral trading system' (MITI, 1999). The key point here is the last part of the sentence referring to the presentation of 'a model to the world.' Multilateral negotiations have in important ways been directly shaped by regional agreements. That is, the existing regional agreements have formed the basis of negotiation for some parts of multilateral agreements. For example, the information technology agreement adopted by the WTO in Singapore in 1996 was based on a similar agreement adopted under US pressure in APEC a few months earlier. Many of the provisions of the ill-fated MAI had as their starting point Chapter 11 of the NAFTA.

Thus, regional agreements have increasingly been used as the point of departure for multilateral negotiations. Such agenda setting mechanisms clearly benefit the United States and the Europeans both of whom have reams of legal text to call upon as a result of their existing regional arrangements. Japan had none and, as a result, found itself debating on other's chosen ground. The need to develop its own 'model' of regional arrangements to 'present to the world' was therefore an important factor in persuading Japan policy-makers of the need to go down the potentially tortuous path of bilateral and regional trade agreements.

The importance of regional economic arrangements as having political pay-offs is also evident from MITI's subsequent analysis. Here Japan's 'multilayered' approach is justified on the grounds that 'recently, interest has emerged in trade liberalization beyond traditional regional frameworks, namely the strengthening of links between regional groupings. Examples include the Free Trade Area of the Americas (FTAA), designed to link the US and Latin America, the Trans-Atlantic Free Trade Area between the United States and the EU, moves to conclude a free trade agreement between Mexico and MERCOSUR, and consensus on a free trade agreement between Mexico and EU.

Factors behind this new trend are as follows: (i) further promotion of free trade liberalization through the creation of frameworks beyond traditional regional groupings; (ii) promotion of access to extra-regional markets; and (iii) the desire to strengthen influence over other regional groupings and negotiating power with these. Japan, as noted, operating without membership of a regional trade agreement, is unable to play and must stand by as the United States and Europe 'strengthen [their] influence over other regional groupings' (MITI, 2000). Japan has signalled that it, too, wishes to enter this game.

Further evidence can be found in the September 2000 Report of the Joint Japan-Singapore Study Group. This Group, set up in December 1999 to look at a possible FTA between the two countries, noted 'there are different motivations for the pursuit of regional economic integration. Some countries see such agreements as strategic alliances, while others leverage on them to obtain more secure and favourable access to important markets. In some cases, they have also helped to promote policy reforms' (MITI, 2000b, Ch. 1: 2). Again the importance of Free Trade Areas (FTAs) as bargaining tools with other countries/regions is evident. Furthermore, the Study Group argued, 'FTAs can be a test bed for new and innovative models of rules governing economic activity. These can subsequently be adapted for global use. FTAs can therefore provide positive complementary pressure for the evolution of WTO agreements' (MITI, 2000b, Ch. 1: 3).

The Study Group, therefore, deliberately proposed an approach that went beyond traditional free trade agreements and which could influence the WTO in areas 'where either there are no rules yet in the WTO or the existing WTO rules can be further improved upon: a) electronic commerce; b) definition of service providers; c) non-tariff measures; d) investment; e) mutual recognition; f) anti-dumping; and g) consultation and dispute settlement' (MITI, 2000b, Ch. 3: 8). The intention to use a bilateral agreement as a springboard for multilateral negotiations is again in evidence with Japan, in consort with other Asian countries, serving notice that they wish to play a larger role in determining the rules that govern the global economy, rules that have to date relied excessively on the United States and Europe for their formulation.

Thus, the view has emerged, stemming directly from the experience of Asian countries in the wake of the financial crisis, that the existing international institutions and the balance of power within the global economy leave Asia vulnerable to the interests of the West, especially the United States. Enhanced regional initiatives offer Asia the possibility to counter these interests.

This has been expressed forcefully by the ASEAN Secretary-General who has argued that a New World Order has not yet arrived, in which the interests are balanced and disputes adjudicated fairly under benign rules that are impartially applied and effectively enforced upon all. It is all too clear that such a utopia remains far from being upon us. Until it arrives, a long, long time from now, if ever, economic power, whether of states or of corporations, will continue to have preponderant advantage. In the face of this, weaker states must band together regionally, strengthening their solidarity and advancing their common interests (Severinto, 1999).

In other words, 'the rules of the game' reflect the interests of those who wrote them and have more the character of 'promoting Empire' rather than 'acting as umpire;' post-crisis Asian regionalism is the response to this.

Conclusion

If, as has been argued in this chapter, Asia's post-crisis regionalism is qualitatively different and is premised on an Asian only vision of economic cooperation forged to counter the power of the United States and Europe, then there are a number of important implications. One concerns the emergence of a 'three bloc world,' a development that has already been noted by Bergsten (2000a). Another concerns the likelihood of such a bloc remaining coherent over the medium term if rivalries between Japan and China resurface and threaten to derail the regional project. Important as these issues are, our attention here is focused on the implications of Asia's post-crisis regionalism for our understanding of the dynamics of the contemporary international political economy.

The widely preferred term of analysis to describe the contemporary world has been that of 'globalization.' While this has spawned an entire academic and popular industry, it can be summarized for our purposes as an analysis of the world that views the current phase of international capitalism as qualitatively different from earlier phases and as being characterized by a shift in power from nation-states to transnational economic actors and forces. It is a story of 'markets' gaining at the expense of 'states.'

For pro-globalists this offers the prospect of a more efficient global allocation of resources and of more effective constraints on interventionist and arbitrary state action. For antiglobalists it offers the prospect of the erosion of sovereignty and the levelling down of social and environmental standards as global corporations gain greater power at the expense of ordinary citizens. While these two groups may disagree about the desirability of the changes, they agree on the basic dynamics at work. Viewed through this lens, the Asian financial crisis can be seen, as Price has argued, as 'a crisis of globalization' (Price, 2000: 187-89). It is about states losing too much power to international financial markets and about the attempts of nation-states to regain lost controls. Certainly, the monetary regionalism of the post-crisis period can be seen exactly in this light, as an attempt by nation-states to re-regulate global finance. This is also evident from MITI's analysis.

Because the Asian currency crisis shares more of the characteristics of 1990s-style currency crises, which are generally sparked by massive capital movements, the usual measures will be inadequate in preventing a recurrence. Rather, consideration of new international financial system reforms (taxes on capital inflows and outflows, etc.) should be promoted in order to open the way for stable real economy development in developing countries, which lack the resilience and flexibility of developed countries (1999: 32).

Apart from the support for international capital taxes, this analysis is interesting precisely for its conceptualization of the problem as one of insufficient state power, particularly, in the case of developing country states. Regional and international regulations are therefore necessary to strengthen the ability of states to confront destabilizing global market forces.

However, this is not the only analytical framework on offer. The subtitle of this paper refers not simply to bringing the state back in to the analysis of regional integration in the Asian region. It also refers more broadly for the need to locate the state centrally in any analysis of the dynamics of the current phase of international capitalism, a phase in which some states have lost power to markets but in which, crucially, some states have not. Laxer (2001) has preferred the term 'global*ism*' to 'globalization,' stressing that globalism is an ideology, one that is based on neoliberalism and the Washington consensus as integral parts of US foreign policy. This theme is developed further by Petras and Veltmeyer (2001) who prefer the term 'imperialism' to 'globalization' as a more accurate description of the contemporary world.

In this analysis it is not the interdependence of economies and the erosion of state power vis-à-vis markets that are the relevant points of reference but the continued domination of global markets by the major powers, most notably the United States but also Europe. It is the use of international financial institutions by these powers and the market-opening strategies of the imperialist powers that are the focus of attention. Asia's post-crisis regionalism also finds resonance with this analysis in the sense that regionalism is being forged to prevent the United States and the IFIs from exercising their power and shaping Asian economies in their interests as they did in the aftermath of the currency crises. That is, a central reason why it is necessary to bring the state back *in* to the discussion of Asian regionalism is precisely because power relations between states are critical to understanding that an important part of the post-crisis regionalism project is to keep the (United) States *out*.

Notes

* First appeared as 'Asia's post-crisis regionalism: bringing the state back in, keeping the (United) States out' in the Review of International Political Economy, (2002) vol. 9 no. 2 pp. 244-270. The editor thanks Taylor & Francis Ltd for permission to edit and republish.

1 APEC originally had 12 members at its formation in 1989 (Australia, Canada, Japan, New Zealand, South Korea, the United States and the six members of ASEAN). Since then China, Taiwan, Hong Kong, Mexico, Papua New Guinea, Chile, Vietnam, Peru and Russia have also joined, bringing membership to 21 'economies.'

2 Quoted in the *Straits Times*, Singapore, 28 January 1992, p. 22.

3 For the most comprehensive set of data and studies on the financial crisis, see the website put together by N. Roubini, http://www.stern.nyu.edu/globalmacro. The discussion here draws upon MacLean, Bowles, and Croci (199x).

4 As an example of such triumphalism see Federal Reserve Chairman Alan Greenspan's comments in 'The Ascendancy of Market Capitalism,' Remarks before the Annual Convention of American Society of Newspaper Editors, Washington D.C., 2 April 1998 at http://www.bog.frb.fed.us/boarddocs/speeches/19980402.htm.

5 For opposition to the AMF see Noland at: http://www.iie.com/TESTIMONY /noljapan.html.

6 See 'China's Policy on Asian Financial Crisis—Interviewing Dai Xianglong, Governor of the People's Bank of China,' *Ta Kung Pao*, Hong Kong, 4 November 1998, as in FBIS-CHI-98-313.

7 See 'Japan Should Shoulder the Responsibility of a Major Power,' *Renmin Ribao*, 29 July 1998 as in FBIS-CHI-98-225.

8 As Hughes (2000: 233) notes, 'Japan's sense of humiliation was . . . compounded during the US-China summit . . . when Presidents Bill Clinton and Jiang Zemin took the extraordinary step of commenting in a bilateral setting on the deficient management of the yen and Japan's economy.'

9 See 'China Makes Preparations for Introduction of Euro; Wang Mengkui Analyses Its Pros and Cons, Saying China Will Not Change All Its US Dollars Into Euro', *Ta King Pao*, Hong Kong, 11 October 1998, as in FBIS-CHI-98-294.

10 See 'Subject of Talks Brought About by Financial Crisis—Senior Official Zhang Yan on '98 APEC Kuala Lumpur Conference,' *Shijie Zhishi*, Beijing, 1 January 1999, p. 33.

11 China's Central Bank Governor Dai Xianglong declared in November 1998 that Thailand and South Korea had 'adopted and properly implemented many of the reform measures recommended by the IMF, which have produced positive results. Besides, the governments' actions have won the understanding and support of the public. In particular, I saw many civilians in the ROK donating their gold rings. This is why the conditions in these two countries are turning for the better.' ('China's Policy on Asian Financial Crisis—Interviewing Dai Xianglong, Governor of the People's Bank of China,' *Ta Kung Pao*, 4 November 1998, as in FBIS-CHI-98-313).

12 China's diplomatic efforts also included a framework for long-term cooperation between China and Thailand, the first time such a framework had been established with an ASEAN country. See K. Chongkittavorn, 'Thai Policy Meets China Challenge,' *The Nation*, Bangkok, 2 February 1999, as in FBIS-EAS-99-033.

PART III

THE DYNAMICS OF ANTIGLOBALIZATION

Chapter Eight

Reflections on Power and Globalization[1]

Noam Chomsky

I would like to set the stage for my reflections on the current dynamics of globalization with a few truisms. It is hardly exciting news that we live in a world of conflict and confrontation. There are lots of dimensions of and complexities to this reality, but in recent years, lines have been drawn fairly sharply. To oversimplify, but not too much, one of the participants in the conflict involves concentrated power centres, state and private, closely interlinked. The other is the general or working population, worldwide. In old-fashioned terms, this situation would have been called 'class war.'

Concentrated power pursues the war relentlessly, and very self-consciously. Government documents and publications of the business world reveal that they are mostly vulgar Marxists, with values reversed of course. They are also frightened—back to 17th century England in fact. They realize that the system of domination is fragile and that it relies on disciplining the population by one means or another. There is a desperate search for such means: in recent years, communism, crime, drugs, terrorism, and others. Pretexts change, policies remain rather stable. Sometimes the shift of pretext along with continuity of policy is dramatic and takes real effort to miss: immediately after the collapse of the USSR, for example. They naturally grasp every opportunity to press their agenda forward: 9/11 is a typical case. Crises make it possible to exploit fear and concern to demand that the adversary be submissive, obedient, silent, distracted, while the powerful use the window of opportunity to pursue their own favoured programmes with even greater intensity. These programmes vary, depending on the society: in the more brutal states, escalation of repression and terror; in societies where the population has won more freedom, measures to impose discipline while shifting wealth and power even more to their own hands. It is easy to list examples around the world.

Their victims should certainly resist the predictable exploitation of crisis, and should focus their own efforts, no less relentlessly, on the primary issues that remain much as they were before: among them, increasing militarism, destruction of the environment, and a far-reaching assault against democracy and freedom, the core of 'neoliberal' programmes.

The Wizards of Davos and the 'Other Davos'

The ongoing conflict is symbolized by the World Social Forum (WSF), to date held in Porto Alegre Brazil, and the more established World Economic Forum (WEF), which, until prior to its 2002 meeting in New York had always met in Davos, Switzerland. The WEF—to quote the national US press—is a gathering of 'movers and shakers,' the 'rich and famous,' 'wizards from around the world,' 'government leaders and corporate executives, ministers of state and of God, politicians and pundits' disposed to 'think deep thoughts' and address 'the big problems that confront humankind in the present conjuncture.' Press reports give a few examples, such as: 'How do you inject moral values into what we do?' Or reference is made to Forum panels with titles such as 'Tell Me What you Eat,' led by the 'reigning prince of the New York gastronomic scene,' whose elegant restaurants will undoubtedly be mobbed by forum participants. There is also mention of an 'anti-forum' where 50,000 people are expected. These are 'the freaks who assemble to protest the meetings of the World Trade Organization.' One can learn more about the freaks from a photo of a scruffy-looking guy, with face concealed, writing 'world killers' on a wall.

At their 'carnival,' as it is described, the freaks are throwing stones, writing graffiti, dancing and singing about a variety of boring topics that are unmentionable or beyond the scope of normal press coverage, at least in the United States: investment, trade, financial architecture, human rights, democracy, sustainable development, Brazil-Africa relations, and other marginal issues. They are not 'thinking deep thoughts' about the 'big problems' or 'critical issues.' That is left to the wizards of Davos in New York, the self-appointed guardians of the 'New World Order.'[2] The infantile rhetoric of the mainstream media pundits is probably a sign of well-deserved insecurity as well as concern for the 'new world order.'

The 'anti-forum' freaks are defined as being 'opposed to globalization,' a propaganda weapon that readers are advised to reject with scorn. 'Globalization' just means international integration and who could be against that. No sane person is 'anti-globalization.' That should be particularly obvious for the labour movement and the left. The WSF is one of the most exciting and promising realization of the hopes of the left and popular movements from their modern origins for a true international, which will pursue an alternative form of globalization concerned with the needs and interests of people rather than of illegitimate concentrations of power. These power-holders, of course, have appropriated as their own the term 'globalization'—to restrict it to their peculiar version of international integration, reflecting their own interests. With this ridiculous terminology in place, those who seek a sane and just form of globalization can be labelled 'antiglobalization,' derided as primitivists who want to return to the stone age, to harm the poor, and other terms of abuse with which we are all too familiar.

The wizards of Davos modestly call themselves the 'international community,' but I personally prefer the term used by the world's leading business journal, the *Financial Times*: 'the masters of the universe.' Since the masters profess to be admirers of Adam Smith, we might expect them to abide by his account of their behaviour, though he only called them 'the masters of mankind' (this was before the space age). Smith was referring to the 'principal architects of policy' in his day—the merchants and manufacturers of England who made sure their own interests were 'most peculiarly attended to, however 'grievous' the impact of others.' At home and abroad, they pursue 'the vile maxim of the masters of mankind; all for ourselves and nothing for other people.' It should hardly surprise us that today's masters honour the same 'vile maxim.' At least they try, though they are sometimes impeded by the freaks—the 'great beast,' to borrow a term used by the Founding Fathers of American democracy to refer to the unruly population that did not comprehend that the primary goal of government is 'to protect the minority from the majority,' as the leading Framer of the Constitution explained in the Constitutional Convention debates.

A World Without War?

I will return to these matters, but first a few words about the theme of the 2001 World Social Forum in Porto Alegre—'a world without war.' We cannot say much about human affairs with any confidence, but sometimes it is possible. We can, for example, be fairly confident that either there will be a world without war or there won't be a world—at least, a world inhabited by creatures other than bacteria and beetles, with some scattering of others. The reason is familiar: humans have developed means of destroying themselves, and much else, and have come dangerously close to using them for half a century. Furthermore, the leaders of the civilized world are now dedicated to enhancing these dangers to survival, in full awareness of what they are doing, at least if they read the reports of their own intelligence agencies and respected strategic analysts, including many who strongly favour the race to destruction. Ominously, the plans are developed and implemented on grounds that are rational within the dominant framework of ideology and values, which ranks survival well below 'hegemony,' the goal pursued by advocates of these programmes, as they frankly insist.

Wars over water, energy and other resources are not unlikely in the future, with consequences that could be devastating. For the most part, however, wars have had to do with the imposition of the system of nation-states, an unnatural social formation that typically has to be instituted by violence. That is a primary reason why Europe was the most savage and brutal part of the world for many centuries, meanwhile conquering most of the world. European efforts to impose state systems in conquered territories are the source of most conflicts underway right now, after the collapse of the formal colonial system. Europe's own favourite sport of mutual slaughter had to be called off in 1945, when it was realized that the next time the game was played would be the last. Another prediction that we can make with fair confidence is that there won't be a war among great powers; the reason is that if the prediction turns out to be wrong, there will be no one around to care to tell us.

Furthermore, popular activism within the rich and powerful societies has had a civilizing effect. The 'movers and shakers' can no longer undertake the kinds of long-term aggression that were options before, as when the United States attacked South Vietnam forty years ago, smashing much of it to pieces before significant popular protest developed. Among the many civilizing effects of the ferment of the 1960s was broad opposition to large-scale aggression and massacre, reframed in the ideological system as unwillingness to accept casualties among the armed forces ('the Vietnam syndrome'). That is why the Reaganites had to resort to international terrorism instead of invading Central America directly, on the Kennedy-Johnson model, in their war to defeat liberation theology, as the School of the Americas describes the achievement with pride.

The same changes explain the intelligence review of the incoming Bush-I administration in 1989, warning that in conflicts against 'much weaker enemies'—the only kind it makes sense to confront—the United States must 'defeat them decisively and rapidly,' or the campaign will lose 'political support,' understood to be thin. Wars since have kept to that pattern, and the scale of protest and dissent has steadily increased. So there are changes, of a mixed nature.

When pretexts vanish, new ones have to be concocted to control the great beast while traditional policies are continued, adapted to new circumstances. That was already becoming clear 20 years ago. It was hard not to recognize that the Soviet enemy was facing internal problems and might not be a credible threat much longer. That is part of the reason why the Reagan administration, twenty years ago, declared that the 'war on terror' would be the focus of US foreign policy, particularly in Central America and the Middle East, the main source of the plague spread by 'depraved opponents of civilization itself' in a 'return to barbarism in the modern age,' as Administration moderate George Shultz explained, also warning that the solution is violence, avoiding 'utopian, legalistic means like outside mediation, the World Court, and the United Nations.' We need not tarry on how the war was waged in those two regions, and elsewhere, by the extraordinary network of proxy states and mercenaries—an 'axis of evil,' to borrow George W. Bush's more up-to-date term.

It is of some interest that in the months since the war was re-declared, with much the same rhetoric, after 9/11, all of this has been entirely effaced, even the fact that the United States was condemned for international terrorism by the World Court and Security Council (vetoed) and responded by sharply escalating the terrorist attack it was ordered to terminate; or the fact that the very people who are directing the military and diplomatic components of the re-declared war on terror were leading figures in implementing terrorist atrocities in Central America and the Middle East during the first phase of the war. Silence about these matters is a real tribute to the discipline and obedience of the educated classes in the free and democratic societies.

It is a reasonable guess that the 'war on terror' will again serve as a pretext for intervention and atrocities in coming years, not just by the United States; Chechnya is only one of a number of examples. In Latin America, there is no need to linger on what that portends; certainly not in Brazil, the first target of the wave of repression that swept Latin America after the Kennedy administration, in a decision of historic importance, shifted the mission of the Latin American military from 'hemispheric defence' to 'internal security'—a euphemism for state terror directed against the domestic population. That still continues, on a huge scale, particularly in Colombia, well in the lead for human rights violations in the hemisphere in the 1990s and by far the leading recipient of US arms and military training, in accord with a consistent pattern documented even in mainstream scholarship.

The 'war on terror' of course, has been the focus of a huge and growing literature during the first phase in the 1980s and since it was re-declared in the past few months.[3] One interesting feature of the flood of commentary, then and now, is that we are not told what 'terror' is. What we hear, rather, is that this is 'a vexing and complex question.' This is curious, given that there are straightforward definitions in official US documents. A simple one takes terror to be the 'calculated use of violence or threat of violence to attain goals that are political, religious, or ideological in nature.' This seems appropriate enough, but it cannot be used in official discourse, for two good reasons. One is that it would also define the official policy of 'counterinsurgency' or 'low-intensity conflict.' Another is that it yields all the wrong answers—facts too obvious to review although suppressed with remarkable efficiency.

The problem of finding a definition of 'terror' that will exclude the most prominent cases is indeed vexing and complex. But fortunately, there is an easy solution: define 'terror' as terror that 'they' carry out against 'us.' A review of the scholarly literature on terror, the media, and intellectual or academic journals will show that this usage is close to exceptionless, and that any departure from it elicits impressive tantrums. Furthermore, the practice is probably universal: the generals in South America were protecting the population from 'terror directed from outside,' just as the Japanese were in Manchuria and the Nazis in occupied Europe. If there is an exception, I have not found it.

Let us return to 'globalization' and the linkage between it and the threat of war, perhaps terminal war.

The version of 'globalization' designed by 'the masters of the Universe' has very broad elite support, as do the so-called 'free trade agreements'—what the *Wall Street Journal*, more honestly, has called 'free investment agreements.' Very little is reported about these issues, and crucial information is simply suppressed; for example, after a decade, the position of the US labour movement on NAFTA, and the conforming conclusions of Congress's own Research Bureau (the Office of Technology Assessment), have yet to be reported outside of dissident sources. And, of course, the issues are off the agenda in electoral politics. There are good reasons for this. The masters know well that the public will be opposed if information becomes available. They are fairly open when addressing one another, however. Thus a few years ago, under enormous public pressure, Congress rejected the 'fast track' legislation that grants the President authority to enact international economic arrangements with Congress permitted to vote 'Yes' (or, theoretically, 'No') with no discussion, and the public uninformed. Like other sectors of elite opinion, the *WSJ* was distraught over the failure to undermine democracy. But it explained the problem: opponents of these Stalinist-style measures have an 'ultimate weapon,' the general population, which must therefore be kept in the dark. That is very important, particularly in the more democratic society, where dissidents cannot simply be jailed or assassinated, as in the leading recipients of US military aid, such as El Salvador, Turkey, and Colombia, to list the recent and current world champions (Israel-Egypt aside).

One might ask why public opposition to 'globalization' has been so high for many years. That seems strange, in an era when it has led to unprecedented prosperity, so we are constantly informed, particularly in the United States, with its 'fairy tale economy.' Through the 1990s, the US enjoyed 'the greatest economic boom in America's history—and the world's,' Anthony Lewis wrote in the *New York Times* a year ago, repeating the standard refrain from the left end of the admissible spectrum. It is conceded that there are flaws: some have been left behind in the economic miracle, and we good-hearted folk must do something about that. The flaws reflect a profound and troubling dilemma: the rapid growth and prosperity brought by 'globalization' has as a concomitant growing inequality, as some lack the skills to enjoy the wondrous gifts and opportunities.

The picture is so conventional that it may be hard to realize how little resemblance it has to reality, facts that have been well known right through the miracle. Until the brief boomlet of the late 1990s (which scarcely compensated for earlier stagnation or decline for most people), per capita growth in the 'roaring 90s' was about the same as the rest of the industrial world, much lower than in the first 25 post-war years before so-called 'globalization,' and vastly lower than the war years, the greatest economic boom in American history, under a semi-command economy. How then can the conventional picture be so radically different from uncontroversial facts? The answer is simplicity itself. For a small sector of the society, the 1990s really were a grand economic boom. That sector happens to include those who tell others the joyous news. And they cannot be accused of dishonesty. They have no reason to doubt what they are saying. They read it all the time in the journals for which they write, and it accords with their personal experience: it is true of the people they meet in editorial offices, faculty clubs, elite conferences like the one the wizards are now attending, and the elegant restaurants where they dine. It is the world that is different.

Let us have a quick look at the record over a longer stretch. International economic integration—one facet of 'globalization,' in a neutral sense of the term—increased rapidly before World War I, stagnated or declined during the interwar years, and resumed after World War II, now reaching levels of a century ago by gross measures; the fine structure is more complex. By some measures, globalization was greater before World War I: one illustration is 'free circulation of labour,' the foundation of free trade for Adam Smith, although not his contemporary admirers. By other measures, 'globalization' is far greater now: one dramatic example—not the only one—is the flow of short-term speculative capital, far beyond any precedent. The distinction reflects some central features of the version of globalization preferred by the masters of the universe: to an extent even beyond the norm, capital has priority, people are incidental.

The Mexican border is an interesting example. It is artificial, the result of conquest, like most borders, and has been porous in both directions for a variety of socioeconomic reasons. It was militarized after NAFTA by Clinton in order to block the 'free circulation of labour.' That was necessary because of the anticipated effects of NAFTA in Mexico: an 'economic miracle,' which would be a disaster for much of the population, who would seek to escape. In the same years, the flow of capital, already very free, was expedited further, along with what is called 'trade,' about two thirds of which is now centrally-managed within private tyrannies, up from half before NAFTA. This is 'trade' only by doctrinal decision. The effects of NAFTA on actual trade have not been examined, to my knowledge.

A more technical measure of globalization is convergence to a global market, with a single price and wage. That plainly has not happened. With respect to incomes at least, the opposite is more likely true. Though much depends on exactly how it is measured, there is good reason to believe that inequality has increased within and across countries. That is expected to continue. US intelligence agencies, with the participation of specialists from the academic professions and the private sector, recently released a report on expectations for 2015. They expect 'globalization' to proceed on course: 'Its evolution will be rocky, marked by chronic financial volatility and a widening economic divide.' This means less convergence, less globalization in the technical sense, but more globalization in the doctrinally preferred sense. Financial volatility implies still slower growth and more crises and poverty.

It is at this point that a clear connection is established between 'globalization' in the sense of the masters of the universe and the increasing likelihood of war. Military planners adopt the same projections, and have explained, forthrightly, that these expectations lie behind the vast expansion of military power. Even pre-9/11, US military expenditures surpassed those of allies and adversaries combined. The terror attacks have been exploited to increase the funding sharply, delighting key elements of the private economy. The most ominous programme involves the militarization of space, also expanded under the pretext of 'fighting terror.'

The reasoning behind these programmes is explained publicly in Clinton-era documents. A prime reason is the growing gap between the 'haves' and the 'have-nots,' which is expected to continue, contrary to economic theory but consistent with reality. The 'have-nots'—the 'great beast' of the world—may become disruptive, and must be controlled, in the interests of what is called 'stability' in technical jargon, meaning subordination to the dictates of the masters. That requires means of violence, and having 'assumed, out of self-interest, responsibility for the welfare of the world capitalist system,' the United States must be far in the lead—quoting here the diplomatic historian Gerald Haines, also the senior historian of the CIA, in a scholarly study of US strategic planning in the 1940s.

But overwhelming dominance in conventional forces and weapons of mass destruction is not sufficient. It is necessary to move on to the new frontier: the militarization of space, undermining the Outer Space Treaty of 1967, so far observed. Recognizing the intent, the UN General Assembly has reaffirmed the Treaty several times; the United States has refused to join, in virtual isolation. And Washington has blocked negotiations at the UN Conference on Disarmament for the past year over this issue—all scarcely reported, for the usual reasons. It is not wise to allow citizens to know of plans that may bring to an end biology's only experiment with 'higher intelligence.'

As widely observed, these programmes benefit military industry, but we should bear in mind that the term is misleading. Throughout modern history, but with a dramatic increase after World War II, the military system has been used as a device to socialize cost and risk while privatizing profit. The 'new economy' is to a substantial extent an outgrowth of the dynamic and innovative state sector of the US economy. The main reason why public spending in biological sciences has been rapidly increasing is that intelligent right-wingers understand that the cutting edge of the economy relies on these public initiatives. A huge increase is scheduled under the pretext of 'bioterror,' just as the public was deluded into paying for the new economy under the pretext that the Russians are coming—or after they collapsed, by the threat of the 'technological sophistication' of third world countries as the Party Line shifted in 1990, instantly, without missing a beat and with scarcely a word of comment. That is also a reason why national security exemptions have to be part of international economic agreements: it does not help Haiti, but it allows the US economy to grow under the traditional principle of harsh market discipline for the poor and a nanny state for the rich—what is called 'neoliberalism,' although it is not a very good term: the doctrine is centuries old, and would scandalize classical liberals.

One might argue that these public expenditures were often worthwhile. Perhaps, perhaps not. But it is clear that the masters were afraid to allow democratic choice. All of this is concealed from the general public, though the participants understand it very well.

Plans to cross the last frontier of violence by militarization of space are disguised as 'missile defence,' but anyone who pays attention to history knows that when we hear the word 'defence,' we should think 'offence.' The present case is no exception. The goal is quite frankly stated: to ensure 'global dominance' or 'hegemony.' Official documents stress that the goal is 'to protect US interests and investments,' as well as control the 'have-nots.' Today that requires domination of space, just as in earlier times the most powerful states created armies and navies 'to protect and enhance their commercial interests.' It is recognized that these new initiatives, in which the United States is far in the lead, pose a serious threat to survival. And it is also understood that these initiatives could be blocked by international treaties. But as already mentioned, hegemony has a higher value than survival, a moral calculus that has prevailed among the powerful throughout history. What has changed is that the stakes are much higher, awesomely so.

The relevant point here is that the expected success of 'globalization' in the doctrinal sense is a primary reason given for the programmes of using space for offensive weapons of instant mass destruction. But let us return to 'globalization' and 'the greatest economic boom in America's history'—in the 1990s.

Since World War II, the international economy has passed through two phases: the Bretton Woods phase from the late 1940s to the early 1970s, and the subsequent period based on, among other things, the dismantling of the Bretton Woods system of regulated exchange rates and controls on capital movement. It is the second phase, associated with the neoliberal policies of what Williamson (1990) termed the 'Washington consensus,' that has been characterized as 'globalization.' The two phases are quite different. The first is often called the 'golden age' of (state) capitalism (Marglin and Schor, 1990). The second phase has been accompanied by marked deterioration in standard macroeconomic measures—the growth of the economy productivity, capital investment, and world trade; much higher interest rates; vast accumulation of unproductive reserves to protect the value of diverse national currencies; increased financial volatility; and other harmful economic, social and environmental consequences have been well documented. There were exceptions, notably the East Asian countries that did not follow the rules: they did not worship at the alter of the 'religion' that 'markets know best,' as Joseph Stiglitz wrote in a World Bank research publication shortly before he was appointed chief economist, later removed (and winning the Nobel prize).

In fact, as acknowledged by, among others, José Antonio Ocampo, director of the Economic Commission for Latin America and the Caribbean (ECLAC), in an address before the American Economic Association in 2001. The 'promised land [of bold neoliberal reforms] is,' he observed, 'a mirage;' growth in the 1990s was far below that of the three decades of 'state-led development' in Phase I. He too noted that the correlation between following the rules and economic outcomes holds worldwide.

Let us return, then, to the profound and troubling dilemma: that the rapid growth and great prosperity brought by globalization has brought inequality because some lack skill. There is no dilemma, because the rapid growth and prosperity are a myth.

Many international economists regard the liberalization of capital as a substantial factor in explaining the poorer outcomes of phase II. But the economy is a complex affair, so poorly understood that one has to be cautious about causal connections. But one consequence of the liberalization of capital is rather clear: it tends to undercut democracy. This was well understood by the framers of the Bretton Woods agreements. One reason why the agreements were founded on the regulation of capital was to allow national governments to carry out social democratic policies that had enormous popular support. Free capital movement creates what has been called a 'virtual Senate' with 'veto power' over government decisions, sharply restricting policy options. Governments, in this context, face a 'dual constituency'—voters, and speculators who 'conduct moment-by-moment referenda' on government policies (quoting technical studies of the financial system). Even in the rich countries, the constituency of private interests prevails.

Other components of investor-rights 'globalization' have similar consequences. Socioeconomic decisions are increasingly shifted to unaccountable concentrations of power, an essential feature of neoliberal 'reforms' (a term of propaganda, not description). An extension of this attack on democracy is presumably being planned, behind closed doors and without public discussion, in the negotiations for a GATS. Like the ill-fated (defeated, that is) efforts a few years ago to establish the MAI (Multilateral Agreement on Investment), GATS is an attack on the idea of democracy. The term 'services' refers to just about anything that might fall within the arena of democratic choice: health, education, welfare, postal and other communications, water and other resources. There is no meaningful sense in which the transfer of such services to private hands could be seen as 'trade' but the term has been so deprived of meaning that it might as well be extended to this travesty as well.

The huge public protests in Quebec in April 2001 at the Summit of the Americas, set in motion by the freaks in Porto Alegre a year ago, were in part directed against the attempt to impose the GATS principles in secret within the planned Free Trade Area of the Americas (FTAA). Those protests brought together a very broad constituency, North and South, all strongly opposed to what is apparently being planned by trade ministers and corporate executives behind closed doors.

The protests did receive coverage of the usual kind: the freaks are throwing rocks and disrupting the wizards thinking about the big problems. But the invisibility of their actual concerns is quite remarkable. For example, *New York Times* economics correspondent Anthony De Palma writes that the GATS agreement 'has generated none of the public controversy that has swirled about [WTO] attempts to promote merchandise trade'—even after Seattle. In fact, it has been a prime concern for years. As in other cases, this is not deceit. De Palma's knowledge about 'the freaks' is surely limited to what passes through the media filter, and it is an iron law of journalism that the serious concerns of activists must be rigidly barred in favour of someone throwing a rock, perhaps a police provocateur.

The importance of protecting the public from information was dramatically revealed at the April Summit. Every editorial office in the United States had on its desk two important studies, timed for release just before the Summit. One was from Human Rights Watch, the second from the Economic Policy Institute in Washington—and neither organization is exactly obscure. Both studies investigated in depth the effects of NAFTA, which was hailed at the Summit as a grand triumph and a model for the FTAA, with headlines trumpeting its praises by George Bush and other leaders, all accepted as Gospel Truth. Both studies were suppressed with near-total unanimity. It is easy to see why. Human Rights Watch analysed the effects of NAFTA on labour rights, which, it found, were harmed in all three participating countries. Its report was comprehensive: it consisted of detailed analyses of the effects of NAFTA on working people, written by specialists on the three countries. The conclusion is that this is one of the rare agreements that have harmed the majority of the population in all of the participating countries.

The effects on Mexico were particularly severe, and particularly significant for the South. Wages had declined sharply with the imposition of neoliberal programmes in the 1980s. This continued after NAFTA, with a 24 percent decline in incomes for salaried workers, and 40 percent for the self-employed—an effect magnified by the rapid increase in unsalaried workers. Although foreign investment grew, total investment declined, as the economy was transferred to the hands of foreign multinationals. The minimum wage lost 50 percent of its purchasing power. Manufacturing declined, and development stagnated or reversed. A small sector became extremely wealthy, and foreign investors prospered.

These studies confirm what had been reported in the business press and academic studies. The *WSJ* (March 8, 1999) reported that although the Mexican economy was growing rapidly in the late 1990s after a sharp post-NAFTA decline, consumers suffered a 40 percent drop in purchasing power, the number of people living in extreme poverty grew twice as fast as the population, and even those working in foreign-owned assembly plants lost purchasing power. Similar conclusions were drawn in a study of the Latin American section of the Woodrow Wilson Center (Bach, 1999), which found that economic power had greatly concentrated as small Mexican companies cannot obtain financing, traditional farming sheds workers, and labour-intensive sectors (agriculture, light industry) cannot compete internationally with what is called 'free enterprise' in the doctrinal system. Agriculture suffered for the usual reasons: peasant farmers cannot compete with highly subsidized US agribusiness, with effects familiar throughout the world.

Most of this was predicted by critics of NAFTA, including the suppressed OTA and labour movement studies. Critics were wrong in one respect, however. Most anticipated a sharp increase in the urban-rural ratio, as hundreds of thousands of peasants were driven off the land. This did not happen. The reason, it would appear, is that conditions deteriorated so badly in the cities that there was a huge flight from them as well to the United States. Those who survive the crossing—many do not—work for very low wages, with no benefits, under awful conditions. The effect is to destroy lives and communities in Mexico and to improve the US economy, where 'consumption of the urban middle class continues to be subsidized by the impoverishment of farm labourers both in the United States and Mexico,' the Woodrow Wilson Center study points out.

These are among the costs of NAFTA, and neoliberal globalization generally, that economists generally choose not to measure. But even by the highly ideological standard measures, the costs have been severe.

None of this was allowed to sully the celebration of NAFTA and the FTAA at the Summit. Unless they are connected to activist organizations, most people know about these matters only from their own lives. And carefully protected from reality by the Free Press, many regard themselves as somehow failures, unable to take part in the celebration of the greatest economic boom in history.

Data from the richest country in the world are enlightening, but I will skip the details. The picture generalizes, with some variation of course, and exceptions of the kind already noted. The picture is much worse when we depart from standard economic measures. One cost is the threat to survival implicit in the reasoning of military planners, already described. There are many others. To take one, the ILO (2001) reported a rising 'worldwide epidemic' of serious mental health disorders, often linked to stress in the workplace, with very substantial fiscal costs in the industrial countries. A large factor, it concludes, is 'globalization,' which brings an 'evaporation of job security,' pressure on workers, and a higher workload, particularly in the US. Is this a cost of 'globalization'? From one point of view, it is one of its most attractive features. When he lauded US economic performance as 'extraordinary,' Alan Greenspan stressed particularly the heightened sense of job insecurity that leads to reduced costs for employers. The World Bank agrees. It recognizes that 'labour market flexibility' has acquired 'a bad name . . . as a euphemism for pushing wages down and workers out.' Nevertheless, 'it is essential in all the regions of the world. The most important reforms involve lifting . . . constraints on labour mobility and wage flexibility, as well as breaking the ties between social services and labour contracts' (World Bank, 1995).

In brief, according to prevailing ideology, pushing workers out, pushing wages down, and undermining benefits are all crucial contributions to economic health.

Unregulated trade has further benefits for corporations. Much—probably most—'trade' is centrally managed through a variety of devices: intra-firm transfers, strategic alliances, outsourcing, and others (UNCTAD, 1994). Broad trading areas benefit corporations by making them less answerable to local and national communities. This enhances the effects of neoliberal programmes, which regularly have reduced labour's share of national income. In the United States the 1990s was the first postwar period when the division of income shifted strongly towards the owners of capital and investors and away from labour and households. Trade has a wide range of unmeasured costs: subsidizing energy, resource depletion, and other externalities that are not counted. But it also brings advantages, although here too some caution is necessary. The most widely hailed is that trade increases specialization, which reduces the capacity to make choices, including the choice to modify comparative advantage, otherwise known as 'development.' The capacity for choice and development (and the UNDP, in its notion of *human development*, defines the first in terms of the second) are values in themselves: undermining them is a substantial cost. If the American colonies had been compelled to accept the WTO regime 200 years ago, New England would be pursuing its comparative advantage in exporting fish, surely not producing textiles, which survived only by exorbitant tariffs to bar British products (mirroring Britain's treatment of India). The same was true of steel and other industries, right to the present, particularly in the highly protectionist Reagan years—even putting aside the state sector of the economy. There is a great deal to say about all of this. Much of the story is masked in selective modes of economic measurement, though it is well known to economic historians and historians of technology.

Upon Further Reflection...

As everyone is aware, at least at the World Social Forum, the rules of the game are likely to enhance deleterious effects for the poor. The rules of the WTO bar the mechanisms used by every rich country to reach its current state of development, while also providing unprecedented levels of protectionism for the rich, including a patent regime that bars innovation and growth in novel ways, and allows corporate entities to amass huge profits by monopolistic pricing of products often developed with substantial public contribution.

Under contemporary versions of traditional mechanisms, half the people in the world are effectively in receivership, their economic policies managed by experts in Washington. But even in the rich countries democracy is under attack by virtue of the shift of decision-making power from governments, which may be partially responsive to the public, to private tyrannies, which have no such defects. Cynical slogans such as 'trust the people' or 'minimize the state' do not, under current circumstances, call for increasing popular control. They shift decisions from governments to other hands, but not 'the people:' rather, the management of collectivist legal entities, largely unaccountable to the public, and effectively totalitarian in internal structure, much as conservatives charged a century ago when opposing 'the corporatization of America.'

Latin American specialists and polling organizations have observed for some years that extension of formal democracy in Latin America has been accompanied by increasing disillusionment about democracy, 'alarming trends,' which continue, analysts have observed, noting the link between 'declining economic fortunes' and 'lack of faith' in democratic institutions (*Financial Times*). As Atilio Borón, an Argentinian political sociologist, pointed out some years ago, the new wave of democratization in Latin America coincided with neoliberal economic 'reforms,' which undermine effective democracy, a phenomenon that extends worldwide, in various forms.

It also applies to the United States. There has been much public clamour about the 'stolen election' of November 2000, and surprise that the public does not seem to care. Likely reasons are suggested by public opinion studies, which reveal that on the eve of the election, three quarters of the population regarded the process as largely a farce: a game played by financial contributors, party leaders, and the Public Relations industry, which crafted candidates to say 'almost anything to get themselves elected' so that one could believe little they said even when it was intelligible. On most issues, citizens could not identify the stands of the candidates, not because they are stupid or not trying, but because of the conscious efforts of the PR industry. A Harvard University project that monitors political attitudes found that the 'feeling of powerlessness has reached an alarming high,' with more than one half saying that people like them have little or no influence on what government does, a sharp rise through the neoliberal period.

Issues on which the public differs from elites (economic, political, intellectual) are pretty much off the agenda, notably questions of economic policy. The business world, not surprisingly, is overwhelmingly in favour of corporate-led 'globalization,' the 'free investment agreements' called 'free trade agreements,' NAFTA and the FTAA, GATS, and other devices that concentrate wealth and power in hands unaccountable to the public. Also not surprisingly, the great beast is generally opposed, almost instinctively, even without knowing crucial facts from which they are carefully shielded. It follows that such issues are not appropriate for political campaigns, and did not arise in the mainstream for the November 2000 elections. One would have been hard-pressed, for example, to find discussion of the upcoming Summit of the Americas and the FTAA, and other topics that involve issues of prime concern for the public. Voters were directed to what the PR industry calls 'personal qualities,' not 'issues.' Among the half of the population that votes, heavily skewed towards the wealthy, those who recognize their class interests to be at stake vote for those interests: overwhelmingly, for the more reactionary of the two business parties. But the general public splits its vote in other ways, leading to a statistical tie. Among working people, noneconomic issues such as gun ownership and 'religiosity' were primary factors, so that people often voted against their own primary interests—apparently assuming that they had little choice.

What remains of democracy is to be construed as the right to choose among commodities. Business leaders have long explained the need to impose on the population a 'philosophy of futility' and 'lack of purpose in life,' to 'concentrate human attention on the more superficial things that comprise much of fashionable consumption.' Deluged by such propaganda from infancy, people may then accept their meaningless and subordinate lives and forget ridiculous ideas about managing their own affairs. They may abandon their fate to the wizards, and in the political realm, to the self-described 'intelligent minorities' who serve and administer power.

From this perspective, conventional in elite opinion, particularly through the last century, the November 2000 elections do not reveal a flaw of US democracy, but rather its triumph. And generalizing, it is fair to hail the triumph of democracy throughout the hemisphere, and elsewhere, even though the populations somehow do not see it that way.

The struggle to impose that regime takes many forms, but never ends, and never will as long as high concentrations of effective decision-making power remain in place. It is only reasonable to expect the masters to exploit any opportunity that comes along—at the moment, the fear and anguish of the population in the face of terrorist attacks, a serious matter for the West now that, with new technologies available, it has lost its virtual monopoly of violence, retaining only a huge preponderance.

But there is no need to accept these rules, and those who are concerned with the fate of the world and its people will surely follow a very different course. The popular struggles against investor-rights 'globalization,' mostly in the South, have influenced the rhetoric, and to some extent the practices, of the masters of the universe, who are concerned and defensive. These popular movements are unprecedented in scale, in range of constituency, and in international solidarity; the meetings here are a critically important illustration. The future to a large extent lies in their hands. It is hard to overestimate what is at stake.

Notes

1 The original form of this chapter was prepared for and presented at the World Social Summit in Porto Alegre, February 1, 2002.
2 Editor's note: For an analysis of these self-appointed guardians as a group, and as a class, see Salbuchi (2000).
3 This literature is too voluminous to cite but see, in particular, the on-line and published writings, such as *Global Outlook*, put out by the Montreal Centre for Research on Globalisation (CRG).

Chapter Nine

The Antiglobalization Movement: Juggernaut or Jalopy?[1]

Adam David Morton

To arrive together at the truth is a communist and revolutionary act
Antonio Gramsci, L'Ordine Nuovo (21 June 1919)

It might seem surprising, amidst a growing interest in globalization as a set of highly contested social relations, to witness Perry Anderson, editor of *New Left Review*, unabashedly declaring that the principal aspect of the past decade, 'can be defined as the virtually *uncontested* consolidation, and universal diffusion, of neoliberalism (Anderson, 2000: 10) Elsewhere, Francis Fukuyama (2001), in typical hyperbolic fashion, has declared that 'modernity is a very powerful freight train that will not be derailed by recent events.' The demonstrations during the 'Carnival Against Capitalism' (London, June 1999), mobilizations against the WTO (Seattle, November 1999), protests against the IMF and World Bank (Washington, April 2000 and Prague, September 2000), and 'riots' during a recent G-8 meeting (Genoa, July 2001) would all seemingly expose the premature logic of these contentions. It was this very series of demonstrations that the UK Prime Minister Tony Blair (2001) dubbed the 'anarchists' travelling circus.'

Elsewhere, rather than critically analysing globalization with a focus on structures from 'above' (Germain, 2000)[2] there is a growing body of literature that attempts to understand and give form to some of the recent resistances against globalization from 'below' (Cockburn and St. Clair, 2000; Gills, 2000; Gunnell and Timms, 2000; Mittelman, 2000; Mittelman and Othman, 2000; Rupert, 2000). As a result, it becomes all the more difficult to suppress the inherent conflicts, struggles and contradictions embedded within globalizing processes of neoliberal restructuring. The aim of this chapter is to focus on some of the crucial facets related to neoliberal globalization and the politics of resistance.

Primarily the issues raised revolve around whether neoliberal globalization should be regarded as a *juggernaut* or a *jalopy*. That is, should it be understood as either a juggernaut—a vehicle or freight train that is on an inexorable path towards consolidating particular social, political and economic priorities—or more of a jalopy whose direction is openly contestable and contested and that, therefore, may even be subject to breakdown. Just as Daniel Singer described his search for alternatives to the inequalities of capitalist society as 'a presumptuous pebble trying to upset the juggernaut' of globalization (Singer, 1999: 2), then it is also my suggestion that the supposed juggernaut of globalization is clearly contestable. Current struggles against the presumed inexorability of globalization may even reveal the jalopy behind the juggernaut. This is evidenced by some of the latest, openly declared, forms of resistance, such as protests once more at Davos (Switzerland, January 2001), the annual rendezvous of the WEF; the recent 10,000-strong WSF meeting at Porto Alegre (Brazil, January 2001); or the demonstrations during the Summit of the Americas initiative promoting the conception of a FTAA (Quebec, April 2001).[3] A focus on such openly declared forms of resistance, of course, does not mean discarding the importance of everyday forms of social struggle at the level of 'infrapolitics' (Scott, 1985, 1990).

To focus, then, on neoliberal globalization as juggernaut or jalopy three issues related to the politics of resistance are worth considering. Firstly, the chapter commences by outlining the understanding of globalization that underpins the argument. It is an understanding entirely consistent with the view that 'globalization is the renewed attempt to impose and extend the rule of capital on a world scale' (Singer, 1999: 186). Secondly, there is a questioning of the tactics and strategies of recent resistances to globalization and, crucially, what tentative conclusions may presently be drawn from such activism. Thirdly, it is questioned what broader implications unfold for the study and practice of resistance to globalization not only in terms of situating issues within an historical perspective but also in terms of rooting the dilemmas of political agency in concrete locations. The conclusion then draws the analysis of globalization as 'juggernaut' or 'jalopy' together and emphasizes normative principles embedded within the search for alternative futures to the present world order confines of neoliberal globalization.

What's in a Word?

From a political economy perspective, neoliberal globalization is best understood as the transnationalization of finance and production through institutions at the level of different state forms and world order. After all, as Marx has put it, 'capital is not a thing, but rather a definite social production relation, belonging to a definite historical formation of society, which is manifested in a thing and lends this thing a specific social character' (Marx, 1998: 801).

Hence, globalization reflects a set of social relations that are constituted by changes to the social relations of production. Social forces, engendered by the social relations of production, are therefore the authors of such neoliberal globalizing processes and have operated through the state itself—which is both shaped by and formative of globalization—as well as through the ideational and material dimensions of institutions in the global political economy (Cox, 1981:

126-155). An emphasis is thus placed on the role state institutions have had in bringing about changes from the national to the global level resulting in globalization. In sum, processes of neoliberal globalization have been authored by, and mediated through, different state forms by the agency of social forces, which has resulted in the restructuring of the state (Panitch, 1994; 2000). Such processes, it has been argued, can be traced to a structural change or crisis in the historical structures of capitalism since the 1970s (Cox, 1987: 273-308; Cox, with Sinclair, 1996; Gill, 1990: Chs. 4-5; Gill 1993). Globalization, then, can be described as 'the response of capital to its structural crisis' (Singer, 1999: 5).

The world economic crisis of 1973-74 followed the abandonment of the US dollar-gold standard link and signalled a move away from the Bretton Woods system of fixed exchange rates to more flexible adjustment measures (Germain, 1997: 95-99). This system was based on a principle of 'embedded liberalism', which allowed the combination of international free trade with the right for governments to intervene in their national economy in order to ensure domestic stability via social security and the partial redistribution of economic wealth (Ruggie, 1982: 379-425). The corresponding form of state was the Keynesian welfare state, characterized by interventionism, a policy of full employment via budget deficit spending, the mixed economy and an expansive welfare system. The underlying social relations of production were organized around a Fordist accumulation regime, characterized by mass production and mass consumption, and tripartite corporatism involving government-business-labour coalitions (Cox, 1996a: 219-30).

The 1970s crisis involved the OPEC-initiated oil price rises and heightened inflation and indebtedness within countries of advanced capitalism which led to the post-World War II order, based on Keynesian demand-management and Fordist industrialism, giving way to a restructuring of the social relations of production. This involved the encouragement of social relations of production based on the priorities of privatization of state-controlled assets, fiscal stability and rectitude, liberalization and deregulation of the economy and little commitment to redistribution or social reform. Hence a shift away from a secure unionized state sector towards the promotion of private business interests and the creation of favourable conditions for internationally and transnationally oriented capital (Gill and Law, 1989: 475-499). A period of structural change therefore unfolded in the 1970s within which there was a tendency to encourage, through different state forms, the consolidation of new priorities.

Although the changes inaugurated by this structural crisis were far from uniform, the rising priorities of monetarism, supply-side economics and the logic of competitiveness nevertheless began to increasingly establish, albeit through prolonged social struggle, a 'hegemonic aura' throughout the world order during the 1980s and 1990s under the banner of Reagan-Thatcherism (Cox, 1996: 196). As Craig Murphy has put it, 'adjustment to the crisis occurred at different rates in different regions, but in each case it resulted in a 'neoliberal' shift in governmental economic policy and the increasing prominence of financial capital' (Murphy, 1998: 159). During the period of structural change in the 1970s, then, the social basis across many different forms of state altered. Whilst some have championed such changes as the 'retreat of the state' (Strange, 1995), or the emergence of a 'borderless world' (Ohmae 1990, 1996), it is argued here that there unfolded a profound restructuring—but not erosion—of the state. After all, the state is not simply supine, it is a social entity that is an active participant at the heart of processes of neoliberal globalization (Singer, 1999: 207). Hence a move beyond the view that globalization is the result of interactions between the state, on the one hand, and the market, on the other, that *separately* interact with one another.

This, for instance, is the view of Robert Gilpin who refers to 'the interaction of the state and market as the embodiment of politics and economics in the modern world.' Additionally he claims that state and market have independent logics and existences of their own influencing the distribution of power and wealth (Gilpin, 1987: 9-10). The result is a treatment of state and market, or politics and economics, as reified (thing-like) abstractions that are separated from specific social relations and material interests that constitute a social (or world) order. Yet, 'state and market are not sheer abstractions . . . they are part of the same social formation' (Singer, 1999: 175). By dividing politics and economics attention is diverted from social (class) struggles over subordination and exploitation that are inextricably embedded within capitalist social relations of production (Meiksins Wood 1995: 19-48). This issue will be developed in more detail shortly. If globalization Is thus understood as a set of social relations, rather than as a thing in itself, it is possible to resist reification as well as avoid the assumption that globalization is an incontestable fact. Globalization is thus a set of social relations through which capitalism and hegemony are expressed.

Tactics and Strategies

The convention of the WTO meeting at Seattle was intended to initiate a so-called Millennium Round of trade talks between the elites of the global political economy. Instead, it presaged a merry-go-round of protests and resistances against neoliberal globalization. In terms of grasping the tactics and strategies of the politics of resistance against globalization several factors are open to discussion. Three key features of resistance against neoliberal globalization are considered: the role of organized labour; a focus on social classes as the agents of political change; and the spread of issues within globalization processes generating resistance.

The Role of Organized Labour?

The post-World War II labour movement has been beset by a history of corporatist structures and reformist institutionalism—a 'politics of productivity' (Maier, 1977: 607-633)—which brings into question its involvement in leading the latest agenda of the politics of resistance against neoliberal globalization. One commentator, for example, has described the gains at Seattle as the result of achievements, 'entirely outside the conventional arena of orderly protest and white-paper activism and the timid bleats of the professional leadership of big labour and environmentalism' (St. Clair, 1999: 81-96). Organized labour, it seems, is not that organized, or rather it is too organized and disciplined to deal with the potential opportunities of resistance because of its concern with the institutionalization of core labour standards, or a seat at the table, within the dominant institutions of the global political economy. Perhaps organized labour is too attracted to hitching a ride on the vehicle of globalization in order to protect jobs and prevent the exit of transnational capital.

However, one must be careful of succumbing to an *a priori* dismissal of the potential role labour might play as a force for historical change in countering neoliberalism. For example, labour organizations have been pivotal in contesting the nature of regional integration or pushing for social protection within, for example, NAFTA or the European Union (Rupert, 1995: 658-92; Bieler and Morton, 2001). Nor should the potential radicalization of labour through contact with other social movements be disregarded (O'Brien, 2000: 533-55). The question of the future role of trade unions as a vestige of resistance is therefore clearly an open one that has to be further researched rather than simply assumed.

Yet, it seems that resistance to neoliberal globalization has, at least most recently, derived from initiatives led by more militant unions and direct-action protesters *outside* legitimacy-creating institutions like the American Federation of Labour-Congress of Industrial Organizations (AFL-CIO) in the US and the International Confederation of Free Trade Unions (ICFTU) concerned with enshrining labour concessions within the WTO. Similarly, the European Trade Union Confederation (ETUC)—described at its inception as 'firmly capitalist' (Van der Pijl 1984: 249)—has been confined to a narrowly circumscribed role within more recent processes of European integration, distanced from broader social movements (Martin and Ross, 1999).

The generally overlooked early writings of Antonio Gramsci can have striking relevance in this sense in connection with the conflict between capital and labour. Arising from political action within the new workers' organizations known as 'Factory Councils' in Turin during the *biennio rosso* (1919-1920), Gramsci rejected the bureaucratic and centralized authority of trade unions. Although trade unions could be important phenomena, as tools or organisms of proletarian mobilization, rather than just a 'slave' to capital, they usually take a more determined rather than determining character (Gramsci, 1977: 103-108, 265, 332). Hence trade unions were ultimately organizations that regulated the relations between capital and labour *within* capitalist society with their function only making sense within capitalist institutions (Schecter, 1991: 137-178). As an integral part of capitalist society they could therefore just as easily become instruments of control achieving only limited reforms:

> *Objectively*, the trade union is nothing other than a commercial company, of a purely capitalistic type, which aims to secure, in the interests of the proletariat, the maximum price for the commodity labour, and to establish a monopoly over this commodity in the national and international fields. The trade union is distinguished from capitalist mercantilism only *subjectively*, insofar as, being formed necessarily of workers, it tends to create among the workers an awareness that it is impossible

to achieve industrial autonomy of the producers within the bounds of trade-unionism (Gramsci, 1977: 76).

In Gramsci's eyes it was more likely that trade unions would tend to represent reformist opportunism, incapable of overthrowing capitalist society, due to their incorporation within the machinery of the bourgeois state (Gramsci, 1977: 103-108, 190-196). Therefore, alternative social institutions were created—Factory Councils—that stood outside the realm of industrial legality to replace those of capitalist society in the endeavour to emancipate labour and create a new form of 'anti-state' organized on a national and ultimately international basis (Gramsci, 1977: 53, 63-68, 80). A dynamic and democratic movement 'from below' was thus envisaged to transform established state, political and social structures created 'from above' (Gramsci as in Clark 1977: 61-62, 72). Resistance, rather than a frontal attack (or war of manoeuvre) on the state, had to therefore be transformed into a war of position which required a concentration of hegemonic activity 'before the rise to power' within the 'fortresses and earthworks' of civil society (Gramsci 1971: 59, 238-239).

Such themes clearly connect with contemporary strands of the politics of resistance against globalization embodied by the Ruckus Society, Reclaim the Streets campaigners, or Earth First!ers. Autonomous forms of peasant mobilizations throughout Latin America—such as the *Ejército Zapatista de Liberación Nacional* (EZLN) in Chiapas, Mexico, or the *Movimento dos Trabalhadores Rurais Sem Terra* (MST) in Brazil—would also seem to confirm the importance of constituting a catalyst of resistance to, and protests against, neoliberal globalization *outside* conventional political parties and institutions that tend to ensure continual absorption, disaggregation and neutralization through the domination of the state (Petras, 1997: 17-47; 1998: 124-133). It is therefore important to problematize the tactics and strategies of resistance by giving further thought to the relationship between 'new' and 'old' social movements in countering neoliberal globalization. Central to this endeavour is the importance of questioning the influence of the working class as the main agency of radical transformation (Panitch, 2000a: 366-70).

Social Classes as the Agents of Political Change?

It is thus essential to appreciate the variety of identities and interests that form in the consciousness of individual and collective actors in resistances to neoliberal globalization, which entails reconstituting class analysis (Veltmeyer, 1997:139-169). The notion, introduced earlier, of social forces engendered by the social relations of production offers the opportunity to capture the essence of class identity without becoming reducible to class agency. Other forms of collective identity and agency are thus included within the rubric of social forces—ethnic, gender, green, national, religious, sexual —with the aim of addressing how, like class, they derive from a common basis of exploitation and marginalization (Cox, 1992: 35). Hence class is used in a heuristic way rather than as a static analytical category (Cox, 1996a: 57). This means that class struggle, as E.P. Thompson

(1978: 133-165) has argued, can be identified within and through historical relationships of economic exploitation even though forms of class-consciousness — involving a conscious identity of common interests—may not be explicitly evident. The analysis of scenarios of inequality is thus best related to struggles between classes that are emerging in contexts of contestation rather than imputing 'class struggle' from a supposed class structure of society. Rather than mechanically deriving objective determinations that have an automatic place in production relations, the focus becomes human relations of exploitation raised by class antagonisms related to the discipline of capital.

> People find themselves in a society structured in determined ways (crucially, but not exclusively, in productive relations), they experience exploitation (or the need to maintain power over those whom they exploit), they identify points of antagonistic interest, they commence to struggle around these issues and in the process of struggling they discover themselves as classes, they come to know this discovery as class-consciousness (Thompson, 1978: 149).[4]

Proceeding from the broader context of instances of exploitation therefore means that issues of class struggle have to be taken seriously. 'Bring back exploitation as the hallmark of class, and at once class struggle is in the forefront, as it should be' (Ste. Croix, 1981: 57). This opens up empirical questions about how class struggle might play out in different contexts.

More generally, the possibility of envisaging common points of convergence between diverse social (class) forces in the struggle over hegemony, centred around the exploitation of the social and natural environment, is afforded. An appreciation of the discipline of capital on the reproductive sphere and the exhaustion of the biosphere is then also promoted (Van der Pijl, 1998: 47-49). Additionally, the possibility of conceptualizing the normative constitution of globalization and the promotion of liberal democratic norms as an expression of a convergence of class interests emerges (Smith, 2000: 26-29). It is then feasible to envision the promotion of narrow definitions of democracy, known as 'low intensity democracy' or 'polyarchy', that confine mass participation in decision-making to leadership choice, as intrinsic to the protection of dominant class interests and the displacement of emancipatory democratic demands (Gills, 1993; Robinson, 1996). Class content thus 'subsists' within the agency *and* conditioning of social forces along with other identities (Foweraker, 1995: 40; Hellman, 1995:170-171).

In terms of strategies and tactics, social forces resisting neoliberal globalization must endeavour to effectively interpellate social subjects by trying to unite heterogeneous forms of identity and interest against the logic of capitalist exploitation. Following Gramsci, an attempt to draw together different ways of being and understanding, by uniting distinct realms of subjectivity, can be understood as an attempt to forge an alliance between oppositional forces based on a 'collective will' (Gramsci, 1977: 125-133). Such counter-hegemonic efforts are being articulated in practice as the cases of new peasant movements in Latin America, such as the EZLN, attest (Morton, 2001). The EZLN have launched a critique of social power relations both located within Mexico as well as targeted towards establishing a more permissive world order by contesting and resisting neoliberal globalization. This stance has influenced movements such as the People's Global Action, a pivot in the Seattle, Washington and Prague protests, as well as *Ya Basta!* an Italian non-violent direct-action Zapatista support group ('Carnivalistas Slink in with a Pink Revolution,' *The Guardian*, 23 September 2000; Chiapaslink 2000: 28-30).

Yet, the basis of shaping a collective will was, according to Gramsci, intrinsically linked to the agency of a modern mass political party: the 'Modern Prince' of the Communist Party. It was a form of political agency that stood as 'the proclaimer and organizer of an intellectual and moral reform, which also means creating the terrain for a subsequent development of the . . . collective will towards the realization of a superior, total form of modern civilization' (Gramsci, 1971: 133).

The party thus had a constructive function in trying to extend emerging forms of resistance to mobilize the mass of the population. 'The modern prince . . . cannot be a real person, a concrete individual. It can only be an organism, a complex element of society in which a collective will, which has already been recognized and has to some extent asserted itself in action, begins to take concrete form' (Gramsci, 1977: 129).

This faith, though, in the guiding role of a 'Modern Prince' is clearly contradicted and rendered more than problematic by the present political organization of movements such as the EZLN and others involved in recent mobilizations against the multilateral institutions of global governance. Contemporary political agency is seemingly more open-ended, plural and inclusive. Hence the need to move beyond notions of the conventional mass political party as the basis for organization within the constraining framework of bourgeois representative democracy. Within such conditions, movements themselves can become the institutional products, or the *interlocuteurs valables*, of the defenders of privilege formed and permeated by the contradictions and metaphysical suppositions of capitalism (Wallerstein, 1999: 27-35; 1999: 152). Nevertheless, contemporary movements do still attempt to converge individual and collective interests and identities even though the practices of conventional mass political parties are rejected. In some ways the recent politics of resistance reaffirms the relevance of Paolo Freire's maxim that a transformative agenda has to be engaged with various spheres of social life: movements have to locate themselves tactically inside and strategically outside the system (Freire, 1970). The aim of such movements, then, can still be described as, 'the attainment of a 'cultural-social' unity through which a multiplicity of dispersed wills, with heterogeneous aims, are welded together with a single aim, on the basis of an equal and common conception of the world' (Gramsci, 1971: 349).

It is, however, worth noting that any unity achieved by such movements is always fragile and subject to antagonisms and that the 'collective will' of any counter-hegemonic appeal can become dispersed and scattered into an infinity of individual wills or identities reduced to separate and conflictive paths (Gramsci,

1971: 128-129). History, after all, is constituted by social subjects in a process of *'becoming* . . . which does not start from unity, but contains in itself the reasons for a possible unity' Gramsci, 1971: 356). New forms of collective political identity and agency, whilst going beyond earlier modernist institutionalized and centralized projects, are therefore seeking novel modes of expression in an attempt to rearticulate provisional notions of 'party' organization within the politics of globalization (Singer, 1999: 255-257; Gill, 2000: 131-140). Such a revelatory agenda will clearly be fraught with difficulties and dilemmas as reports about divisions between peaceful ('fluffies') and violent ('spikies') protesters within direct action groups, such as Reclaim the Streets, suggest (*The Guardian*, 14 April 2001).

Spread of Issues?

The spread of issues within the remit of institutions concerned with global governance, balancing everything from human rights to social, economic, environmental as well as civil and political rights, may also mean that activists can build broader coalitions in response to neoliberal globalization. Increasingly, the mobilization of various elements of civil society across different forms of state also encompasses reaction against transnational corporations with high brand-name recognition. This has increasingly promoted a new kind of anti-corporate politics so that, 'rather than dividing communities into factions, corporations are increasingly serving as the common thread by which labour, environmental and human-rights violations can be stitched together into a single political ideology' (Klein, 2000: 266). This spread of issues resulting from neoliberal globalization raises the opportunity to further unite diverse social forces with emancipatory potential. It may, for instance, provide a basis to include additional social processes of resistance such as those related to precarious 'unprotected workers'—involved in social relations ranging from unpaid household work to subcontracting in small enterprises—that have become increasingly central to (re)producing the global political economy (Harrod, 1987). Hence, according to one view, 'it is in the ranks of the millions of temp workers that the true breeding ground of the anticorporate backlash will most likely be found' (Klein, 2000: 269). However, two cautionary remarks are worth making.

First, the prospect that wider resistances to neoliberal globalization could be coopted and de-radicalized by a global governance framework of multilateral institutions should not be disregarded (O'Brien, et al., 2000: 209-210, 231). Attempts to revive a new round of trade talks at the ministerial meeting of the WTO in Doha, Qatar (November 2001) should be seen in this light. So, too, should the recent UK government's policy stance on supposedly 'making globalization work for the poor' (UK Government, 2000). Embedded within this policy is the rhetoric presented by figures such as Claire Short, the UK government's Secretary of State for International Development, that *marginalization* rather than *globalization* is the main threat to developing countries, thereby further validating inclusion within the dominant institutions of the global political economy (Short,

2001). Allied to this is the bid to generate wider consensual support for the GATS)—aimed at codifying the privatization of public services—which, according to Mike Moore, the director general of the WTO, 'offers benefits for every part of the world' (Moore, 2001). Secondly, there is also a danger that social cleavages might rekindle more invidious movements based on authoritarian populism, which may equally threaten progressive objectives. The nationalist and reactionary response of extreme-right parties, such as the Austrian Freedom Party, poses one such danger. The question therefore remains open as to what form resistance to neoliberal globalization may take or which contending views may vie for hegemony in the wider world order (Rupert, 2000: 94-118).

Broader Implications for the Practice and Study of Resistance

Three further inter-related issues arise as a result of the above argument concerning the broader context of the practice and study of resistance to neoliberal globalization. Namely, the importance of situating issues within an *historical perspective*, the significance of considering the possibilities of collective *agency* in relation to prevailing—constraining and enabling—structures, and the merit of relating such factors to concrete *locations*.

Historical Perspective

Firstly, rather than reifying globalization as an incontestable fact or unstoppable juggernaut, it is crucial to acknowledge that political strategies *are* presently contesting neoliberal globalization. Even this simple concession, however, escapes major authorities such as Perry Anderson (2000: 17) who has declared that, 'whatever limitations persist to its practice, neoliberalism as a set of principles rules undivided across the globe: [it is] the most successful ideology in world history.' Most recently Anderson has added that there has been 'the disappearance of any programmatic alternatives to the scene of neoliberalism' (Anderson, 2000: 6). To counter, with the words of Naomi Klein (2000: 107), 'we may be able to see a not-so-brave new world on the horizon, but that doesn't mean we are already living in Huxley's nightmare.' As further protests during the international workers' May Day demonstrations have made clear, anti-capitalist activists, non-governmental organizations, rank-and-file militant labour and social movements are articulating a common political agenda and raising the possibility of alternatives to neoliberal globalization, albeit faced with the challenge—at least in Britain—of building wider socially-rooted support. This poses the question of whether ameliorative, rather than transformative strategies, are more likely in founding sustainable social relations (Langley and Mellor, 2002: 49-65). Hence, rather than a canonization, it is meaningful to set diverse forms of resistance to neoliberal globalization within a thorough historical perspective. Only by considering the divergent and contingent historical circumstances of various resistances to neoliberal globalization can the commonalities and transformative possibilities of collective agency be realized.

Recognizing Agency

Secondly, it becomes imperative to recognize the creative capacities of historically situated social agents *within* specific structural constraints. After all, if we do not have the structures clearly in mind then our so-called recognition of agency is at risk of being blind (Wallerstein, 1999: 218). Hence, rather than invoking vague and salutary notions of 'global civil society,' it is essential to try and connect collective human agency to the structural frameworks that constrain and enable such action within specific conditions (Bieler and Morton, 2001: 5-35). A realization of agency-structure can thus promote an understanding of the hegemony of neoliberal globalization not as an immutable structure, edifice, or juggernaut but as an active, formative and transformative process of political struggle that is fragile, tenuous and subject to challenges.

Location

Finally, the analysis of resistances to neoliberal globalization has to be grounded within the detail of actually existing locations. However controversial it may be, it is argued that the terrain of state-civil society relations remains the immediate concrete location and framework for political struggle, although resistance to globalization cannot be successful unless it is also prosecuted beyond national boundaries (Jameson, 2000: 49-68). 'The advantages as well as the disadvantages which large sectors of populations experience in different national contexts,' according to Anne Showstack Sassoon, 'must be taken as a starting point for alternative strategies' (Sassoon, 2001: 14). Or, as Leo Panitch has put it, 'any adequate strategy to challenge globalization must begin at home, precisely because of the key role of states in making globalization happen' (2000a: 374-275). This is not to lapse into a defence of the state system or a version of 'progressive nationalism,' meaning the promotion of an agenda restricted to the national arena (Radice, 2000: 5-19).⁵ Nor is it a collapse into the 'cosmopolitan fancy' of exalting global civil society. It is merely to recognize that state-civil society relations are still important in shaping the structures through which forms of resistance emerge, advance and negotiate concessions (Brennan 2001: 75-84). Overall, then, it is argued that an appreciation of the specific and general admixture of history, agency and location is essential in order to understand present resistances to neoliberal globalization.

Conclusion: Towards a Utopian Realism?

Within the above argument there is clearly a commitment to considering the conditions for and furthering historical change, although this need not entail establishing specific criteria for a future society or possible utopia. There is no blueprint for an alternative society, no specific policy programme, underlying such a critical purpose but simply an emphasis on building new means for collective action informed by new understandings of society and polity (Cox, 1996a: 393-394). It is an approach, therefore, that is particularly infused with the belief that knowledge of the social world is charged with social and political commitments. There is, then, an insistence upon an ethical dimension to analysis so that 'questions of justice, legitimacy and moral credibility are integrated sociologically into the whole and into many of its key concepts' (Gill, 1993: 24). This means that, however controversial and difficult it may be, there is an emancipatory basis to the overall argument. There is an overall normative element that 'allows for a normative choice in favour of a social and political order different from the prevailing order, but it limits the range of choice to alternative orders which are feasible transformations of the existing world' (Cox, 1981: 130).

This emphasis is echoed within various undertakings that are also attempting to establish normative principles as the basis for historical change. For example, Ken Booth (1991: 527-45) has sketched a 'utopian realism' that aims to set goals that have practical efficacy in order to establish a praxis of emancipation within more stable security relations. Similarly, Immanuel Wallerstein (1998 I: 4-5, 90) has coined the neologism 'utopistics' to refer to the serious assessment of possible utopias and their limitations and constraints as real historical alternatives in the present, which includes reconsidering prevailing structures of knowledge. Furthermore, Daniel Singer has attempted to develop a perspective on a 'realistic utopia'—*realistic* 'since it must be rooted in current conflicts and in the potentialities of existing society' and *utopian* 'because that is how any attempt to look beyond the confines of capitalism is branded' (Singer, 1999: 6-7).

This conception is akin to the complex political realism sketched by Antonio Gramsci. 'No one can be expected to imagine new things,' Gramsci wrote, 'but one can expect people…to exercise fantasy so as to round out the full living reality on the basis of what they know' Gramsci (1994, Vol. 1: 105). Political action, then, has to begin and take place on the terrain of 'effective reality' rather than idle fancy, yearning or daydreaming. These voluntarist traits were compared by Gramsci (1994, Vol. 2: 372) to the folly of building skyscrapers on a pinhead. In addition, tidy utopian social constructions were deemed prone to collapse because of a lack of efficacy within the terrain of 'operative ideals.' Yet it was maintained that the endeavour to give shape and coherence to particular social forces within 'effective reality' necessarily involves concern about issues of 'concrete fantasy' within the extant equilibrium of forces. 'What *ought to be* is therefore concrete; indeed it is the only realistic and historicist interpretation of reality; it alone is history in the making and philosophy in the making, it alone is politics' (Gramsci, 1971: 172). This is, then, far from a simple 'utopian' conception of politics.

Such a 'utopian realist' agenda, as Panitch discerns, could give further consideration to the following four central issues that might be crucial in stimulating theoretical and practical debate about the kinds of institutions and strategies that can promote historical change. Firstly, rather than simply articulating resistance against the status quo, there is a need to offer a strategic vision for a different order which would entail establishing democratic control over investment and, one can add, subordinating the control of the economy to social purpose by ensuring that production and consumption are more compatible with a sustainable biosphere. Secondly, it is imperative to transform labour itself as a more inclusive social agent and thereby widen understandings of the relationship between democracy and class consciousness. Thirdly, there is a need to promote forms of political organization beyond traditional parties whilst nevertheless providing the basis for a 'structured movement' of broad-based coalitions. Finally, there is an overriding necessity to converge and coordinate pressures in and beyond specific national contexts to engender wider internationalist challenges to neoliberal globalization (Panitch, 2000a: 381-389).

To come full circle, then, in relation to the opening epigraph, any derivation of the 'truth'—in this case in terms of an assessment of neoliberal globalization—lies within the fit between ideas and the social forces that shape history because 'for the purpose of human history, the only *truth* is the truth embodied in human action, that becomes a passionate driving force in people's minds' (Gramsci, 1977: 185). 'This must mean,' Robert Cox (1996b: 30) remarks, 'that *truth* changes with the movement of history.' Hence the importance of indicating how theoretical issues have practical efficacy (or some 'truth' in human action) and how they are finding concrete expression. 'Objective' means this and only this: that one asserts to be objective, to be objective reality, that reality which is ascertained by all, which is independent of any merely particular or group standpoint' (Gramsci, 1977: 291).

Gramsci here echoes Marx's sentiment that 'theory . . . becomes a material force as soon as it has gripped the masses' (Marx, 1975: 182). Yet, to cite Marx again, 'this does not mean that we shall confront the world with new doctrinaire principles and proclaim: Here is the truth, on your knees before it!' It simply means developing 'new principles from the *existing* principles of the world' (Marx, 1975: 208). Hence the importance of following Gramsci (1977: 385-6) in giving 'precedence to practice' and the 'real history of the changes in social relations.'

The crux is to give 'precedence to practice' by unravelling particular changes within different forms of state and world order shaped by social forces engendered by changes within the social relations of production. In short, providing insight into the antagonisms, conflicts and contradictions of capital that are expressed through historical and contemporary conditions of class struggle. It is the practical expression of class struggle and consciousness that is today in question and requires further consideration. The purpose of this argument is to provide a starting point for thinking about such questions by attempting to develop an understanding of processes of neoliberal globalization as well as the intensifying resistance against such forces that can be advanced in particular cases as part of general trends.

To conclude, it has been argued that globalization—at least as a rhetorical move—can be understood as a vehicle that is not always successful in following its desired route, it is more of a *jalopy* that is constantly contested rather than an unstoppable *juggernaut*. Indeed, as a jalopy it is suspect to hijack by new drivers that may also retune the engine, take on new passengers, even embark on a bit of progressive 'road rage,' to drive politics in a quite different direction. Thereby posing questions about the conditions for a just world order within the global political economy, the forms democracy may take and, ultimately, considering how future world social power relations will be constituted.

Notes

1　The title and the metaphor used throughout the chapter owes a debt to Alan Knight, 'Cardenismo: Juggernaut or Jalopy?' *Journal of Latin American Studies*, Vol. 26, No. 1 (1994: 73-107). An earlier version of this chapter was presented on the roundtable 'Globalization and the Politics of Resistance' at the 42nd Annual Convention of the International Studies Association, Chicago (20-24 February, 2001). I would particularly like to thank Barry Gills for his original invitation to participate in the roundtable and all the participants for their comments and criticisms. I am also grateful to Andreas Bieler, Pauline Ewan, Randall Germain, Steve Hobden and Stuart Shields for comments on this chapter in draft. The support of an Economic and Social Research Council (ESRC) Postdoctoral Fellowship is acknowledged.

2　Both collections of studies allude to issues of 'collective agency operating through established institutions,' or to 'the insertion of subjects' within globalization processes, yet there is a reluctance to develop an account of identity formation in terms of resistance to globalization. There is no account of *who* the agents are, *what* collective agency is, or *where* such agency is effective.

3　See the World Economic Forum's own newspaper for reports on the most recent protests, Forum News Daily, 'Swiss barricade Davos to prevent protesters from reaching centre,' http://www.earthtimes.org/forumnewsdaily.htm; Internet; accessed 28 January 2001; and *Le Monde diplomatique*, 'The Promise of Porto Alegre,' (January 2001) English print edition, http://www.monde-diplomatique.fr/en; Internet; accessed 12 January 2001; or *Le Monde diplomatique*, 'Towards a 'Free Trade Area of the Americas,' (April 2001) English print edition, http://www.monde-diplomatique.fr/en; Internet; accessed 20 April 2001.

4　Also see Thompson (1968: 8-9) where it is noted that 'class happens when [people], as a result of common experiences (inherited or shared), feel and articulate the identity of their interests as between themselves, and as against other [people] whose interests are different from (and usually opposed to) theirs.' In this understanding, whilst class experience appears determined by the social relations of production, class consciousness is a historical question arising from processes that have to be considered in an open-ended fashion.

5　For a recent variant, calling for the revival of such progressive nationalism, see Laxer, (2001: 1-32).

Chapter Ten

The Antinomies of Antiglobalization

Henry Veltmeyer

The object of this concluding chapter is to unmask globalization as imperialism and to point out the limits of the antiglobalization movement. As I see it, this movement is fundamentally flawed in ways that will limit its capacity to bring about fundamental change. For one thing, movement activists fail to recognize that the issue is not globalization in one form or another; it is *imperialism*—the projection of state power under conditions of a renewed form of US-led imperialism. Until this problem is grasped and dealt with in thought and practice the forces of resistance cannot be fully mobilized in the struggle for social change.

My argument is constructed as follows. First, I turn towards the ubiquitous search for an alternative form of development and globalization. I argue that there is both more to and less than meets the eye in the movement on which the political Left has pinned its hopes and expectations. I then turn towards the concept of 'imperialism' as a more useful tool for analyzing the dynamics of global developments and of the forces of resistance. In the following section I address, and challenge, the mythical notion of a powerless state, undermined by a process of globalization.

This chapter then moves into a discussion of the form that imperialism is taking in the current world context. To this end I begin by discarding the notion, advanced by Hardt and Negri, of an 'empire without imperialism.' Then I turn towards various alternative conceptions of the 'new' imperialism—neomercantilist and 'postmodern.' In this intellectual and ideological context, and with reference to arguments advanced by James Petras in this volume, I argue that imperialism is very much on the agenda—that the US state is leading this project.

In the following two sections I examine the question of 'democracy' and its meaning for both the agents (and ideologists) of imperialism and its opponents in the popular movement. At issue here is the nature of the state and its relation to 'civil society'—and the different forms taken by 'democracy' as well as its alternate uses. For the most part, the idea of 'democracy' has served as an ideology, to obfuscate and camouflage the interior design (and fascistic fist) of the imperialist project. At the same time, 'democracy' has served the popular movement in creating spaces for the accumulation, and mobilization, of the forces of opposition and resistance. In this sense—that is, as development 'from below'—democracy can be viewed as a two-edged sword, with a progressive side.

In the last two parts of this argument I turn back towards the Antiglobalization Movement before reviewing the form that the struggle against neoimperialism is taking on the Latin American periphery of the system. Here we bring into focus three waves of sociopolitical movements in the mobilization of the popular forces of opposition and resistance. I argue that these movements provide the best opportunity for progressive change and the forces of social transformation in the struggle against capitalism and imperialism. However, the political problems involved in this process are considerable. I conclude that the Left needs to overcome its penchant for sectarian politics and unite in a common struggle.

Neoliberalism and the Dynamics of Antiglobalization

In the wake of the financial crisis, which hit Mexico in 1995 and then spread to Asia and elsewhere in 1997, the neoliberal model of capitalist development has been seriously tarnished, abandoned by all except for a few ideological diehards. Even erstwhile ideologues of free market capitalism such as Carlos Salinas de Gortari, the now disgraced ex-president of Mexico but once the darling of the international neoliberal jet set; George Soros, self-appointed guardian of the world capitalist system, President of the Quantum Fund and the Soros Foundation, and 'retired' financier, expert manipulator of the free market in speculative capital; Joseph Stiglitz, formerly chief economist at the World Bank; and—most surprisingly perhaps—Michel Camdessus, until a few years ago managing director of the IMF, all have turned against or distanced themselves from neoliberalism (Soros in Bordegaray, Soledad and Toti Flores, 2001: 66-67; Stiglitz, 1998; Salinas and Mangabeira Unger, 1999). These and other erstwhile advocates of capitalism in its neoliberal form, while wedded to the notion of globalization in its diverse dimensions, have joined critics in the search for an alternative form of organizing and developing the economy.

The shared concern—not to put too fine a point to it and to exaggerate only slightly—is *not* with globalization per se (globalization or antiglobalization) but the form that the alternative to neoliberalism should take. At stake, as George Soros (in Bordegaray, Soledad and Toti Flores, 2001: 67) notes, is the survival of global capitalism. To prevent its destruction, he further notes, fundamental reforms are required—and not those that have dominated economic and political developments over the past two decades. These neoliberal reforms, designed to take the state out of the process of economic development, to reduce its weight and role (and power); to restore the power of private property and the workings of the free unregulated market, as argued by so many critics in the Antiglobalization Movement, in fact constitute the 'problem'—the source of the crisis that besets the system as a whole. The issue, in other words, is: what form the alternative to neoliberalism should take? What changes, for example, are needed in the financial architecture that supports the international flows of productive and speculative capital? What sort of regime should there be put into place to control the ballooning free flow of speculative and volatile short-term capital? What should be the institutional framework of this new regulatory regime and what connections should there be to the broader institutionality of the system? And within this framework what sort of policies should be pursued and implemented vis-à-vis 'good governance'—and the neoliberal programme of stabilization and structural adjustment and measures? That is, how are we to move beyond and away from the tarnished 'Washington Consensus' identified by Williamson (1990)?

The problem behind these questions was first clearly posed, in 1996, by Robert Kapstein, Director, at the time, of the trilateralist US Council on Foreign Relations.[1] As Kapstein (1996) saw it, the problem was rooted in a tendency of neoliberal or free market capitalism, freed from all constraints and state regulation, towards excessive social inequalities in the distribution of global resources, and income, leading toward social discontent the forces of which could be mobilized politically in ways that are destabilizing for democratic regimes and the system as a whole. However, on the Left of the political spectrum, within the Antiglobalization Movement the concern is not so much with the (potential) political instability as with the moral issue of unfairness or injustice represented by a system in which, as the UNDP, in its 1996 *Human Development Report*, pointed out, some 385 individuals could receive (or appropriate) as much of the world's wealth and income as 1.4 billion of the world's poorest, and the top 10 percent of income 'earners' receives over 40 percent of world income.

Most critics within the Antiglobalization Movement see this maldistribution of wealth and income not as Kapstein sees it, that is, as a political problem; nor as more radical critics on the Left see it—also as a *political* problem but one of 'the North robbing the South' or exploitation (and oppression, to boot)—but as a *moral* issue, that is, as inequitable or unfair, a matter of social justice. In fact, this was by far the dominant theme of the vast majority of 28 conferences, 200 or so seminars and close to 800 workshops that made up the second WSF in 2002. According to Martin Khor, director of the Malaysia-based Third World Network and a keynote speaker at the WSF, among the diverse ways in which countries in the south are 'cheated' are through the predatory operations of speculative capital, the siphoning off of profits by transnational corporations and the protectionist trading measures adopted by the industrialized countries. On these issues also see, among many others, Falk (2000) and the Canadian columnist Naomi Klein (2000), who not only provide a moral critique of the corporate agenda but address directly or indirectly the question of 'democracy' or 'good governance'—holding the corporations accountable, if not to some electorate then at least to a more representative 'global civil society' (Corpwatch, 2001). The securing of good governance is, in fact, the remedy proposed by both the advocates and opponents of 'globalization.'

Despite their concerns about 'globalization' the guardians of the NWO, who meet annually at the WEF, count on the Antiglobalization Movement to provide the broad contours and critical elements, if not the actual design, of a solution to the 'problem' that has beset the 'system'—a problem (ungovernability, lack of good governance) that in some contexts has reached critical proportions. This is one reason why the World Bank and other sponsors of multilateral 'aid' and global development finance, as well as the governments in the G-8 and, more broadly, the

OECD, are prepared to finance the activities of its critics in the antiglobalization movement—up to 80 percent, it has been estimated (Okonski, 2001).

Another reason for this funding is that it provides a mechanism of what could be termed 'controlled opposition and dissent'—to contain the forces of opposition and resistance, and to direct them towards a system-bound solution, a respect of its fundamental institutionality and seeking alternatives 'within,' on the basis of acceptable (because necessary) reforms achieved through dialogue. A case in point is the World Bank's sponsorship, funding and use of many albeit selected nongovernmental organizations as a 'sounding board' of possible opposition to, and changes in, its policies—as a forum for dialogue and critical engagement with dissenting opinion and alternative ideas. Another example of such a mechanism of controlled opposition and informed dissent can be found in the WSF. Held for the first time in January 2001 (WSF I) and again in 2002 (WSF II), in Porto Alegre, Brazil, it represents a major advance in the Antiglobalization Movement—in the tracking, from Seattle to Genoa and Qatar, of policies set and decisions made by the economic and political elite of what Leslie Sklair (1997) among others, define as the 'international capitalist class.'

The WSF provides an organizational context for the opponents of 'globalization' not as such but in its manifest neoliberal form (the world 'as it is')—to discuss, and debate, the alternative ('another world is possible'). These opponents and critics represent a broad array of nongovernmental organizations and a spectrum of ideas that is at once broad and narrow—broad in its agreed-upon principles (social justice and equity, popular participation and democracy, etc.) and diverse proffered solutions (ideas for a new more humane and socially just world) yet narrow in its political scope (liberal, state-led reforms to the existing system impelled by an emerging (and growing) 'global civil society').

In this connection, 'radical' solutions predicated on systemic transformation, viz. its basic institutionality (private property, wage labour, markets, state, etc.), and 'confrontationalist politics' (as opposed to humanizing social reforms and a pacifist politics of nonviolence and dialogue) are explicitly ruled out. This is one reason why with few exceptions (the MST, for one) organizations of the 'Revolutionary Left' (for example, FARC) that call for and espouse such a path towards change were expressly excluded from the WSF-II. In practice, as well as theory, the 'other world' sought by the directorate of the Antiglobalization Movement ('Another World is Possible') is predicated on the principles of a renovated social democracy—on what after Anthony Giddens (1995) has been termed 'the third way.'

In the 1980s, in the context of a widespread restructuring of the state—and its ostensible retreat from the conduct (planning, regulation, etc.) of economic affairs—there was a veritable explosion of NGOs, formed in the concern with not only the provision of basic human needs (shelter, food, health, security, etc.), the major concern of the grassroots organizations of civil society, but with diverse issues ranging from human rights, the environment, the exclusion of women, widespread urban poverty and the lack of economic development or 'democracy.'

The nongovernmental (social or civic) organizations that were formed in this process, and that generally cast themselves into the role of 'critical opposition'—to globalization in its neoliberal form as well as associated government policies—were (and are) widely (and alternatively) perceived to represent either a 'new social movement,' 'grassroots postmodernism,' 'democracy without social movements,' or, more recently, an emerging 'global civil society,' and, as such, the latest expression of a popular or grassroots movement against the structures of economic and political power.

In practice, however, many of these NGOs have been pushed into an effective, if (often) undeclared, partnership with the operating institutions and agents of the system, particularly the World Bank and other agents of 'overseas development assistance' or international finance. In this partnership, the keystone of a strategy designed by the World Bank but soon adopted by virtually all of the multilateral and bilateral institutions as well as the other operating agencies of the undoubtedly unjust global economic system, the NGOs cast themselves (and were cast) into the role of intermediary between the donor agencies and the target of the international development or donor organizations, the poor and their communities.

In effect, these NGOs were converted into the executing agencies of government policy or the donors' agenda. Although widely (and erroneously) identified with, and seen as part of 'the grassroots organizations' of civil society, many of these NGOs could be viewed as 'agents of imperialism,' unconsciously (for the most part) serving the 'interests of capital' just as surely—albeit more obliquely—as the international financial institutions and restructured reformist states in Latin America and elsewhere.

In any case, the NGOs within 'civil society' are positioned somewhere in between those agencies seeking to promote development or initiate projects 'from above and the outside' and those who do so 'from below and within.' In this somewhat ambiguous position they are also part of two seemingly contradictory 'projects.' On the one hand, they are conscious participants in the broad search for an alternative form of 'development' (to neoliberal capitalism) and 'globalization'—to 'improve [the lives] in the world's poorest countries' (Gerry Barr, President of the CCIC, *Reality of Aid*, a semi-annual *Review of ODA*, 2002).

In this search they are part of an emerging global network of individuals and organizations that make up 'civil society'—a complex configuration that like all structures has an influence vastly greater than the sum of its parts and tends to take on a life of its own. On the other hand, this 'global civil society' is also part of something quite different, a more nefarious network of which many of the participant individuals and organizations are not even aware. To understand how this can be, by way of an analogy, consider the parasitic wasp, of the genus *Hymenoepimecis*, which, unknown to the spider that it targets and penetrates, lays its eggs in the spider's abdomen. The spider goes to work oblivious of the growing larvae in its abdomen, which, nourished on the spider's fluids, chemically induces the spider to modify or change its behaviour. In fact, the spider is induced to spin a cocoon web that is useless to the spider but necessary to the larvae. As soon as the spider has finished its work, the larvae consume the spider and hang the pupal cocoon in the special web constructed unwittingly by the spider for the wasp. Nourished on the fluids of the unknowing host organism whose behaviour it has manipulated, the larvae are transformed into wasps capable of stinging their prey in its global reach for sustenance and—to extend our analogy—profits on their invested capital. To complete this analogy, in the process of 'development' or 'globalization' the parasite might not consume its host as long as it does not need to do so; that is, as long as the host organization, a global network of anti-globalization forces, continues to serve as means of manipulating the broader apparatus of civic governance into building the web that serves their purpose and as a means of derailing the forces of opposition to its globalization project—to channel these forces into acceptable forms or, even better, to demobilize them.

Development, Globalization or Imperialism?

Few words have gained as much currency in such a short period of time (since around 1986) as 'Globalization.' Although used in different ways it generally denotes a multifaceted process characterized by increased international flows of capital, goods and services, information and cultural values, and ways of doing things—and an associated 'interconnectedness of social phenomena' (Therborn, 2000) and, at a different level, 'economic integration.' However, in these terms, the term 'globalization' explains little of what is actually going on across the world and, as noted by most contributors to a special theme issue of the *Cambridge Review of International Affairs* (Desai, et al., 2000), serves better as an *ideology*, a means of masking what is going on or to promote a certain desired form of action or thought, than as *theory*, an explanatory device—or even as a means of describing well the dynamics of a supposed paradigmatic (and historical) shift.

For one thing, the term entirely eludes reference to the structures of political and economic power or the practice (foreign policy) in which these structures are imposed by some states, or peoples, on others. The reality of this institutionalized practice is better described, and explained, by use of a term given to Marxist discourse but abandoned by many: 'imperialism.' Oddly enough, this point has been grasped well by some supporters and advocates of neoliberal capitalism than by the many critics of 'corporate capital' or 'neoliberal globalization' in the AGM. In this connection, Martin Wolf (*Financial Times*, February 5, 2002) writes of the 'ritualistic concern with unbridled corporate power' expressed by the critics and protesters at this year's meeting in New York of the World Economic Forum (WEF) as 'paranoid delusion.'

However, in defence of the many critics and opponents of corporate global power it could be said that if it can be demonstrated that these corporations do indeed have command of a large measure of economic, if not political, power, which is used in the (their own) interest (profits), then the concern with corporate global power of critics such as Anderson and Cavanagh, Susan George, Martin Khor, David Korten, and closer to home (Canada, that is), Maud Barlow and Tony

Clarke, among many others, denotes neither paranoia nor delusion. However, Wolf is also correct in pointing out that 'corporations are not unchallenged masters of the universe;' nor are they 'autonomous' agents of the system or 'as powerful as critics claim.' Indeed, '[t]he change . . . seen over the past twenty years . . . is market-driven globalization unleashed, consciously and voluntarily by governments.' Wolf makes an important point here. But where the defenders of 'market-driven globalization' such as Wolf are remiss (and knowingly so) is in failing to point out that some 'governments' indeed do have the will and capacity to unleash such power, and that they do so on the basis of an imperialist agenda. On this point see the discussion in the following two sections.

The Myth of the Powerless State

One of the biggest myths propagated in the double ideological turn towards a discourse on *globalization* and *civil society*[2] is that of a powerless state, hollowed out and stripped off its functions vis-à-vis the economic development process, prostrate before unbridled global corporate power (Weiss, 1998). But in actual fact, the welfare states in the North and the developmentalist states in the South while partially 'dismantled' have been neither weakened nor reduced in terms of its various 'powers;' rather, they have been restructured to better serve the interests of the transnational capitalist class.

In the post World War II period, the nation-state was widely regarded, and generally used, as an instrument for advancing the interests of diverse economic groups and incorporating, by degrees, both the middle and working classes into the development process as well as the political system. In the North (the OECD) this resulted in the evolution of what was dubbed the 'Keynesian' and 'welfare state,' characterized by the growth of the public sector both in the economy and the provision of social services (welfare, education and health); in the South (developing countries in Latin America, Asia and Africa), under different conditions (inter alia, nationalization—of industrial enterprises in strategic sectors) it entailed both this 'development' and the consolidation of the state as an agency of economic development—at the level of ownership, planning and the regulation of private capitalist enterprise.

Nowhere in Latin America was this process as advanced as in Chile, where, under Salvador Allende, the working class managed to reach into the state apparatus, compelling the propertied classes to at least acknowledge and respond to some of its claims and concerns, if not share actually state power. However, with the intrusion of Agusto Pinochet into Chilean politics ('We will teach the world a lesson in democracy') and the institution of a military dictatorship, one of a number fomented by the US in its battle against 'international communism,' Chile also represents a critical turning point in this non-revolutionary (in the case of Chile) development: a counterrevolution in development thought and practice— and (a U-turn) in the relation of capital to labour (Crouch and Pizzorno, 1978; Davis, 1984; Toye, 1987).

In the North, this counterrevolution was part of a series of structural and strategic responses of the capitalist class and the state to a systemic crisis;[3] in the South it involved the arrest, and reversal, of the process of incorporating the working class into the processes of development and political—and the recapture of the state apparatus by the propertied and capitalist classes. This process would take close to two decades to unfold but by the end of the millennium the state, with diverse permutations North and South, had been duly restructured to serve the imperial agenda and interests of capital.

Not only has the state been restructured to advance the agenda and more clearly reflect the interests of transnational capital but also in the case of the United States, it has been reshaped so as to advance the imperialist design, and foreign policy agenda (to reassert its declining hegemony over the whole system), of the new regime. The formation of what could well be termed the 'imperial state' has been years in the making but it took a giant step forward in 2001 after the events of 9/11. As it turns out, these events created conditions not only for the concentration of presidential power over the state apparatus but in the projection of imperial power in various areas of strategic geopolitical interest to the United States.

The 1980s and 1990s saw an erosion of US economic and political power both in the Middle East, Europe, and Asia and, despite gains in Central America, in Latin America. In the Middle East, in a major area of strategic interest viz. the supply of petroleum, both Iran and Iraq have been able to escape efforts of the US to assert its power and trade directly with the European Community. In Europe itself, a series of unilateral actions by the US state had not been able to circumvent the relative ascendancy of the Europeans in the region. Only in the Balkans did US foreign policy and the projection of [naked or well-clothed] political and military power bear fruit. In Latin America most governments had been reduced into submissive client states on the basis, and through the actions, of the functionaries of the World Bank, the IMF and other international organizations dominated by the United States. However, the policies foisted on Latin American states by these institutions, or adopted by servile client regimes, have not only undermined these regimes but have generated formidable forces of opposition and resistance in the most important countries, particularly as relates to the 'strategic triangle' of Colombia, Venezuela and Ecuador that control the access of US TNCs to strategic resources (petroleum and energy, etc.). And the same applies to Argentina and Brazil, and Bolivia, and, in the immediate backyard of the US, Mexico and Central America.

9/11 was by no means responsible for the form that US imperialism has taken in this historic conjuncture. However, it did allow President George W. Bush to launch a brutal offensive against Afghanistan and to extend it into a global war without specific location or end in sight—against 'international terrorism;' and it also provided his regime a considerable supply of political capital for dealing with possible dissent and advancing an imperialist agenda without the encumbrance of democracy. But two of the characteristic features of US imperialism in this conjuncture—unilateralism in decision-making and increased reliance on, and use of, the repressive apparatus—were in response to a general erosion of US economic and political power, especially vis-à-vis the EC, which had been making considerable gains vis-à-vis the United States in regards to Latin America (for example, in the takeover of lucrative state enterprises).

This turn towards unilateralism and militarism—and towards what could be termed 'neomercantilism' (the projection of imperial state power in lieu of reliance on the functionaries of the World Bank, the IMF and other IFIs)—is also (in part) a response to the onset and conditions of an economic crisis 'at home' (in the US), the conditions of which for some time (1995-2000) had been masked by a speculative boomlet. By 9/11, however—certainly by October 7—it was evident that the US economy was in crisis. The signs were serious enough and increasingly evident, exposing cracks that went to the very foundations of the system. In the manufacturing sector, for example, a 'recession' (declines in output) had been officially registered for fifteen consecutive months and continued for another six, up to a New York meeting of the WEF to seek ways of activating the economy by raising the confidence of investors and consumers.

At the level of the national accounts, a trade deficit of US$430 billion (representing 4 percent of GNP in 2000) reflected a growing weakness in the export sector of industrial production while a huge mass of functioning capital (hundreds of billions of dollars) invested in the high-tech industries of fibreoptics, informatics and biotechnology had evaporated. By 2001, only four out of twenty leading informatics firms in the United States had achieved profitability, recovering returns on huge investments. Under such conditions, the US imperial state could hardly afford to provide what was demanded (or rather, timorously requested) of it by its client states and regimes such as Argentina or Colombia—a new Marshall Plan (or, at least, an IMF bailout) that would provide an economic development fund of a sufficient size to activate economies that are everywhere in decline or crisis.

But the US state, under pressure and with the imperative need to activate its own economy, responded instead with a plan to convert the entire region into one free market (LAFTA) and, at a different level, to extend 'Plan Colombia' (to the Andean countries of Ecuador, Peru and Bolivia; Venezuela and the Brazilian Amazon). Deploying some US$40 billion of largely military 'aid'—constituting, after Israel, the largest programme of US 'overseas development assistance'—this imperialist counteroffensive is aimed squarely at the most powerful force of opposition and resistance to US power in the region: the FARC. Officials of the US state, in this geopolitical and strategic context, view the FARC as the largest (and most effective) insurgent force in the region (with an armed force of 20,000 with a projected power in at least 40 percent of the national territory, including in the oil-rich strategic region), to be the major threat to its interests in the region.

Not only does it threaten the stability, even the survival, of the regime in Colombia, an important client state, but, it is calculated, as FARC goes so does the Left (other forces of opposition and resistance in the region, mostly social movements based in the peasantry or indigenous communities). The forces of Leftist opposition to US imperialism in the region would be seriously undermined and demoralized by a victory of the United States and the Colombian state over FARC.

Empire and the State

'*Building an empire is not a tea party*'—Lieutenant Colonel US Marine Corp.

In the debate as to the impact of globalization on the nation-state, a number of theorists such as Antonio Negri (Hardt and Negri, 2000) have argued that the state is becoming, or has become, increasingly a less important factor in both the regulation and management of the global economy and in mobilizing the forces of resistance into (in Gramscian terms) a 'counter-hegemonic force' or (in Negri's own terms) a 'counter-power' based on 'the multitude' within 'civil society.' The state, in this analysis, is no longer a significant actor on the world scene.

To take the case of Argentina: once upon a time the state was a powerful instrument for advancing the national interest; but today state officials, from the president down, are unable to exercise any crucial state powers with regard to the economy—they can execute strategic decisions but do not make them. These are largely made, as it happens, in Washington—by members of the Trilateral Commission or the Council of Foreign Relations, Wall Street, the White House or the Secretary of State, the IMF, the World Bank, etc. This might be somewhat of an exaggeration, but recent (as yet on-going) events in Argentina related to pressures exerted by the IMF on the government—to have it 'face reality' as relates to the requirements of the 'international financial community' (financiers, investors, etc.)—suggest that governments such as Dualde's Argentina in the current context have no room to manoeuvre, or to make any independent decisions, in the setting of macroeconomic policy.

Notwithstanding the erosion of certain powers experienced by many governments and states, the problem in this analysis, and with the conclusions drawn by Negri and others, is at once both a lack of specificity and over-generalization. The fact is while the power of some states might be reduced or circumscribed that of others, in what could be viewed as the centre of the system, has been reinforced. Nothing could be further from the truth than Hardt and Negri's notion of an 'empire without imperialism.' The US State, in particular, is a powerful instrument for the projection of both economic and political—not to speak of military—power. The facts here are too numerous and obvious to warrant discussion (see our discussion above). However, in this connection we can—and do—note that the state is but one of a complex of institutions that serve the interests of, and are controlled by, the transnational capitalist class—the economic, political and other members of the elite that represent the interests of this class.

As to who this elite might be, or the class that it is a part of, the facts are not hard to discern. The US Council on Foreign Relations (CFR), for example, like the WTO, the latest addition to the global power structure of this elite, might make decisions behind closed doors but they do not operate in secret. Nor are the major nodal points of the complicated and broad network of institutions set up and controlled by this class difficult to identify, notwithstanding the fact that many are hidden (and like all structures visible only in their effects). They include various institutional networks and forums that bring together representatives and members of this class that run the TNCs and financial institutions that dominate the world economy. On this point we need but look at and examine the membership of the CFR (Salbuchi, 2000) and regular participants in the WEF.

The entire debate as to whether these TNCs, as argued by Korten and so many others in the Antiglobalization Movement, are free to operate globally over and above the nation-state, whose powers they supposedly exceed, is misplaced. The fact is that these TNCs do not roam the world at will, free from state control and regulation; they generally have their home-base and decision-making centres in the industrially advanced or 'developed' societies at the centre of the system—the G-8—and, to a considerable extent, are still subject to government control and regulation. The vast majority of the top TNCs (*Financial Times*' or *Forbes*' Top 100) are located in the United States (49 percent), the European Community (37 percent) or to a lesser degree, Japan (9 percent). The leading directors and CEOs of these TNCs are integrated into a network of institutions, including the US imperial state, controlled by the transnational capitalist class, whose members are also largely located in these societies.

In this context, the US State still serves as the major source of imperial power, particularly in its political and military dimensions but also economic. It is the US State that backstops the institutions of economic power, paving the way for the operation of these institutions and creating the facilitating conditions. For example, the IMF might well be the force behind the policies adopted by virtually every government in Latin America but behind the IMF and other such international organizations can be found the power of the imperial state system, particularly the US. It is also this power that lies behind the imposition of tariffs and other free trade barriers that protect US capital in its home market operations from foreign competition.

It is the US State that has levied a 27 percent import duty on Canadian lumber. It is the US State that levies prohibitive duties on the import of steel and other goods and services from Europe, Asia and Latin America whenever producers in these countries 'threaten' the interests of the United States—that is, out-perform uncompetitive US producers on the domestic market. In short, there is no question of an 'empire without imperialism.' Any such intellectual construction is both misleading and politically dangerous, leading minimally to a failure to understand the forces at play in the so-called globalization process.

The Contradictions of Imperialism: From Neoliberalism to Neomercantilism

In the turn towards what has been termed the 'short twentieth century' (1917-1989) Lenin identified five structural features of imperialism, regarded not as an adjunct to but as the most advanced phase of capitalist development at the time.

One of these features was the exchange of raw materials produced in the non-capitalist world in exchange for goods manufactured in a process of capitalist development—what would become 'the old imperialism.' In the 1970s, however, history took a new turn in the context of, and response to, a deep systemic crisis.

As in Lenin's time, at a critical conjuncture of modernization, we can at this point identify five major structural features of capitalist development arising out of diverse strategic responses made to this crisis. The first is what has been described alternatively as a New International Division of labour (Fröebel, et al., 1980) and a 'Second Industrial Divide' (Piore and Sabel, 1984), a structure arising out of strategic decisions of the TNCs to relocate their labour intensive operations closer towards sources of cheaper labour. A second feature of the 'new imperialism' is a shift in, or transformation of, the dominant mode of regulating labour at the point of production—from Fordism to Postfordism (Boyer, 1989; Lipietz, 1982, 1987). A third feature is based on a process of productive transformation and technological conversion, characterized by the evolution of new production technologies as well as the shedding of vast numbers of workers, replenishing thereby what Marx had termed the 'industrial reserve army'—a huge and growing reserve of surplus labour. A fourth feature is a major change in the structure formed by the relation of capital to labour. The defining characteristic feature of this new structure is a qualitative shift in labour's participation in the process of economic production—in its share of income and value added to production.

The effects of this shift—the compression and dispersal of wages, a fall in their real value and a decline in the purchasing power and consumption capacity of workers—have been well documented and analyzed, particularly in regards to Latin America (see, for example, Veltmeyer, 1999). As with the associated restructuring of the labour market they generally relate to conditions of 'social exclusion' that can be directly traced back to a process of class struggle—the assault of the capitalist class on labour (Gazier, 1996; Paugam, 1996). The fifth characteristic feature of the new imperialism, defined as Lenin did, that is, not in strategic or political but in structural terms, is precisely a tendency towards globalization and the integration of country after country into an extended capitalist economy.

Although often defined in 'structural' terms imperialism in any form entails a relation of domination between states at the 'centre' of the system and those on its 'periphery.' And the structure of this relation is maintained by a projection of political—and military—power, concentrated in the imperial state system, which, in the current context, is made up of the state apparatus of the United States and the major 'powers' in the European Community.

Notwithstanding the theorizing of Hardt and Negri about the end of imperialism, on the one hand, and, on the other, the ideology of globalization, the *reality* of this power structure is evident and not just in its effects. However, just as evident is the fact that the system as a whole is in trouble, rift by internal contradictions. First, in the global workings of this system, more and more direct producers are being separated from their means of social production. At the same time, large numbers of workers are subjected to diverse conditions of 'exploitation' or 'social exclusion'—unemployment, precarious forms of labour and employment, and low income. Under these and other such conditions the process of capital accumulation, although extended on a global scale, is reaching its structural—and political—limits. Although it is sustained by the productive capacity of the leading capitalist enterprises and established markets at the centre of the system as well as a number of 'emerging markets,' the capital accumulation process is, at the same time, undermined by the growth of large sectors of the world population without any productive capacity or insufficient purchasing power. As we have noted, there are signs that this problem is generating cracks in the very foundation of the system. And, at the political level, it is giving rise to forces of opposition and resistance that are being mobilized against the system and its supports. In all of the leading countries on the Latin American periphery of the US Empire both the status quo and the system itself are under attack.

The current US imperial worldwide offensive, launched in the wake of 9/11, faces two types of contradictions with both conjunctural and structural features. First, in regard to the 'war against international terrorism' the military build-up and campaign against Afghanistan, the Al-Qaeda network, Iraq (and possibly Iran, the other threat to US interests in the Gulf region); and, in Latin America, against the FARC and other forces of subversion ('narcotrafficking,' 'terrorism,' etc.) and opposition to US interests, each projection of military power has resulted in a 'blowback' (Chalmers, 2000) and over the medium and long-term is very costly; and these costs of necessity will escalate. In this regard, the officials of the US imperial state have not learnt an elemental historical lesson—that the military costs of defending the empire sooner or later will undermine, and irrevocably damage, the imperial economy that it is designed to protect. In this connection, it might be expected that an expansion of the military apparatus would dynamize an important sector of the economy—the industrial enterprises that service this apparatus.

However, this idea is misplaced. The costs of 'defending the empire'—military expansion in a time of deepening economic recession, both locally and worldwide. Military Keynianism—increased war spending—has not and will not reverse the current recession, as few sectors of the economy are affected and the industries such as aerospace that could receive some economic stimulus are hard hit by the recession in the civilian airline market. In addition, the military apparatus of the imperial state is not a cost-efficient service provider, far from it. Expenditures on this apparatus far exceed the immediate benefits to the US-based corporations and has not reversed the tendency towards declining rate of profits or opened up new markets, particularly in the regions of maximum military engagement. Military intervention tends to expand the scale and scope of colonization without increasing returns to capital. Imperial wars tend to undermine non-speculative capitalist investment, even as it symbolically assures overseas investors.

As in Central America, the Balkans and now in Afghanistan and Colombia, the United States is more interested in destroying adversaries and establishing client regimes than in large-scale, long-term investments in 'economic reconstruction.' After high military spending for conquest, budget priorities have shifted to subsidizing US-based corporations, and lowering taxes for the wealthy: there can be no more 'Marshall Plans.' The US State can no longer afford this possibly successful resolution of economic problems generated by imperial policies in the subjugated areas of 'pre-modern states.' Instead, Washington leaves it to its allies in Europe and Japan to 'clean up the human wreckage' left in the wake of US military actions. Post-war reconstruction does not intimidate possible adversaries; B-52 carpet-bombing does.

Any military victory in the present conjuncture leaves unsettled the consolidation of a pro-imperial client regime. Just as the United States financed and armed the Islamic fundamentalists in their war against the secular nationalist Afghan regime in the 1980s and then withdrew, leading to the ascendancy of the anti-western Taliban regime, last year's 'victory' and subsequent withdrawal is likely to have similar results within the next decade. The gap between the high war-making capacity of the imperial state and its incapacity to revitalize the economies of the conquered nations is a major contradiction.

Another even more serious contradiction is found in the aggressive effort to impose neoliberal regimes and policies when the export markets that they were designed to service are collapsing and external flows of capital are drying up. In this connection, the recession in the United States, Japan and the EU has severely damaged the most loyal and subservient neoliberal client-states, particularly in Latin America. The prices of the exports that drive the neoliberal regimes in the region have fallen and in some cases collapsed: exports of coffee, petrol, metals, sugar, as well as textiles, clothes and other goods manufactured in the 'free trade zones' have suffered from sharp drops in prices and glutted markets. The US as an imperial power has responded to this by pressing for greater 'liberalism' (free markets) in the South while raising protective tariffs at home and increasing subsidies for exports.

In this connection, tariffs in the Northern imperial countries on imports from the South are four times higher than those on imports from other imperial countries (World Bank, 2002). At the same time (2000, that is) support for agricultural TNCs in the imperial countries was $245 billion in 2000 (*Financial Times*, Nov. 21, 2001: 13). In May 2002 the Bush administration announced US$73 billion of subsidies to the agricultural sector. As the World Bank (2002: 7) has pointed out, with regard to these and such protections against the forces of the world market, 'the share of subsidized exports has even increased [over the past decade] for many products of export interest to developing countries.'

In effect, the neoliberal doctrine of the 'old imperialism' is giving way to the neomercantilist practice of the 'new imperialism.' State policies dictate a structure of economic exchanges and delimit the role of the market—all to the benefit of the imperial economy. However, the highly restrictive nature of neomercantilist policies tends to polarize the economy between local producers and the imperial state-backed monopolies. While the erosion and destruction of domestic markets under neoliberal policies marginalize large sectors of the economically active population, the collapse of overseas markets negatively affects 'neoliberal' export sectors and weakens the position of the bourgeoisie in the client states of the empire. In this situation, imperial free market policies have threatened to 'kill the goose that lays the golden eggs'—creating conditions that make it difficult, if not impossible, for the imperial economy to generate needed 'resource flows'—in the form of interest payments on loans, profit remittances on direct investments, royalty and license fee payments, dividends on portfolio investments, and 'unequal exchange' as well as trade imbalances (Petras and Veltmeyer, 2001).

In addition to undermining the economies of its client states, the highly visible role of the imperial state in imposing what amounts to a neomercantilist system is politicizing the growing army of unemployed and poorly paid workers, peasants and public employees. Take, for example, the case of Argentina, one of the most compliant clients of the United States throughout the 1990s. The collapse of both overseas and domestic markets over the past four years has meant less foreign exchange to service foreign debts. In December of 2001, in the throes of the worst economic and political crisis in its history and days after a massive social 'upheaval' of the working and middle classes, the newly formed government announced that it could not and would not service its foreign debt obligations. Fewer exports have also meant a lower capacity to import essential foodstuffs and capital goods to sustain production. Thus the entire export and free market strategy upon which the whole imperial edifice in Latin America is built has been undermined. Unable to import, countries like Argentina will be forced to produce locally or do without—and revert to a domestic market that has been opened up to the forces of 'globalization.'

However, the definitive rupture with the export-oriented strategy of neoliberal capitalist development and subordination to empire will not come about because of internal contradictions: it requires political intervention. What form shall this intervention take? How has the 'system' responded to these (structural) contradictions and (political) challenges? Indications are that rather than, as Hardt and Negri would have it—the disappearance of imperialism—it is leading to what some have termed its 'renaissance,' a new form, described by some (Robert Cooper, for example) as 'postmodern,' and by others (the author, as it happens) as 'neomercantilism.'

On the New Imperialism in the Postmodern Era—Empire Without Imperialism?

> . . . in dealing with more old-fashioned kinds of states outside the postmodern
> continent of Europe [and North America] we need to revert to the rougher methods
> of an earlier era—force, pre-emptive attack, deception, whatever is necessary to
> deal with those who still live in the nineteenth century world of every state for
> itself [in the pre-modern world of developing countries]. Among ourselves
> [postmodern states] we keep the law but . . . in the jungle we must also use the laws
> of the jungle (Robert Cooper, Foreign Policy Advisor of Tony Blair, 2000b: 7).

The need for a new form of 'liberal' imperialism has been placed on the agenda on both sides of the Atlantic that separates the postmodern states of Europe and

North America. While the Left is caught up and lost in the struggle for and against globalization, the Right is advancing its project to redesign and restore imperialism. Very few have stated the problem as forthrightly and clearly as Robert Cooper and, on the other side of the Atlantic, the journalist Martin Wolf (*Financial Times*, Oct. 10, 2001: 13) who also sees the need for a 'new' more direct form of 'imperialism' that does not hesitate to use force when and where necessary. In Wolf's words, 'To tackle the challenge of the failed state [in an impoverished Third World] what is needed is not pious aspirations but an honest and organized coercive force.'[4]

For the trilateralists in the foreign CFR and elsewhere (World Bank, other IFIs and Washington-based Foundations such as the Heritage Foundation) that constituted the Washington Consensus the issue is not imperialism but a better management of the forces of globalization, even if it means a new form of regulating global movements of capital or capital controls (Stiglitz, 1998; Wade and Veneroso, 1998). This is, in fact, the essence of the globalization project, both in its neoliberal and alternative forms. However, for Cooper and others searching for a new post-Washington Consensus what is required is a new form of imperialism that is not circumscribed by 'humanitarian interventionism'—the 'theology of aid for countries seeking to insert themselves into the global economy' (Cooper, 2002b).

This form of 'multilateral imperialism,' to date led and protagonized by the World Bank and the other members of the 'international financial community,' according to Cooper (2002b), is predicated on the enlightened ('humanitarian') 'interference' of the international organizations and states that make up the world of 'postmodern states' (the OECD). Such interference has been standard procedure as of the mid 1980s under the globalization project but the rationale for it has been restated in the clearest possible terms by MIT economists Rudiger Dornbusch and Ricardo Caballero in the context of recent developments in Argentina. However, Cooper argues, it is clear enough that the multi- or trilateral institutions have been unable to manage the forces of 'globalization'—to establish the conditions of 'good governance' (governability) and thereby prevent the outbreak or to control the forces of resistance and opposition generated by the 'cycle of poverty, instability and violence' that characterize the 'pre-modern states' (in the developing world of failed and weak states). 'If there were other ways of resolving the problem,' (the threat presented by these conditions to the citizens and states [members] of the postmodern and modern world, Cooper notes, the 'renaissance of imperialism' would not have been necessary.

This is clear enough. But it is also clear that 'overseas development assistance' has not 'born fruit' and all other efforts to improve conditions for the countries in the pre-modern world of backward states have failed. As a result, Cooper adds, what is needed is a new form of 'colonialism' and an imperialism that does not hesitate to use force—to project power in political and economic forms and military if and where needed—but a force that is 'acceptable to all, both weak and strong' ('the weak need the strong and the strong need order'); that rests, in other words, on 'voluntary acceptance' or a new consensus (the consent of the governed)—or, in Hardt and Negri's (2000) abstracted conception of the search for hegemony, an 'empire without imperialism.' Cooper, in this context, notes that order or stability generally depends on a balance of power—a balance in the 'power of aggression'—but that this balance is rare; states in the pre-modern world are generally weak, having lost legitimacy and/or their 'monopoly in the legitimate use of force.'

In this situation, the state is unable to contain the forces of opposition among 'non-state actors' which threaten not only stability in these countries but in 'the postmodern world,' which, in this circumstance,' have the right, and the need, to react—to 'defend' themselves. Thus, the US invasion of Afghanistan, for example. And, for another, the war against 'subversion' in Colombia and elsewhere.

Development, Democracy and the Empire

In the 1980s, the idea of democracy was advanced in the form of (i) the return to power of civilian elected and constitutional regimes, and the restoration of an electoral mechanism in the transition from one regime to another; (ii) the decentralization of government of services and some powers; and (iii) the strengthening of civil society within the framework of government initiated political and social reforms (Reilley, 1995). In the 1990s, however, in Latin America, the idea of democracy was assumed by the popular movement, initiating 'from below' or within 'civil society,' on the basis and in the form of social movements and popular or direct (as opposed to liberal and representative) democracy.

At the base of these grassroots social movements are urban communities, citizens groups or neighbourhood associations, or, in the rural sector, indigenous communities of peasant farmers. In general these organizations tend to be profoundly detached from what is perceived to be the 'old politics'—a phenomenon mistakenly theorized in diverse contexts as an abandonment of the search for political power and the struggle against the holders of political power (see, for example, Benasayag and Sztulwark, 2000; Holloway, 2001; Negri, 2001).

Thus, the EZLN has been conceptualized as 'the first postmodern movement in history' (Burbach, 1994). And in similar terms Esteva and Prakash (1998), among others (Escobar and Alvarez, 1992) write of Latin American 'new' social movements in terms of 'grassroots postmodernism.' There is an element of truth that is misconstrued in these conceptions: the movements that they seek to describe are characterized by an almost fatal distrust of [the old] 'politics,' politicians and their 'parties.'

Democracy versus Authoritarianism—Hegemony, Terror and Intimidation

What defines the new imperialism in its most recent offensives is not only unilateralism in the projection of state power but an increased use of its repressive apparatus with an aggressive reliance on military force in 'defence' of the empire. However, naked power is always destabilizing. To secure the conditions of order, which, Cooper pointed out, are needed by the powerful, a degree of consensus or hegemony is also needed, and—in terms analyzed by Noam Chomsky—duly manufactured. Until recently (viz. The War against International Terrorism), such a consensus was generally sought on the basis, and in terms of, a battle of 'democracy' against 'international communism.' At issue in this ideological struggle was the idea of 'democracy'—that decision-making power is exercised, directly or indirectly, by 'the people;' that the holders of power represent the people and are held accountable to them; and that politics take the form of dialogue and negotiation of conflicting interests rather than violent confrontation—channelling of grievances and demands through forms of 'peaceful and civil struggle' (UNRISD, 2000).[5] Alternatively, Bultman and colleagues (1995) write of the emergence in Latin America of 'democracy without a social movement.'

In this context, it was even asserted and argued (by ideologues and scholars alike), despite historical evidence to the contrary, that democracy and capitalism in the (neoliberal) form of private enterprise and the free market were intrinsically connected; that the marriage between free markets (capitalism, economic liberalism) and free elections (democracy, political liberalism) was not one of convenience or historic accident but organic (Dominguez and Lowenthal, 1996).

Thus, liberal scholars, both political scientists and economists, have theorized that the institutionalization of democracy (political liberalization) would create the necessary or facilitating conditions of capitalist development (political liberalization) or vice versa. Thus, at the level of practice, within the context of euro American imperialism in the post Second World War, the iron fist of armed force and political repression has often been cloaked with the idea of democracy and a concern for associated 'human rights.' However, democracy in this (liberal) form has proven to be a two-edged sword. As Samuel Huntington, a well-known but best forgotten conservative but trilateralist political scientist and author of *The Clash of Civilizations*, recognized as early as 1974, the year to which the capitalist counteroffensive (and the conservative counterrevolution in development theory and practice) can be traced, that democracy provides conditions under which forces of opposition and resistance can expand and prosper—and be mobilized against the system (Huntington, et al., 1975).

The issue, from Huntington's view, was the generation of pressures and demands for inclusion that exceeded the institutional capacity of the system and that cannot be accommodated or contained. Thus, in the shared context of conditions under which the globalization project was launched and policies of structural adjustment were implemented, a redemocratization process in Latin America and elsewhere in the Third World[6] generated widespread forces of opposition to, and resistance against, the projects of globalization and imperialism.

How have the guardians of economic and political order responded to the threat of organized and mobilized forces of resistance and opposition? The record here is clear, particularly as relates to the current regime headed by

George W. Bush. Whenever and wherever the institution of democracy has proven to be dysfunctional for the system—in securing hegemony—it is jettisoned.

Thus, in the 1960s and 1970s the state either invaded, otherwise intervened or sponsored military coups against one democratically elected constitutional regime in Latin America after another. In this projection of political power a democratic façade was nevertheless maintained (for example, President Johnson's congratulation of the Brazilian military in 1964, hours after their coup against the democratically elected nationalist Goulart regime, for 'restoring democracy'). However, where and when necessary this façade is dropped, as, for example, it was in recent efforts of the US state to orchestrate a civilian-military coup against the democratically elected Chavez regime in Venezuela.

The coup failed largely as a result of a mass popular uprising in support of Chavez who had been removed from power and held in detention, prior to being forced to leave the country. But a significant feature of the dynamics preceding and surrounding the coup was the behaviour and position of the US administration. The coup was without doubt a rupture of the democratic institutionality to which the US state pays rhetorical homage and which the OAS is committed to protect. But it is just as clear that the US itself engineered the *coup* attempt through the agency of a right-wing coalition of groups and organizations, the machinations of its ambassador and other US officials, and a part of Venezuela's Armed Forces. However, the United States was totally isolated within the OAS in refusing to see the attempted coup as a rupture with democracy, and in viewing Chavez as the author of his own misfortune.

Despite the lies and counter images projected by both the mass media inside Venezuela, a major source of anti-government agitation, and the US media, generally an instrument of imperial doublespeak, it was transparently clear that the US state sponsored this as so many other antidemocratic actions in the region and was its architect. No one outside the White House, and likely no one inside, believed for a moment in the weak and failed efforts of the US state to put a democratic gloss on the attempted military coup in Venezuela. As with the lukewarm and failed efforts of George W. Bush to manufacture popular or political consent for its imperialist project, viz. the projection of military power in the form of a fight against the 'axis of evil,' this particular effort to hide the relations of power and to obfuscate the issues involved did not work. No one believes in it.

Atilio Borón, a well-known Argentine political sociologist, among other analysts, has drawn the not surprising but important conclusion from this and other such failures that 'US imperialism might be powerful but not omnipotent.' The matter is not only of the limits of political and military power but of the capacity of the US imperial state to secure 'hegemony' over the system. In this regard, it is clear enough that despite support from the mass media for its anti-terrorist campaign the US imperial state is moving towards a serious legitimation crisis, which perhaps helps explain the lack of apparent concern, in Bush's administration of the empire, to maintain a democratic façade for his policies.[7] An appeal to respect for human rights and democracy is simply no longer functional or necessary in the new world order called for by Bush the elder and being brought about by Bush junior.

Antiglobalization or Anti-imperialism?

Despite its global extension and its ability to mobilize forces of resistance against, and opposition to, the agenda (and neoliberal programme) of global corporate capital the Antiglobalization Movement is very limited in its capacity to derail the system—or to induce the radical reforms that would be needed to implement its agenda of 'creating another (that is, better) world—of social justice, greater equity and more democracy.' Adam Morton, a political scientist from Wales, in chapter 8 interprets this situation metaphorically by questioning whether the Antiglobalization Movement can best be viewed as a 'juggernaut' ('a vehicle on an inexorable path toward consolidating particular social, political and economic priorities') or as a 'jalopy' ('whose direction is openly contested and that may even be subject to breakdown') and, as such, a 'presumptuous pebble' (Singer, 1999).

However, in realistic rather than metaphorical terms, the AGM can better be viewed as a vehicle that is not going anywhere fast and will likely stall or be derailed rather than overpower the globalization project. The major reasons for this include the fact that the theorists and activists of the Antiglobalization Movement misconstrue the nature or scope of the problem (fail to see it as systemic) and are unwilling to directly confront the formidable forces mobilized in support of the globalization project with the equally (if potential) formidable forces of opposition and resistance at the disposal of this project. It is not recognized that at issue is a class war waged on a global scale in diverse theatres and with a growing concentration of armed force—and all of the instrumentalities of an imperial state in control of the enemy.

The fact is, the globalization project is part of an ideological counteroffensive in a class war that has been waged by capital against labour at different levels and in different forms since the early 1970s. A politics of peaceful resistance, dialogue and partnerships, and other forms of 'civil' responses will not change the structure of the system or emancipate working people.

The only way to bring about the end and transformation of the capitalist system is to directly confront the structure of political, economic and military power and to mobilize the forces of resistance and opposition against this structure. What is needed is not an antiglobalization but an anti-imperialist movement—the mobilization of forces of opposition and resistance against capitalism in its current form; to exploit the opportunities made available by the contradictions of this system. The point is that any given structure—and the structure of the new imperialism no less—provides not only challenges and 'constraints' but both opportunities and resources for effective action. This is perhaps the one useful insight achieved by Anthony Giddens (1990), the architect of Tony Blair's 'third way' towards political change, in his various theoretical constructions—his 'restructuration' theory and that of the consequences of 'modernity.'

Organizing for Change: Opportunities for the Left within the Empire

US imperialism in its recent and current offensives and counteroffensives is far from omnipotent and, as we have noted, is fraught with contradictions that are generating forces of opposition and resistance.

In terms of these 'contradictions,' what then are the organizational forms of possible or effective opposition and resistance against the US counteroffensive in the current context of neoliberal capitalist development and neoimperialism—in the conjuncture of the general and specific conditions of the situation in which people in Latin America find themselves today? Unfortunately, several decades of sociological and political studies into the dynamics of these social movements have yielded little information and fewer ideas.[8] Nevertheless, a review of these movements suggests that they have been formed in three distinct but overlapping 'waves' of organized resistance.

The first wave hit Latin America in the late 1970s and the early to mid 1980s in the context of a region-wide debt crisis, a redemocratization process and the implementation of the 'new economic model' of macroeconomic stabilization and structural adjustment measures. It took the form of what appeared to some as a 'new social movement' that brought onto the centre stage of resistance and opposition new 'social actors' in the urban areas (Assies, 1990; Calderón, 1995; Calderón and Jelín, 1987; Castells, 1983; Slater, 1985).

The social or civic organizations at the base of these movements were formed around concern over a wide range of specific issues that ranged from day to day survival and the predations of military dictatorship to respect for human rights, the environment and the situation of women, as well as the search for human dignity and social or cultural 'identity' (Calderón, 1995; Escobar and Alvarez, 1992; Esteva and Prakash, 1998; Scott, 1990). It involved both grassroots, community-based and civic organizations that sought not social transformation but redress of a wide range of specific concerns and the expansion of local spaces within the existing structure—a direct rather than liberal form of democracy.

These so-called 'new social movements' dominated the urban landscape in the late 1980s but the social forces that they had mobilized by and large had dissipated at the turn of the next decade. Only recently, have some analysts detected their reappearance in the popular assemblies and social movements formed by diverse neighbourhood associations and groups of unemployed workers in the poor *barrios* of Buenos Aires and other urban centres in Argentina. According to the theorists of this sociopolitical 'development'—a group of sociologists, political scientists and philosophers with a 'postmodernist, non- or poststructuralist optic—these movements are 'new' in that are totally disenchanted with 'politics as practiced to date (*¡Que se Vayan Todos!*) and that in their practice they seek a new way of 'doing politics,' not in the pursuit of power but, on the contrary, a 'counterpower' (Benasayag and Sztulwark, 2000; Colectivo de Situaciones, 2000; Holloway, 2001; Negri, 2000).

A second wave of more antisystemic movements was formed by associations of peasant producers and indigenous communities in the late 1980s. In the 1990s, however, these peasant-based—and led—sociopolitical movements took their struggle to the cities and urban centres, mobilizing, in the process, other forces of opposition and resistance to both government policy and the broader system behind it.

One of the earliest movements established in this process is the Landless Rural Workers Movement (MST) in Brazil. Although currently facing a serious counteroffensive by the government, the MST has managed to maintain one of the most dynamic social movements in Latin America, occupying and settling on the land in the process of fifteen years of struggle and direct action, upwards of 400,000 families since 1995; and organizing agricultural production on this land 'expropriated' from its owners in the landed oligarchy.

Other such sociopolitical organizations with both its social based and leadership in the peasantry or indigenous communities in the rural society include: the Confederación Nacional Indígena de Ecuador (CONAIE); the EZLN; the Confederación Nacional Campesino de Paraguay; the Cocaleros of Bolivia; and, to some extent, the FARC, which, as noted above, unlike the other 'new peasant sociopolitical movements' formed in this second wave, was formed much earlier—in the 1960s.

As of the mid 1990s it has been possible to identify the emergence of a third wave of sociopolitical movements formed in opposition to both government policies and against the 'system.' In this case, the social base of the movement is found in the urban working class, restructured under conditions of 'productive transformation' (technological conversion) and structural adjustments in government policy under the 'new economic model.' The working class, formed in this process by and large, and increasingly, is located not in factories and plants in diverse centres of industrial production; nor in government offices, but in the streets under conditions of marginality (precarious forms of employment), social exclusion, unemployment, low income and poverty. Nowhere has this process advanced to the point that it has in Argentina, with an uninterrupted and deepening crisis in production that has already lasted four years, rates of unemployment that exceed 20 percent in official statistics—in many areas from 30 to 60 percent—and over half of the population subsisting on incomes below conservatively defined poverty lines.

In response to the objectively defined and experienced conditions of the failed attempts by the government to insert the national economy into the process of 'globalization,' to position itself advantageously in the NWO, a broad array of workers, both unemployed and unemployed, have taken their antigovernment and antisystemic struggle into the streets, with a combination of strikes, plant takeovers, demonstrations and marches on government buildings, and, most importantly, the tactic of *cortas de ruta*—cutting off, with barricades and pickets (piquetes), road and highway access. In 1997, under conditions of an impending production crisis there were on average eleven 'cortas de ruta' or 'piquetes' a month. By 1999 this number had doubled while in 2002 it climbed to an estimated 70 or so a month.

The *piqueteros* have clearly established themselves as a beachhead at the crest of a new wave of Leftist opposition and sociopolitical movements directed against government policies and against the system (US imperialism), which they see to be behind it. Whether this movement can advance on the rising tide of this wave, or whether the social forces of opposition that it has mobilized will once more be dissipated in the ebb and flow of struggle remains to be seen. The organizational and political challenges involved are considerable, perhaps unsurmountable. But they certainly will not be surmounted in the new politics of anti-power, dissolving as it does in thought the political dynamics of the existing power structure. At the same time, there is little to no doubt that the new social movements formed in the second and third 'wave' of Leftist or antisystemic opposition have greater mobilizing capacity and political potential than the 'juggernaut' (or 'jalopy') of the Anti-Globalization Movement. The struggle against imperialism needs of necessity take an anti-imperialist form.

Conclusion

Globalization, often presented as an irresistible force, is a scam. For one thing, it is designed as an ideology and as such, does not explain 'what is going on;' rather, it serves to direct action towards an end desired by the apologists, and supporters, of the existing system. In this connection, the Antiglobalization Movement, notwithstanding its considerable capacity to mobilize intellectual and political forces of opposition and resistance, in political terms is very limited. Much more significant in these terms are the sociopolitical movements being formed in the countryside and urban centres of Latin America and elsewhere on the 'periphery' of the world capitalist system. Imperial policies, in fact, are undermining and weakening the middle classes in these societies and polarizing them between the propertied and the working classes—what Hardt and Negri choose to term 'the multitude'—and between the forces of reaction and sociopolitical movements for revolutionary change. Some of these movements are community-based or formed by grassroots forms of organization. However, the most significant of these movements have to be understood in class terms: as involved in a class war, a struggle that is waged worldwide, in diverse contexts, between capital and labour—between member organizations and individuals of the capitalist class and the mass of direct producers and workers that make up the bulk of the world's economically active population.

To gauge the weight and dynamism of the forces for evolutionary or revolutionary change, that is, for social or systemic transformation, and to appreciate what these forces are up against, the notion of 'globalization' should be abandoned. More useful in this connection is to conceive of world developments in terms of 'neoimperialism,' a project designed and put into effect by agents of the system. In the projection of imperial power the international capitalist class has at its disposal diverse instruments and institutions, most notably the state apparatus in the United States and the EC, and to some extent, Japan. The United States is the major power within this system, both in economic and political, as well as military, terms. Notwithstanding evidence of a continuing interimperialist rivalry, and of the manifest difficulties experienced by the US in the search for 'good governance' and hegemony, US imperialism remains a powerful force.

But US imperialism is by no means omnipotent. Indeed, the entire system is rift by a series of contradictory developments that provide the Left both space and 'opportunities' for successful political intervention. The question is whether the Left is positioned to take advantage of these opportunities or what form political organization and action should take? The answer to this question is not clear but this is a major challenge for the Left—to assess, and help mobilize, the available forces for change. To this end, the Left needs to escape 'the old politics' of sectarian partisanship in the struggle for political power without, at the same time, succumbing to the virus of postmodernism or otherwise falling in the trap of the 'new politics'—the struggle for democracy and the politics of identity. At issue are class power and systemic transformation.

Notes

1 The Council on Foreign Relations, and its executive Trilateral Commission, constitutes, it could be argued (Salbuchi, 2000), the 'brain of the world,' 'the hidden side of globalization.' It is composed of the biggest makers and shakers of US foreign policy. But it also part of a broader network that involves an international 'advisory board' that includes Canada's (now Britain's) Conrad Black and Muhammad Yunus, founder of the Graneen Bank. Also part of this network is an 'International Crisis Group' that includes Graca Machel, Managing Director of Mozambique's Foundation for Community Development and Carlos Salinas de Gortari, ex-President of Mexico, as well as George Soros, also a key member of the Davos-based WEF.

2 On the parallel (to globalization) 'civil society' discourse, see Howell and Pearce (2001). In the 1990s, both bilateral and multilateral organizations of 'overseas development assistance' turned away from the 'third sector' discourse towards one based on the 'strengthening civil society.' As Mitlin (1998) points out, this shift has to do with a new agenda of incorporating the 'private sector' into the development process. For a critical perspective on this agenda see Karliner (1999).

3 There are a number of diverse interpretations of this crisis, which, by most accounts was evidenced in a slowdown of system-wide economic activity, a drop in productivity growth, conditions of a 'profit crunch' and a systemic tendency towards a fall in for average profits (Marglin and Schor, 1990).

4 Another exponent of the need for a new imperialism is the *Washington Post* editorial writer and columnist Sebastian Mallaby, who notes that in the past whenever a great power was threatened by some power vacuum in some corner of the world that this power had at its disposal diverse weapons—an 'imperial solution.' But, he adds, since the Second World War 'well-ordered' societies (in the North) out of political weakness have refused to 'impose its own institutions.' Nevertheless, he further adds, in today's

world of increasingly 'repulsive and prolonged wars' this attitude of self-restraint is increasingly more difficult to sustain.

5 Thus also the notion that democracies do not go to war—that conditions of war and the violent settling of social conflicts—have been banished in democratic regimes.

6 This process took the form of the decentralization of government; the return to state power of civilian constitutional regimes; and the strengthening of 'civil society.' On the complex dynamics of this process in the Latin American context see Veltmeyer and Petras (1997).

7 The attempted coup against the democratically elected Chavez regime in Venezuela is a clear indication of this. Given the alacrity with which the IMF expressed its support for the short-lived government instituted by the coup-makers, and the absence of any condemnation on the part of the Bush administration, it is, according to a number of analysts in the region (Luzani, 2002: 2), 'the first sign of a change in US doctrine . . . [raising the spectre of] a return to the nightmare of coups in the region.' Bruce Bagley, Director of Graduate Studies at the University of Miami, has expressed a similar concern, noting that the Bush administration has 'returned once more to the unacceptable . . . tactics [designed to] overthrow foreign governments [without regard to democratic norms and procedures]' (*Clarin*, Suplemento 'Zona,' April 21: 2).

8 There is, in fact, a fairly large literature on the 'new' social movements in Latin America's urban and rural landscape (see, inter alia, Foweraker, 1995; Assies, 1990). But as noted by Munck (1997) in this literature there is a dearth of comparative analysis—at best a series of country case studies and theoretical debates that by and large appears to be disconnected from these studies; that is, they tend to be descriptive and not analyzed within the various theoretical frameworks at issue in these debates.

Conclusion

After several decades of rapid growth and development in the post-World War II period—what French historians have dubbed 'the thirty glorious years' (and economic historians more generally as 'the golden age of capitalism')—the world economic order was in disarray and the underlying system in crisis. The first cracks in the foundation of this system were manifest as early as the late 1960s, in the wake of 1968, which in retrospect can be viewed as the last offensive of labour in its struggle for higher wages and better working conditions (Crouch and Pizzorni, 1978). However, by 1974, in conditions of a system-wide production crisis, manifest in a slowdown in productivity growth, a fall in profits on invested capital and a general decline in the rate of economic growth, capital struck back.

The subsequent thirty years can be viewed as a period of crisis and restructuring—diverse efforts to find a way out of the crisis that besets the capitalist system in its global projection. Major 'developments' in this period include:

- the emergence of a major new dynamic growth pole ('newly industrializing countries') in East Asia and an associated 'new international division of labour';
- a technological revolution in the form of global production and means of communication—and an associated growth of a new information-rich society and economy;
- a shift towards a new regime of accumulation and mode of regulation ('Postfordism');
- the collapse of the socialist model used to direct policies and underpin the institutional structure of societies and economies in the 'East';
- a crisis in the development project and reformist policies pursued by many governments in the capitalist 'North';
- the implementation of a 'new economic model' and an associated process of 'globalization'—the integration of economies across the world into one system based on free market capitalism;
- a widespread change in the economic policies of governments, both in the North and the South, on the basis of this new economic model; and
- a direct offensive by capital against the advances made by labour over the years—halting (and then reversing) the gains of the working and producing classes, and inducing in the process conditions of a new global divide in wealth and incomes.

By 1980, the development project, offered to workers, peasant producers, women, indigenous communities and the poor as an alternative to the demands for radical change and social revolution, stalled and, to a large degree, was abandoned.

In its place, the self-appointed guardians of the world economic order proceeded with a project to restructure their economic system. The aim, in terms of George W. Bush's new National Security Doctrine, was to create a new world economic order in which the 'forces of freedom' could flourish.

Like 'development' and other such geoeconomic or geopolitical 'projects' the changes associated with the new economic model have the appearance of a 'process', that is, as the products not of conscious design but of structural force beyond human or rational control. However, one conclusion that the various authors in this book have come to is that the dynamics of both globalization and antiglobalization can only be understood in terms of the conscious decisions made by people in their collective interest. What we have in the globalization-antiglobalization movement, in effect, is a class war with two opposing sides and alternative projects to restructure the existing world economic system or to dismantle and change it.

Unfortunately, there is no balance of forces in this situation and the custodians of the world economic order have a virtual monopoly on the instruments of armed force. However, various authors in this volume such as James Petras makes the point, and allows us to conclude, that the forces in support of the system are by no means impotent. For one thing, the system is rift with contradictions. For another, in its 'development', the 'system' generates conditions and gives rise to forces that might well lead to its destruction if not its overthrow. Karl Marx in an earlier historic context wrote of the capitalist system as generating its own gravediggers. The antiglobalization movement in the current context appears to have this potential. Although the social and political forces mobilized in this movement seem to be pointed towards reforms to the existing system—a new world within capitalism and globalization—a significant sector is mobilized not only against capitalism in its neoliberal and globalized form but against capitalism as such.

There is no systemic evidence of any imminent collapse in the capitalist system. At the same time the economic, social and environmental—and political—costs of the capitalist globalization process are reaching crisis proportions and are just as clearly generating the political conditions of a worldwide global movement of resistance and opposition. This movement is divided and the forms of this resistance are difficult to unify but at the same time the potential for systemic change is considerable. What is required in this regard is a close understanding of the forces at play and of their dynamics.

The editor shares the hope of the various authors in this volume that their reflections on these dynamics might make a modest contribution in this regard. Marx said long ago that what would be needed in bringing about a new world is not to reinterpret reality but to change it. But effective change requires as clear as possible an understanding of what is to be changed and how. It is to this end that we constructed this volume of writings.

Bibliography

AAWH—American Association for World Health (1997), *Denial of Food and Medicine: The Impact of the U.S. Embargo on Health & Nutrition in Cuba. Executive Summary*, Washington, DC, AAWH, March.

Agacino, Rafael and Gonzalo Rivas (1995), "La industria Chilena despues del ajuste: evaluación y perspectives," Proyecto Regional: *Cambio Tecnológico y mercado de Trabajo, Santiago*, ILO, Office for Latin America and the Caribbean.

Aglietta, M. (1979), *Theory of Capitalist Regulation*. London: New Left Books.

_____ (1982), "World Capitalism in the 1980s," *New Left Review* 136.

Alimir, Oscar (1994), "Distribución del ingreso e incidencia de la pobreza a lo largo del ajuste," *Revista de CEPAL*, 52, Abril.

Amin, Samir (1994), *Re-Reading the Postwar Period*, New York, Monthly Review Press.

Anand, S. and A. Sen (2000), "The Income Component of the Human Development Index," *Journal of Human Development*, Vol. 1, No. 1.

Anderson, Perry (2000), "Renewals," *New Left Review* (II), No. 1, January-February.

_____ (2001), "Testing Formula Two," *New Left Review* (II), No. 8, March-April.

Angell, Marcia (2000), "Pockets of Poverty," in Joshua Cohen and Joel Rogers (eds.), *Is Inequality Bad for Our Health?* Boston, Beacon Press.

Arellano, Sonia and James Petras (1997), "Non-governmental Organizations and Poverty Alleviation in Bolivia," pp. 165-178 in H. Veltmeyer and J. Petras, *Neoliberalism and Class Conflict in Latin America*, London, Macmillan.

Arrida Palomares, Joaquín (1995), "Economía y sindicalismo. Significado económico del marco de relaciones laborales Salvadoreño," *ECA*, No. 551.

Arrighi, Giovanni (1994), *The Long 20th Century: Money, Power and the Origins of Our Times*, London, Verso.

Arrighi, Giovanni and Beverly Silver (2001), *Caos e governabilidade*, Rio de Janeiro, Contraponto.

Assies, William, et al. (eds.) (1990), *Structures of Power, Movements of Resistance: An Introduction to the Theories of Urban Movements in Latin America*, Amsterdam, Centre for Latin American Research and Documentation.

Aulakh, Preet and Michael Schecter (2000), *Rethinking Globalizations: From Corporate Transnationalism to Local Interventions*, New York, St. Martin's Press.

Bairoch, P. (1996), "Globalization. Myths and Realities. One Century of External Trade and Foreign Investment," in R. Boyer and D. Drache (eds.), *States Against Markets: The Limits of Globalization*, London, Routledge.

Bamuamba, Clement (2001), "Political Corruption in Congo-Zaire: Its impact on Development," MA Thesis, St. Mary's University, Halifax.

Barrett, Kathleen (1993), "The Collapse of the Soviet Union and the Eastern Bloc: Effects on Cuban Health Care," *Cuba Briefing Paper*, Series 2, Washington, DC, Georgetown University, Cuba Project, May.

Bauer, P. T. (1971), *Dissent on Development: Studies and Debates in Development Economics*, London, Weidenfeld and Nicolson.

Bellamy Foster, John (2002), "Monopoly Capital and the New Globalization," *Monthly Review*, Vol. 53.

Benasayag, Miguel and Diego Sztulwark (2000), *Política y situación: de la potencia al contrapoder*, Buenos Aires: Ediciones Mano en Mano.

Bengoa, José (2000), *La emergencia indígena en América Latina*, México/Santiago, Fondo de Cultura Económico.

Bergsten, Fred (2000), "Towards a Tripartite World," *The Economist*, July 15-21.

Bhagwati, J. (1998), "The Capital Myth: The Difference Between Trade in Widgets and Trade in Dollars," *Foreign Affairs*, 77, 3, 7-12.

Bieler, Andreas and Adam David Morton (eds.) (2001), *Social Forces in the Making of the New Europe: The Restructuring of European Social Relations in the Global Political Economy*, New York, Palgrave, 2001.

Bienefeld, Manfred (1995), "Assessing Current Development Trends: Reflections on Keith Griffin's 'Global Prospects for Development and Human Security,'" *Canadian Journal of Development Studies*, Vol. XVI, No. 3.

Blair, Tony (2001), "Travel ban to block 'anarchists,'" *The Guardian* (London), 18 June.

Booker, Salih and William Minter (2001), "Global Apartheid," *The Nation*, July 9.

Boom, Gerard and Alfonso Mercado (eds.) (1990), *Automatización flexible en la industria*, Mexico: Editorial Limusa Noriega.

Booth, Ken (1991), "Security in Anarchy: Utopian Realism in Theory and Practice," *International Affairs*, Vol. 67, No. 3.

Bordegaray, Soledad and Toti Flores (eds.) (2001), *El Foro Social Mundial desde los desocupados*, Buenos Aires, MTD Editora (de la Matanza).

Borón, Atilio (2001), "El nuevo orden imperial y como desmontarlo," in José Seoane and Emilio Taddei (eds.), *Resistencias Mundiales. De Seattle a Porto Alegre*, CLACSO, Buenos Aires.

Bounds, Andrew (2001), "Costly Lessons of Central America Bank Reform," *Financial Times*, 11 July.

Bowles, Paul, (2000), "Regionalism and Development After (?) the Global Financial Crisis," *New Political Economy*, Vol. 5, No. 3.

Bowles, Paul and B. MacLean (1996), "Regional Blocs: Will East Asia Be Next?" *Cambridge Journal of Economics*, 20.

Boyer, Robert (1989), La teoría de la regulación: un análisis crítico, Buenos Aires, *Ed. Humanitas*.

Boyer, Robert and Daniel Drache (eds.) (1996), *States Against Markets: The Limits of Globalization*, London, Routledge.

Brennan, Timothy (2001), "Cosmopolitanism and Internationalism," *New Left Review*, II, No. 7, Jan-Feb.

Brenner, Robert (2000a), "The Boom and the Bubble," *New Left Review*, II, No. 6.

_____ (2000b), *The Economics of Global Turbulence*, London, Verso.

Brown, Flor and Lilia Domínguez (1989), "Nuevas tecnologias en la industria maquiladora de exportación," *Comercio Exterior* (Mexico), Vol. 39, Num. 3, Marzo.

Bulmer-Thomas, Victor (1996), *The Economic Model in Latin America and its Impact on Income Distribution and Poverty*, New York, St. Martin's Press.

Bultman, Ingo, et al. (eds.) (1995), *¿Democracia sin movimiento social?* Caracas, Editorial Nueva Sociedad.

Burbach, Roger (1994), "Roots of the Postmodern Rebellion in Chiapas," *New Left Review* 205.

Burbach, Roger and William Robinson (1999), "Globalization as Epochal Shift," *Science & Society*, Vol. 63, No. 1.

Calderón, Fernando (1995), *Movimientos sociales y política*, Mexico: Siglo XXI.

Calderón, Fernando and Elizabeth Jelín (1987), *Clases y movimientos sociales en América Latina. Perspectivas y realidades*, Buenos Aires, Cuadernos CEDES.

Carriles, Luis (2001), "Contratos sin riesgo y territorio a transnacionales," *Milenio*. No. 222, December 17.

Castañeda, Jorgé (1993), *Utopia Unarmed*, New York, Vintage Books.

Castañeda, Nora and Calixto Ávila (1998), "Venezuela. Two Dimensions: Health and Gender," PROVEA, Annual Report 1-6, Instituto del Tercer Mundo—Social Watch, www.socwatch.org.

Castells, Manue (1983), *The City and the Grassroots: A Cross-Cultural Theory of Urban Social Movements*, Berkeley, University of California Press.

CEPAL—Comisión Ecónomica de America Latina y el Caribe (1991), *Internacionalización y regionalización de la economia mundial: sus consequencias para Latina America*, LC/L 640, September 3.

_____ (1994), *Panorama Social*, Santiago, CEPAL.

_____ (1998), "Progresos realizados en la privatización de los servicios públicos relacionados con el agua: reseña por países de México, América Central y el Caribe" (LC/R. 1697; restricted document).

Chalmers, Johnson (2000), *Blowback: The Costs and consequences of American Empire*, Metropolitan Books, New York.

CIA—Central Intelligence Agency (1998), *The World Factbook: Cuba*, www.cia.gov/cia/publications/factbook/geos/ve.html.

_____ (2000), *Global Trends 2015*; cited in *Does Globalization Help the Poor?* International Forum on Globalization, August 2001, San Francisco.

_____ (2002), *The World Factbook: Venezuela*, www.cia.gov/cia/publications /factbook /geos/ve.html.

Clark, Martin (1977), *Antonio Gramsci and the Revolution that Failed*, Yale University Press.

Coatsworth, John H. (1998), "Poverty Blocks Economic Growth," *DRCLAS News*, Boston, David Rockefeller Center of Latin American Studies, Harvard University, Spring.

Cockburn, Alexander and Jeffrey St. Clair (2000), *Five Days That Shook the World: Seattle and Beyond*, London, Verso.

Cohen, Joshua and Joel Rogers (2000), *Is Inequality Bad for Our Health?* Boston, Beacon Press.

Colectivo Situaciones de Buenos Aires (2001a), "Conversaciones con el MTD en Solano," *Situaciones 4*, Buenos Aires, Deciembre.

_____ (2001b), *Contrapoder: una introducción*, Buenos Aires, Ediciones de Mano en Mano.

Cooper, Robert (2000a), "The Post-Modern State, Reordering the World; the Long Term Implications of September 11," The Foreign Policy Centre, www.info@fpc.org.uk.

_____ (2000b), "The New Liberal Imperialism," *The Guardian*, April 7.

Coronil, Fernando and Julie Skurski (1991), "Dismembering and Remembering the Nation: The Semantics of Political Violence in Venezuela," *Comparative Studies in Society and History*, Vol. 33, No. 2, April.

Corpwatch (2001), *Holding Corporations Accountable*, November 5, www.corpwatch.org.

Cox, Aidan and John Healey (2000), *European Development Cooperation and the Poor*, London, Macmillan; New York: St Martin's Press, in association with the Overseas Development Institute.

Cox, Robert W. (1981), "Social Forces, States and World Orders: Beyond International Relations Theory," *Millennium: Journal of International Studies*, Vol. 10, No. 2.

_____ 1987, *Production, Power and World Order: Social Forces in the Making of History*, Columbia University Press.

_____ (1992), "Global Perestroika," in Ralph Miliband and Leo Panitch (eds.), *The Socialist Register: New World Order?*, Merlin Press.

_____ (1996), "The Global Political Economy and Social Choice," in Cox, with Sinclair, *Approaches to World Order*, Cambridge University Press.

_____ (1996a), "Production, Power and World Order" and "Realism, Positivism and Historicism," in Cox with Sinclair, *Approaches to World Order*.

_____ (ed.) (1997), *The New Realism: Perspectives on Multilateralism and World Order*, London, Macmillan.

_____ (1999), "Civil Society at the Turn of the Millennium. Prospects for an Alternative World Order," *Review of International Studies*, No. 25.

Cox, Robert W. with Timothy J. Sinclair (1996), *Approaches to World Order*, Cambridge University Press.

Crouch, C. and A. Pizzorno (1978), *Resurgence of Class Conflict in Western Europe Since 1968*, London, Holmes & Meier.

Cuba, Government of (2000), "Salud Publica y Asistencia Social," *Anuario Estadistico de Cuba 2000*, Chapter X1V.

Cumings, B. (1993), "Rimspeak; or The Discourse of the 'Pacific Rim,'" in A. Dirlik (ed.), *What's In a Rim? Critical Perspectives on the Pacific Region Idea*, Boulder, Colorado, Westview Press.

Davis, Mike (1984), "The Political Economy of Late-Imperial America," *New Left Review*, No. 143, Jan-Feb.

Deffeyes, K. S. (2001), *Hubbert's Peak: the Impeding World Oil Shortage*, Princeton University Press, Princenton, Oxford.

De Long, J. Bradford (2001), "Globalization" and "Neoliberalism," www.j-bradford-delong.net/ (accessed May 31).

De Soto, Hernando (2000), *The Mystery of Capital: Why Capitalism Triumphs in the West and Fails Everywhere Else*, New York, Basic Books.

Desai, Meghnad, James Petras and Henry Veltmeyer, Robert Scrire, Leslie Sklair, Ghautam Sen, and Deepak Lal (2000), Essays in *Cambridge Review of International Affairs*, Vol. XIV, No. 1, Autumn-Winter.

Díaz González, Elena (1995). "The Quality of Life in Cuba's Special Period: Examining the Impact of U.S. Policies," in José Bell Lara and Richard A. Dello Buono (eds.), *Carta Cuba: Interdisciplinary Reflections on Development and Society*, Havana, FLACSO, Universidad de la Habana.

Díaz-Polanco, Héctor (2002), "Renovación de la crítica en la era de la globalización," *Memoria*, No. 156, México.

Dicken, Paul (1992), *Global Shift: The Internationalization of Economic Activity*, New York, Guilford Press.

Dieter, H. (2000), "Asia's Monetary Regionalism," *Far Eastern Economic Review*, 6.

Dominguez, Jorge and A. Lowenthal (1996), *Constructing Democratic Governance in Latin America and the Caribbean in the 90s*, Baltimore, John Hopkins University Press.

Doremus, Paul et al. (1998), *The Myth of the Global Corporation*, Princeton, Princeton University Press.

Drake, Paul W. (1994), "Introduction. The Political Economy of Foreign Advisors and Lenders in Latin America," in Paul W. Drake (ed.), *Money Doctors, Foreign Debts, and Economic Reforms in Latin America from the 1890s to the Present*, Wilmington Delaware, Scholarly Resources.

Du Boff, Richard and Edward Herman (1997), "A Critique of Tabb on Globalization," *Monthly Review*, Vol. 49, No. 6.

Eckstein, Susan (1997), "The Limits of Socialism in a Capitalist World Economy: Cuba Since the Collapse of the Soviet Bloc," in Miguel A. Centeno and Maurecio Font (eds.), *Towards a New Cuba? Legacies of a Revolution*, Boulder, Lynne Rienner.

Eckstein, Susan (2000), "Resistance and Reform: Power to the People?" *DRCLAS News*, Harvard University, Winter.

ECLAC—United Nations Economic Commission for Latin America and the Caribbean (1996), *Economic Survey of Latin America and the Caribbean 1994-1995*, Santiago, ECLAC.

_____ (1998), *Social Dimensions of Economic Development and Productivity: Inequality and Social Performance*, 29 December. Santiago, ECLAC.

_____ (2001), *Preliminary Overview of the Economies of Latin America and the Caribbean*, Santiago, ECLAC.

Escobar, Arturo (1995), *Encountering Development: The Making and the Unmaking of the Third World*, Princeton University Press.

Escobar, Arturo and Sonia Alvarez (eds.) (1992), *The Making of Social Movements in Latin America: Identity, Strategy, and Democracy*, Boulder, Westview Press.

Esteva, Gustavo and Madhu Suri Prakash (1998), *Grassroots Post-Modernism*, London, Zed Books.

Falk, Richard (2000), "The Quest for Human Governance in an Era of Globalization," in D. Kalb, et al. (ed.), *The End of Globalization, Bringing Society back In*, Lanhan, Rowland & Littlefield.

Ferriol Muruaga, Angela (2000), "External Opening, Labor Market and Inequality of Labor Incomes," *Working Paper*, Series 1, New York: New School University, Center for Economic Policy Analysis (CEPA), February.

Filgueira, Fernando and Jorgé Papadópulos (1997), "Putting Conservatism to Good Use? Long Crisis and Vetoed Alternatives in Uruguay," in Douglas A. Chalmers. et al. (eds.), *The New Politics of Inequality in Latin America*, New York, Oxford University Press.

Foweraker, Joe (1995), *Theorising Social Movements*, Boulder, Pluto Press.

Freire, Paulo (1970), *Pedagogy of the Oppressed*, Penguin Books.

French, Howard (1993), "Cuba's Ills Encroach on Health," *New York Times*, A.3, July 16.

Friedman, Milton (1982), *Capitalism and Freedom*, Chicago, University of Chicago Press.

Fröbel, Folker; Jürgen Heinrichs, and Otto Kreye (1980), *The New International Division of Labour, Structural Unemployment in Industrialised Countries and Industrialisation in Developing Countries*, Cambridge, Cambridge University Press.

Fukuyama, Francis (2001), 'The west has won,' *The Guardian* (London), 11 October.

FUSADES (1996), *Boletin Economico y Social*, No. 128, Julio, San Salvador, FUSADES.

Gachúz Maya, Juan C. (2000), *La Globalización de las Empresas Petroleras Multinacionales: Alternativas para Pemex*, Mexico, FCPS, UNAM.

Ganuza, Enrique and Lance Taylor (1998), "Macroeconomic Policy, Poverty and Equality in Latin America and the Caribbean," Working Papers on Globalization, Labor Markets and Social Policy," *Working Paper*, No. 6, New York, Center for Economic Policy Analysis, New School University, March.

Garfield, Richard and Sarah Santana (1997), "The Impact of the Economic Crisis and the U.S. Embargo on Health in Cuba," *American Journal of Public Health*, Vol. 87, No. 1, January.

Garfield, Richard and Timothy H. Holtz (2000), "Health System Reforms in Cuba in the 1990s," in Peter Lloyd-Sherlock (ed.), *Healthcare Reform and Poverty in Latin America*, London: Institute of Latin American Studies, University of London.

Gasper, Des (2002), *Is Sen's Capabililty Approach an Adequate Basis for Considering Human Development?* The Hague, Institute of Social Studies, February.

Gazier, Bernard (1996), "Implicites et incompletes: les théories économiques de l'exclusion," in Serge Paugam, (ed.), *L'exclusion. L'Etat des savoirs*, Paris, Ed. La Découverte.

George, Susan (1994), *Faith and Credit: the World Bank's Secular Empire*, Boulder, CO, Westview Press.

_____ (1999), *The Lugano Report: On Preserving Capitalism in the 21ˢᵗ Century*, London, Pluto Press.

Germain, Randall (1997), *The International Organisation of Credit: States and Global Finance in the World Economy*, Cambridge University Press.

_____ (ed.) (2000), *Globalisation and Its Critics: Perspectives from Political Economy*, London, Macmillan.

Giddens, Anthony (1990), *The Consequences of Modernity*, Cambridge, Polity Press.

_____ (1995), *Beyond Left and Right: The Future of Radical Politics*, Cambridge, Polity Press.

Gill, Stephen (1990), *American Hegemony and the Trilateral Commission*, Cambridge University Press.

_____ (ed.) (1993), *Gramsci, Historical Materialism and International Relations*, Cambridge University Press.

_____ (2000), "Toward a Postmodern Prince? The Battle in Seattle as a Moment in the New Politics of Resistance," *Millennium: Journal of International Studies*, Vol. 29, No. 1.

Gill, Stephen and David Law (1989), "Global Hegemony and the Structural Power of Capital," *International Studies Quarterly*, Vol. 33, No. 4.

Gills, Barry, K. (ed.) (2000), *Globalisation and the Politics of Resistance*, London, Macmillan.

Gills, Barry K., Joel Rocamora and Richard Wilson (eds.) (1993), *Low Intensity Democracy: Political Power in the New World Order*, Pluto Press.

Gilpin, Robert (1987), *The Political Economy of International Relations*, Princeton University Press.

Glynn, A., A. Hughes, A. Lipietz, and A. Singh (1990), "The Rise and Fall of the Golden Age," in Stephen Marglin and Juliet Schor (eds.), *The Golden Age of Capitalism: Reinterpreting the Post-War Experience*, Oxford, Clarendon Press.

González Casanova, Pablo (1999), *La Explotación Global*, Mexico, CEIICH, UNAM.

Goodwin, Neva (2001), "Civil Economy and Civilized Economics: Essentials for Sustainable Development," *Working Paper* No. 01-01, Tufts University, Global Development and Environment Institute.

Gordon, Robert (1999a), "Has the New Economy Rendered the Productivity Slowdown Obsolete," http://faculty-web.at.nwu.edu/education/gordon/researchhome.htm.

_____ (1999b), "U.S. Economic Growth Since 1870: One Big Wave?" *The American Economic Review*.

Gramsci, Antonio (1971), *Selections from the Prison Notebooks* (ed.), Quintin Hoare, Lawrence and Wishart.

_____ (1977), *Selections from Political Writings, 1910-1920* (ed.) Quintin Hoare, London, Lawrence and Wishart.

_____ (1994), "Letter to Tatiana Schucht" (25 April 1927), in Frank Rosengarten (ed.), *Letters from Prison*, Vol. 1, New York, Columbia University Press.

Griffin, Keith (1995), "Global Prospects for Development and Human Security," *Canadian Journal of Development Studies*, Vol. XVI, No. 3.

Griffin, Keith and Rahman Khan (1992), *Globalization and the Developing World*, Geneva, UNSRID.

Gunn, Gillian (1992), "Cuba's Search for Alternatives," Current History, February.

Gunnell, Barbara and David Timms (eds.) (2000), *After Seattle: Globalisation and Its Discontents*, Catalyst.

Haq, Mahbub (1994), "New Imperatives of Human Security: Barbara Ward Lecture," *Development*, No. 2.

Hardt, Robert and Antonio Negri (2000), *Empire*, Cambridge, Harvard University Press.

Harrod, Jeffrey (1987), *Power, Production and the Unprotected Worker*, Columbia University Press.

Hawkins, J. J. (1991), "Understanding the Failure of IMF Reform: the Zambian Case," *World Development*, Vol. 19, No. 7.

Hayter, Teresa (1971), *Aid as Imperialism*, Harmondsworth, Penguin Books.

Helleiner, G. K. (1992), "The IMF, the World Bank and Africa's Adjustment and External Debt Problems: an Unofficial View," *World Development*, Vol. 20, No. 6.

Hellinger, Daniel (1991), *Venezuela: Tarnished Democracy*, Boulder CO, Westview Press.

Hellman, Judith Hellman (1995), "The Riddle of New Social Movements: Who They Are and What They Do," in Sandor Halebsky and Richard L. Harris (eds.), *Capital, Power and Inequality in Latin America*, Boulder CO, Westview Press.

Hernández-Cata, Ernesto (2000), "The Fall and Recovery of the Cuban Economy in the 1990s: Mirage or Reality?" *Cuba in Transition*, No. 10.

Herrera, Gonzalo (1995). "Tendencias del cambio tecnológico en la industria Chilena," *Economía y Trabajo en Chile 1994-1995*, Santiago, ILO—Programa de Economía del Trabajo (PET).

Higgott, R. (1998), "The Asian Economic Crisis: A Study in the Politics of Resentment," *New Political Economy*, Vol. 3, No. 3, November.

Higgott, R and R. Stubbs (1994), "Competing Conceptions of Economic Regionalism: APEC Versus EAEC in the Asia Pacific," *Review of International Political Economy*, Vol. 2, No. 2, Summer.

Hirst, Paul and Graham Thompson (1996), *Globalization in Question*, Cambridge, Polity Press, London.

Holloway, John (2001), *Contrapoder: una introducción*, Buenos Aires, Ediciones de Mano en Mano.

Holm, Hans-Henrik and Georg Sorensen (eds.) (1995), *Whose World Order? Uneven Globalization and the End of the Cold War*, Boulder CO, Westview Press.

Howard, M. and J. King (eds.) (1976), *The Economics of Marx: Selected Readings*, Harmondsworth, Penguin Books.

Howell, Jude and Jenny Pearce (2001), *Civil Society and Development: A Critical Exploration*, Boulder CO, Lynne Rienner.

Hughes, C. (2000), "Japanese Policy and the East Asian Currency Crisis: Abject Defeat of Quiet Victory?" *Review of International Political Economy*, 7 (2).

Human Rights Watch (2001), *Trading Away Rights*, April.

Huntington, Samuel (1996), *The Clash of Civilizations and the Remaking of the World Order*, New York, Simon & Schuster.

Huntington, Samuel, Micher Crozier and Joji Watanuki (1975), *The Crisis of Democracy: A Report to the Trilateral Commission*, No. 8, New York.

IDB—Inter-American Development Bank (1991), *Economic and Social Progress in Latin America. 1991 Report*, Washington DC.

ILO—International Labor Organisation (1996), *World Employment 1996*, Geneva, ILO.

_____ (2000), *Mental Health in the Workplace*, Geneva, ILO Office.

_____ (2001), *Annual Report*, Geneva, ILO.

International Forum on Globalization (2001), "Does Globalization Help the Poor," San Francisco, August.

Jameson, Fredric (2000), "Globalisation and Political Strategy," *New Left Review* II, No. 4, July-August.

Johnson, Chalmers (2000), *Blowback*, New York, Metropolitan Books.

Jorgenson, Dale and Kevin Stiroh (1999), "Information Technology and Growth," *American Economic Review*, May.

Kapstein, Ethan (1996), "Workers and the World Economy," *Foreign Affairs*, Vol. 75, No. 3, May-June.

Karliner, Joshua (1999), "A Perilous Partnership: the UNDP's Flirtation With Corporate Collaboration," TRAC-Transnational Resource & Action Center.

Kawachi, Ichiro, Bruce P. Kennedy and Richard G. Wilkinson (eds.) (1999), *The Society and Population Health Reader*, Vol. I, New York, The New Press.

Kenen, Peter (1994), *Managing the World Economy*, Washington DC, Institute for International Economics.

Keohane, Robert and Joseph Nye (2000), "Globalization: What's New? What's Not? (And so What?)," *Foreign Policy*, No. 118, Spring.

Khor, Martin (1995), *States of Disarray: The Social Effects of Globalization*, Geneva, United Nations Research Institute for Social Development.

Kiely, Ray (2000), "Review of Global Transformations: Politics, Economics and Culture," *The Journal of Development Studies*, Vol. 36, No. 4. April.

Kirkpatrick, Anthony F. and Harry E. Varden (1997), "The U.S. Embargo and Health Care in Cuba. Assessing the May 1997 State Department Report," *LASA Forum*, Vol. XXVIII, No. 2, Summer.

Klare, Michael (2001), *Resource Wars*, New York, Metopolitan Books.

Klein, Naomi (2000), *No Logo. Taking Aim at the Brand Bullies*, Flamingo.

_____ (2001), "May Day's lessons for the rootless," *The Guardian* (London), 3 May.

Kolko, Gabriel (1974), *Politicas de Guerra*, Barcelona, Ediciones Grijalbo.

Kolko, Gabriel and Joyce Kolko (1972), *The Limits of Power: the World and United States Foreign Policy, 1945-1954*, New York, Harper & Row.

Korten, David (1995), *When Corporations Rule the World*, West Hartford, Kumarian Press.

Krueger, Anne, C. Michalopoulos, and V. Ruttan (1989), *Aid and Development*, Baltimore, Johns Hopkins University Press.

Krugman, P. "What happened to Asia?" www.web.mit.edu/krugman/www/DISINTER.html.

Labonte, Ronald (2000), "International Health Presence in Future World Trade/Investment Talks," in A. Bambas, J. A. Casas, H. A. Drayton and A. Valdés (eds.), *Health and Human Development in the Americas: The Contributions and Perspectives of Civil Society in the Americas*, Washington DC, PAHO.

Laibman, David (1997), *Capitalist Macrodynamics*, London, Macmillan.

Langley, Paul and Mary Mellor (2002), "Economy, Sustainability and Sites of Transformative Space," *New Political Economy*, Vol. 7, No. 1.

Lawrence, R (1994), "Regionalism: An Overview," *Journal of Japanese and International Economics*, Vol. 8, No. 4.

Laxer, Gordon (2001), "The Movement that Dare Not Speak Its Name: The Return of Left Nationalism /Internationalism," *Alternatives*, Vol. 26, No. 1.

Leiva, Fernando and Rafael Agacino (1995), *Mercado de trabajo flexible, pobreza y desintegración social en Chile, 1990-1994*, Santiago, Chile, Universidad ARCIS.

Levins, Richard (2000), "Is Capitalism a Disease?" *Monthly Review*, Vol. 52, No. 4, September.

Lipietz, Alain (1982), "Towards Global Fordism," *New Left Review*, No. 132, March-April.

_____ (1986), "Behind the Crisis: The Tendency of the Profit Rate to Fall. Considerations About Some Empirical French Works," *Review of Radical Political Economics*, Vol. 18, Nos. 1-2.

_____ (1987), *Mirages and Miracles: The Crisis in Global Fordism*, London,Verso.

Lodoño, Juan Luis and Miquel Székely (2000), "Persistent Poverty and Excess Inequality: Latin America, 1970-1995," *Journal of Applied Economics*, Vol. III, No. 1, May.

Lopez de Blanco, Mercedes (1997), "El Problema Nutricional en Venezuela," *SIC*, Vol. LX, No. 600, Diciembre.

Lucas, Kintto (2002), "Ecuador: IMF wants Future Oil Revenues to Service Debt, Not Health," *Inter Press Service*, May 29.

Lustig, Nora (ed.) (1995), *Coping with Austerity: Poverty and Inequality in Latin America*, Washington DC, The Brookings Institution.

Luzani, Telma (2002), "El Viejo fantasma que agito a Latinoamerica: la democracia en guardia," Suplemento Zona, *Clarin*, April 21.

MacEwan, Arthur (1999), *Neo-Liberalism or Democracy? Economic Strategy, Markets, and Alternatives for the 21st Century*, London, Zed Books.

MacLean, B (1999), "The Transformation of International Economic Policy Debate 1997-98," in B. MacLean (ed.), *Out Of Control*, Toronto, James Lorimer.

Magdoff, Harry (1969), *The Age of Imperialism*, New York, Monthly Review Press.

_____ (1978), *Imperialism: From the Colonial Age to the Present*, New York, Monthly Review Press.

_____ (1992), *Globalization: To What End?* New York, Monthly Review Press.

Maier, Charles (1977), "The Politics of Productivity: Foundations of American International Economic Policy After World War II," *International Organisation*, Vol. 31, No. 4.

Manzo, José Luis (1996), *¿Qué Hacer con Pemex?* México, Grijalbo.

Marglin, Stephen and Juliet Schor (eds.) (1990), *The Golden Age of Capitalism: Reinterpreting the Postwar Experience*, Oxford, Clarendon Press.

Márquez Mosconi, Gustavo and Carola Alvarez (1996), "Poverty and the Labor Market in Venezuela 1982-1985," in Inter-American Development Bank, No. SOC96-101, Washington DC, December.

Márquez, Gustavo (1995), "Venezuela: Poverty and Social Policies in the 1980s," in Nora Lustig (ed.), *Coping with Austerity: Poverty and Inequality in Latin America*, Washington DC. Brookings Institute.

Márquez, Patricia (1999), *The Street is My Home: Youth and Violence in Caracas*, Stanford University Press.

Martin, Andrew and George Ross (1999), "In the Line of Fire: The Europeanisation of Labour Representation," in Andrew Martin and George Ross et al. (eds.), *The Brave New World of European Labour: European Trade Unions at the Millennium*, Berghahn.

Marx, Karl (1975), *Texts on Method*, Oxford, Basil Blackwell.

Marx, Karl (1998), *Capital*, Vol. III, in Karl Marx and Frederick Engels, *Collected Works*, Vol. 37, Lawrence and Wishart.

McMichael, Philip (1996), *Development and Change: A Global Perspective*, Thousand Oaks CA, Pine Gorge Press.

Meiksins Wood, Ellen (1995), *Democracy Against Capitalism: Renewing Historical Materialism*, Cambridge University Press.

Mekay, Emad (2002), "Jeffrey Sachs to Poor Nations: Forget Debt, Spend on AIDS," *Inter Press Service*, August 2.

Melcher, Dorothea (2000), "Seguridad Social y Derechos Laborales en Las Reformas Neoliberales en Venezuela." Paper presented at the Congreso Internacional de Americanistas, Warszawa, July 10-14.

Miranda Parrondo, Patricia de and Carlos J. Tabraue Castro (2000), "Impacto social de la crisis económica en la Cuba de los noventa," Presented at the Latin American Studies Association Conference.

MITI (1999), "White Paper on International Trade 1999," English Executive Summary, Tokyo, MITI.

_____ (2000a), "Japan-Singapore Economic Agreement for a New Age Partnership," Released 29 September, Tokyo, MITI.

_____ (2001b), "The Economic Foundations of Japanese Trade Policy – Promoting a Multi-Layered Trade Policy," White Paper, Tokyo, Released 22 August.

Mitlin, Diana (1998), "The NGO Sector and its Role in Strengthening Civil Society and Securing Good Governance," in Armanda Bernard, Henry Helmich and Percy Lehning (eds.), *Civil Society and International Development*, Paris, OECD Development Centre.

Mittelman, James (2000), *The Globalisation Syndrome: Transformation and Resistance*, Princeton, Princeton University Press.

Mittelman, James and Norani Othman (eds.) (2000), "Special Issue: Capturing Globalisation," *Third World Quarterly*, Vol. 21, No. 6.

Montesinos, Mario and Roberto Góchez (1995), "Salarios y productividad," *ECA* 564, Octubre.

Moore, Mike (2001), "Liberalisation? Don't Reject it Just Yet," *The Guardian*, February 6.

Morales, Josefina (1992). "La reestructuración industrial," in Josefina Morales (ed.), *La Reestructuración industrial en México*. Mexico: IIE, UNAM; Editorial Nuestro Tiempo.

Morales-Gómez, Daniel (ed.) (1999), *Transnational Social Policies: The New Development Challenges of Globalization*, London, Earthscan Publications.

Morley, Samuel (2000), "Efectos del crecimiento y las reformas ecónomicas sobre la distribución del ingreso en América Latina," *Revista de la CEPAL*, No. 71, Agosto.

Morton, Adam David (2001), "'La Resurrección del Maíz": Some Aspects of Globalisation, Resistance and the Zapatista Question," Paper presented at the 42nd Annual Convention of the International Studies Association, Chicago, February 20-24.

Mosley, Paul, Jane Harrigan and John Toye (1991), *Aid and Power: The World Bank and Policy-Based Lending*, London and New York, Routledge.

Munck, Gerardo (1997), "Social Movements and Latin America: Conceptual Issues and Empirical Applications," Paper presented to the Latin American Studies Association, Guadalajara, April 17-19.

Murphy, Craig (1998), "Globalisation and Governance: A Historical Perspective," in Roland Axtman (ed.), *Globalisation and Europe: Theoretical and Empirical Investigations*, Pinter.

Naim, Moisés (1993), *Paper Tigers and Minotaurs: The Politics of Venezuela's Economic Reforms*, Washington DC, The Carnegie Endowment for International Peace.

Naughton, B. (ed.) (1997), *The China Circle: Economics and Technology in the PRC, Taiwan and Hong Kong*, Washington DC, Brookings Institution Press.

Negri, Toni (2001), "Contrapoder," in *Colectivo Situaciones de Buenos Aires, Contrapoder: una introducción*, Buenos Aires, Ediciones de Mano en Mano.

Noland, M. (2000), "Japan and the International Economic Institutions," paper prepared for the Centre for Japanese Studies, Macquarie University, Fifth Biennial Conference on "Can the Japanese Change? Economic Reform in Japan," Sydney, Australia, 6-7 July.

Nudler, Julio (2002), "Imperialismo para poner orden," *Página 12* (Buenos Aires), April 13.

O'Brien, Robert (2000). "Workers and World Order: The Tentative Transformation of the International Union Movement," *Review of International Studies*, Vol. 26, No. 4.

Ohmae, Kenichi (1990), *The Borderless World*, Fontana.

_____ (1996), *The End of the Nation State: The Rise of Regional Economies*, Free Press.

Okonski, Kendra (2001), "Riots Inc. The Business of Protesting Globalization," *The Wall Street Journal*, The editorial page, August 14.

Ominami, Carlos (ed.) (1986), *La tercera revolución industrial, impactos internacionales el actual viraje tecnológico*, Mexico, RIAL-Anuario-Grupo Editorial Latinoamericano.

Ostry, Silvia (1990), *Government and Corporations in a Shrinking World: Trade and Innovation Policies in the US, Europe and Japan*, New York, Council on Foreign Relations.

PAHO—Pan American Health Organization (1994), *Health Conditions in the Americas*, Vol. II, Scientific Publication, No. 549, Washington DC.

_____ (1998), *Health in the Americas*, Vol. II, Washington DC.

_____ (1999), *Cuba. Profile of the Health Services System*, Washington DC.

_____ (2001), *Profile of the Health Services System of the Bolivarian Republic of Venezuela*, 2nd edition, May 14.

Panitch, Leo (1994), "Globalisation and the State," in Ralph Miliband and Leo Panitch (eds.), *The Socialist Register: Between Globalism and Nationalism*, Merlin Press.

_____ (1996), "Rethinking the Role of the State in an Era of Globalization," in J. Mittelman (ed.), *Globalization: Critical Reflections. Yearbook of International Political Economy*, Vol. 9, Boulder, Lynne Rienner.

_____ (2000), "The New Imperial State," *New Left Review* (II), No. 2, March-April.

_____ (2000a), "Reflections on Strategy for Labour," in Leo Panitch and Colin Leys, with Greg Albo and David Coates (eds.), *The Socialist Register: Working Classes, Global Realities*, Merlin Press.

Paugam, Serge (ed.) (1996), *L'exclusion. L'Etat des savoirs*, Paris, Ed. La Découverte.

Petras, James (1987), *Latin America: Bankers, Generals and the Struggle for Social Justice*, New York, Rowman & Littlefield.

_____ (1997), "Latin America: the Resurgence of the Left," *New Left Review*, No. 223.

_____ (1998), "The Political and Social Basis of Regional Variation in Land Occupations in Brazil," *The Journal of Peasant Studies*, Vol. 25, No. 4.

_____ (2001), "Globalización: un análisis crítico," in Saxe-Fernández et al., *Globalización, imperialismo y clase social*, Buenos Aires/México: Lúmen-Humanitas.

Petras, James and Soñia Arellano-Lopez (1997), "Non-Government Organisations and Poverty Alleviation in Bolivia," pp. 180-194 in Henry Veltmeyer and James Petras, *Neoliberalism and Class Conflict in Latin America*, London, MacMillan Press.

Petras, James and Henry Veltmeyer (1999), "Latin America at the End of the Millennium," *Monthly Review*, Vol. 51, No. 3, July-August.

_____ (2000), *Ascensão da Hegemonia dos Estados Unidos no Nova Milênio*, Petrópolis, VOZES.

_____ (2001a), *Globalization Unmasked: Imperialism in the 21st Century*, London, ZED Press / Halifax, Fernwood Books.

_____ (2001b), *Brasil de Cardoso: Expropriação de un pais*, Petrópolis: VOZES.

Piore, Michael and Charles Sabel (1984), *The Second Industrial Divide*, New York, Basic Books.

Price, J. (2000), "Economic Turmoil in Asia: A Crisis of Globalization," in S. McBride and J. Wiseman (eds.), *Globalization and Its Discontents*, London, Macmillan.

PROVEA—Programa Venezolana de Educación y Acción (2001), *El Derecho a la Alimentación Adecuada en Venezuela*, Caracas, PROVEA / FIAN.

Pronk, Jan (2000), "Development for Peace," in Kamalesh Sharma (ed.), *Imagining. Tomorrow. Rethinking the Global Challenge*, New York.

Radelet, S. and Sachs J. (1998), "The East Asian Currency Crisis: Diagnosis, Remedies, Prospects," *Brookings Papers on Economic Activity*, Vol 1, Washington DC.

Radice, Hugo (2000), "Responses to Globalisation: A Critique of Progressive Nationalism," *New Political Economy*, Vol. 5, No. 1.

Ramonet, Ignacio, "The Other Axis of Evil," *Le Monde Diplomatique*, March 2002.

Reilley, Charles (1995), *New Paths to Democratic Development in Latin America: the Rise of NGO-Municipal Collaboration*, Boulder, Lynne Rienner.

Reuss, Alejandro (2000), "Cause of Death: Inequality," *Dollars & Sense*, May/June.

Robinson, William (1996), *Promoting Polyarchy: Globalisation, US Intervention and Hegemony*, Cambridge University Press.

Rocha, Alberto (2002), "Silencioso Proceso para Privatizar Pemex: Trabajadores," *Excelsior* (Mexico), May 7.

Romero Gómez, Antonio F. (2001), "Crisis, Economic Restructuring and International Reinsertion," in Claes Brundenius and John Weeks (eds.), *Globalization and Third World Socialism*, New York, Palgrave.

Rose-Ackerman, Susan (1998), "Corruption and Development," in B. Pleskovic and J. Stiglitz (eds.), *Annual Conference on Development Economics*, Washington, The World Bank.

Rosen, Fred and Jo-Marie Burt (2000), "Hugo Chavez: Venezuela's Redeemer?" *NACLA*, Vol. 33, No. 6, May/June.

Rosenau, James (1990), *Turbulence in World Politics*, Princeton, Princeton University Press.

Rosenbluth, Guillermo (1994), "Informalidad y pobreza en America Latina," *Revista de CEPAL*, 52, Abril.

Ruggie, John G. (1982), "International Regimes, Transactions and Change: Embedded Liberalism in the Postwar Economic Order," *International Organisation*, Vol. 36, No. 2.

Rupert, Mark (1995), "(Re-)Politicising the Global Economy: Liberal Common Sense and Ideological Struggle in the US NAFTA Debate," *Review of International Political Economy*, Vol. 2, No. 4.

_____ (2000), *Ideologies of Globalisation: Contending Visions of a New World Order*, Routledge.

Salbuchi, Adrian (2000), *El cerebro del mundo: la cara oculta de la globalización*, Córdoba, Ediciones del Copista.

Salinas de Gortari, Carlos and Roberto Mangabeira Unger (1999), "The Market Turn Without Neoliberaliam," *Challenge*, 42 (1), January-February.

Salop, Joanne (1992), "Reducing Poverty: Spreading the Word," *Finance & Development*, Vol. 29, No. 4, December.

SAPRIN—Structural Adjustment Participatory Review International Network (2002), "Executive Review, Multi-Country Participatory Assessment of Structural Adjustment."

Sassoon, Anne Showstack (2001), "Globalisation, Hegemony and Passive Revolution," *New Political Economy*, Vol. 6, No. 1.

Saxe-Fernández, John (1989), "Carta de Intención: Convergencia subordinada," Excelsior, April 18.

_____ (1994), "The Chiapas Insurrection: Consequences for Mexico and the United States," *International Journal of Politics, Culture and Society*, Vol. 8. No. 2.

_____ (1998), "Ciclos Industrializadores y desindustrializadores," *Nueva Sociedad*, No. 158, noviembre-diciembre.

_____ (1998), "Neoliberalismo y TLC: ¿Hacia Ciclos de Guerra Civil?" Paper presented for the Asociación Latinoamericana de Sociología Rural, Conference on "Globalización, Crisis y Desarrollo Rural en América Latina," Universidad Autónoma de Chapingo.

_____ (1999), "Globalización e Imperialismo," in Saxe-Fernández (ed.), *Globalización: crítica a un Paradigma*, México, Plaza & Janés.

_____ (2002), *La Compra Venta de México*, México, Plaza James.

Saxe-Fernández, John, James Petras and Henry Veltmeyer (2001), *Globalización, imperialismo y clase social*, Buenos Aires/Mexico City, Editorial Lumen.

Saxe-Fernández, John and Omar Núñez (2001), "Globalización e Imperialismo: La transferencia de Excedentes de América Latina," in Saxe-Fernández et al. *Globalización, Imperialismo y Clase Social*, Buenos Aires/México, Editorial Lúmen.

Schaefer, Brett D. (2001), *Priorities for the President: Reforming International Financial Institutions*, New York, Heritage Foundation.

Schecter, Darrow (1991), *Gramsci and the Theory of Industrial Democracy*, Avebury.

Scott, James C. (1985), *Weapons of the Weak: Everyday Forms of Peasant Resistance*, Yale University Press.

_____ (1990), *Domination and the Arts of Resistance: Hidden Transcripts*, New Haven, Yale University Press.

Sen, Amartya (1999), *Development as Freedom*, New York, Alfred A. Knopf.

Severinto, Rodolofo C. (1999), "Regionalism: The Stakes for South-East Asia," Address delivered in Singapore at ASEANWEB, 24 May.

Shepard, Stephen (1997), "The New Economy: What it Really Means?" *Business Week*, November 17.

Shields, David (1996), "Sobreexplotación de yacimientos de petróleo; pérdida de reservas," *El Financiero*, 24 de junio. México.

Short, Claire (2001). "Globalisation, Trade and Development in the Least Developed Countries," Speech delivered to the Ministerial Roundtable on Trade and the Least Developed Countries (London, 19 March), http://www.globalisation.gov.uk/.

Sinclair, Minor and Martha Thompson (2001), *Cuba: Going Against the Grain*, Boston, Oxfam America, June.

Singer, Daniel (1999), *Whose Millennium? Theirs or Ours?* New York, Monthly Review Press.

Sivanandan, A and Ellen Meiksins Wood (1997), "Globalization and Epochal Shifts: An Exchange," *Monthly Review*, Vol. 48, No. 9.

Skirbekk, Gunnar and Asunción St. Clair (2001), "A Philosophical Analysis of the World Bank's Conception of Poverty. A Critical View of the World Bank Report: World Development Report 2000/2001. Attacking Poverty," Bergen, Norway, Comparative Research Programme on Poverty.

Sklair, Leslie (1997), "Social Movements for Global Capitalism: The Transnational Capitalist Class in Action," *Review of International Political Economy*, Vol. 2, No. 3.

Slater, David (1985), *New Social Movements and the State in Latin America*, Amsterdam, CEDLA.

Snow, Anita and Paul Elias (2002), "Cuba Seeks New Drug Markets," *Seattle Times*, July 8.

St. Clair, Jeffrey (1999), "Seattle Diary: It's a Gas, Gas, Gas," *New Left Review* I, No. 238, Nov.-Dec.

Stalker, Peter (2000), *Workers Without Frontiers*, Boulder CO, Lynne Rienner.

Ste. Croix, G. E. M. (1981), *The Class Struggle in the Ancient Greek World from the Archaic Age to the Arab Conquests*, Duckworth.

Stiglitz, Joseph (1998), "More Instruments and Broader Goals: Moving Toward the Post-Washington Consensus," The 1998 WIDER Annual Lecture, Helsinki, Finland.

_____ (2002), *Globalization and Its Discontents*, New York, W. W. Norton.

Stillwagon, Eileen (1998), *Stunted Lives, Stagnant Economies: Poverty, Disease and Underdevelopment*, New Brunswick NJ, Rutgers University Press.

Strange, Susan (1995), *The Retreat of the State: The Diffusion of Power in the World Economy*, Cambridge University Press.

Stubbs, Richard (1995), "Asia-Pacific Regionalization and The Global Economy: A Third Form of Capitalism?," *Asian Survey*, XXXV(9), 785-97.

Sunkel, Osvaldo (1991), "Del desarrollo hacia adentro al desarrollo dede adentro," *Revista Mexicana de Sociologia*, 1: 3-42.

Sweezy, Paul (1997), "More (or Less) on Globalization," *Monthly Review*, Vol. 49, No. 4.

Tabb, William (1997), "Contextualizing Globalization: Comments on Du Boff and Herman," *Monthly Review*, Vol. 49, No. 6.

Tanzer, Michael (1993), Seminario de Teoría del Desarrollo, Instituto de Investigaciones Económicas, UNAM, México.

Therborn, Goran (2000), "Globalizations: Dimensions, Historical Waves, Regional Effects, Normative Governance," *International Sociology*, Vol. 15, No. 23, June.

Thompson, E. P. (1968/1991), *The Making of the English Working Class*, New York, New Press.

_____ (1978), "Eighteenth Century English Society: Class Struggle Without Class?" *Social History*, Vol. 3, No. 2.

Toye, John (1987), *Dilemmas of Development: Reflections on the Counter-Revolution in Development Theory and Policy*, Oxford, Basil Blackwell.

Tulchin, Joseph and Allison Garland (eds.) (2000), *Social Development in Latin America*, Boulder CO, Lynne Rienner.

UNCTAD—United nations Commission on Trade and Development, Division of Transnational Corporations (1994), *World Investment Report: Transnational Corporations, Employment and the Workplace*, New York and Geneva, UN.

UNDP—United Nations Development Programme (2000), *Investigación sobre desarrollo humano y equidad en Cuba 1999*, Havana, UNDP.

_____ (1990, 1992, 1993, 1996, 1997, 1999, 2000, 2001), *Human Development Report*, New York, UNDP / Oxford University Press.

UNICEF—United Nations Children's Fund (1995, 1998, 2001), *The State of the World's Children*, Geneva, UNICEF.

United Kingdom Government (2000), "Eliminating World Poverty: Making Globalisation Work for the Poor," White Paper on International Development, At http://www. Globalisation.gov.uk/, Internet accessed December 11.

UNRISD—United Nations Research Institute for Social Development (1994), *States of Disarray: The Social Effects of Globalization*, Geneva, UNRISD.

_____ (2000), "Civil Society Strategies and Movements for Rural Asset Redistribution and Improved Livelihoods," UNRISD, Civil Society and Social Movements Programme, Geneva, UNRISD.

Valdés Paz, Juan (1997), "Voices on the Left," *NACLA Report on the Americas*, Vol. XXXI, No. 1, July-August.

Van der Pijl, Kees (1984), *The Making of an Atlantic Ruling Class*, London, Verso.

Veltmeyer, Henry (1997), "Class and Identity: The Dynamics of New Social Movements in Latin America," *Journal of Peasant Studies*, Vol. 25, No. 1.

_____ (1999), "Labour and the World Economy," *Canadian Journal of Development Studies*, XX, Special Issue.

_____ (2001), "The Politics of language: Deconstructing Postdevelopment Discourse," *Canadian Journal of Development Studies*, Vol. XX11, No. 3.

Veltmeyer, Henry and James Petras (1997), *Economic Liberalism and Class Conflict in Latin America*, London, Macmillan Press.

Verdezoto, Maria Elena (2002), "Dow Jones Newswires" (August 2), 50 Years Is Enough Network. http://50years.org.

Wade, Robert (2001), "Winners and Losers," *The Economist*, April 26.

Wade, Robert and Frank Veneroso (1998), "The Asian Crisis: the High Debt Model vs. the Wall Street-Treasury-IMF Complex," *New Left Review*, March-April.

Wald, Karen (1999), "Widespread organic farming could help boost Cuba's sagging agricultural sector," *Cuba News*, November.

Wallerstein, Clare (2000), "Venezuela Struggles with Surplus Plastic Surgeons," *The Lancet* 355, June 10.

Wallerstein, Immanuel (1998), *Utopistics, Or Historical Choices of the Twenty-First Century*, New York, The New Press.

_____ (1999), *The End of the World As We Know It: Social Science for the Twenty-First Century*, University of Minnesota Press.

Washington Office on Latin America (WOLA) and Oxfam America (1997), "Myths and Facts About the U.S. Embargo on Medicine and Medical Supplies," Press Release, June 26.

Watkins, Kevin (2002), "Making Globalization Work for the Poor," *Finance & Development*, Vol. 39, No. 1, March.

Weeks, John (2001), "A Tale of Two Transitions: Cuba and Vietnam," in Claes Brundenius and John Week (eds.), *Globalization and Third World Socialism: Cuba and Vietnam*, New York, Palgrave.

Weisbrot, Mark (2002), "The Mirage of Progress," The American Prospect, Vol. 13, No. 1, January 1-14.

Weiss, Linda (1998), *The Myth of the Powerless State: Governing the Economy in a Global Era*, Cambridge, Polity Press.

Welder, Michael and David Rigby (1996), *The Golden Age Illusion: Postwar Capitalism*, New York, Guilford.

Whiteford, Linda (1998), "Children's Health as Accumulated Capital. Structural Adjustment in the Dominican Republic and Cuba," in Nancy Scheper-Hughes (ed.), *Small Wars: The Cultural Politics of Childhood*, Berkeley, University of California Press.

Williams, Robin C. (1997), "In the Shadow of Plenty, Cuba Copes with a Crippled Health Care System," *Canadian Medical Association Journal*, Vol. 157, No. 3, August 1.

Williamson, J. (ed.) (1990), *Latin American Adjustment. How Much Has Happened?* Washington DC, Institute for International Economics.

WOLA—Washington Office on Latin America and Oxfam (1997), Myths and Facts about the U.S. Embargo on Medicine and Medical supplies," October, Washington, WOLA.

Wolf, Martin (1999), "Not So New Economy," *Financial Times*, August 1.

_____ (2002), "Countries Still Rule the World," *Financial Times*, February 5.

Wolfe, Marshall (1996), *Elusive Development*, London, Zed Press.

Woods, Adèle (2000), *Facts about European NGOs Active in International Development*, Paris, OECD.

Woodside, A. (1993), "The Asia-Pacific Idea as a Mobilization Myth," in A. Dirlik (ed.), *What's In a Rim? Critical Perspectives on the Pacific Region Idea*, Boulder CO, Westview Press.

World Bank (1989a), *Report of the Trade, Finance and Industry Division*, Washington DC.

_____ (1989b), *Report and Recommendation to the Executive Directors*, Washington DC.

_____ (1990), *AGSAL 1*, Report No. 8310-ME, Washington DC.

_____ (1992), *Global Economic Prospects and the Developing Countries*, Washington DC.

_____ (1994), *Adjustment in Africa: Reforms, Results, and the Road Ahead*, Washington DC, The World Bank.

_____ (1995), *Country Strategy Paper—Mexico, Mexican Division*, Country Department II, Mexico and Central America, Washington DC.

_____ (1995a), *World Development Report. Workers in an Integrating World*, New York, Oxford University Press.

_____ (1997, 2000/01), *World Development Report*, New York, Oxford University Press.

_____ (1998), *Assessing Aid. What Works, What Doesn't, and Why*, New York, Oxford University Press.

_____ (2002), *Global Economic Prospects and the Developing Countries*, www.worldbank.org.

_____ (no date), *Mexico-PCR PERL (First Draft) and Hybrid Loans*, Washington DC.

WHO—World Health Organization (2001), Globalisation, Diet and Health: An example from Tonga. Cited in Aziz Choudry, "Killing Me Softly," www.zmag.org/sustainers/content/2002-08/03choudry.cfm.

_____ (2001a), "Macroeconomics and Health: Investing in Health for Economic Development," Report of the Commission on Macroeconomics and Health, chaired by Jeffrey Sachs, Geneva.

Index

Notes: page numbers in italics indicate tables. Numbers in brackets preceded by *n* are note numbers.